CATHERINE THE GREAT

AN ENLIGHTENED EMPRESS

CATHERINE THE GREAT

AN ENLIGHTENED EMPRESS

CATHERINE
THE GREAT

Published by
NMS Enterprises Limited – Publishing
a division of NMS Enterprises Limited
National Museums Scotland
Chambers Street
Edinburgh EH1 1JF

Text, photographic images
(unless otherwise credited)
© The State Hermitage Museum,
St Petersburg 2012

Catalogue format and additional material
© National Museums Scotland 2012

Text of chapter VIII © Antony Cross 2012

Ownership of exhibits
(unless otherwise credited)
The State Hermitage Museum, St Petersburg

**British Library Cataloguing in Publication
Data**
A catalogue record for this book
is available from the British Library.

ISBN (CASED): 978 1 905267 68 2
ISBN (PAPER): 978 1 905267 74 3

Book layout and design by Mark Blackadder.
Printed and bound in the United Kingdom
by Bell & Bain Limited, Glasgow.

Image on title page shows a carnival sledge
used by the Imperial court during winter
carnival celebrations (CATALOGUE NO. 161).

www.nms.ac.uk
www.hermitagemuseum.org

EXHIBITION SPONSORED BY

INVESTMENT MANAGERS

National Museums Scotland would like to thank
Baillie Gifford Investment Managers
for their generous sponsorship of the exhibition.

The Museum is extremely grateful for their support.

CONTENTS

COVER IMAGE

The Empress
Catherine II appears in
magnificent coronation
robes, with all the symbols
of Russian Imperial power.

*Attributed to
Vigilius Eriksen*
(1722–82)

CATALOGUE NO. 38

EXHIBITION CREDITS

CATHERINE THE GREAT: AN ENLIGHTENED EMPRESS

National Museums Scotland
Chambers Street
Edinburgh EH1 1JF
13 July to 21 October 2012

EXHIBITION

*Concept and co-organization
of the exhibition:*
National Museums Scotland
and State Hermitage Museum,
St Petersburg

*Ownership of exhibits
(unless otherwise credited):*
State Hermitage Museum,
St Petersburg

NATIONAL MUSEUMS SCOTLAND

Maureen Barrie
Dr Godfrey Evans

STATE HERMITAGE MUSEUM, ST PETERSBURG

Exhibition organizing committee:
Professor Dr M. Piotrovsky
Director, State Hermitage Museum

Professor Dr G. Vilinbakhov
Deputy Director,
State Hermitage Museum

Dr V. Matveyev
Deputy Director,
State Hermitage Museum

Dr S. Adaksina
Deputy Director, Chief Custodian,
State Hermitage Museum

Dr V. Fedorov
Head of the Department of History
of Russian Culture,
State Hermitage Museum

Curator of the exhibition:
Dr V. Fedorov

Working group:
N. Bakhareva
Yu. Efimov
M. Garlova
I. Garmanov
Yu. Gudimenko
D. Lazarevskaya
A. Miklayeva
I. Nikulina
E. Sagdtdinova

FOREWORD

Dr Gordon Rintoul

DIRECTOR, NATIONAL MUSEUMS SCOTLAND

National Museums Scotland is delighted to be collaborating once again with our good friends and colleagues, Professor Piotrovsky and the staff of the State Hermitage Museum in St Petersburg.

In 2005, and again in 2006, we mounted two highly successful exhibitions – one on the subject of the last Tsar and Tsarina and the other about Islamic art – using the wonderful collections of the State Hermitage Museum. We are now very pleased to be able to stage an even more spectacular exhibition about the Empress Catherine the Great in our new and much larger special exhibition gallery.

The year 2012 is the 250th anniversary of the year Catherine ascended the throne. It is thus a highly appropriate moment to examine the remarkable life of this minor German princess, who overthrew

her husband in a *coup*, brought the Enlightenment to Russia, and transformed her vast adopted country through great vision, commitment and hard work. The 600 items in the exhibition enable us to explore and understand Catherine's personal and family life, her links with intellectuals of the day, the spectacular victories of her military commanders, and her outstanding achievements as a builder, patron and collector.

For many people, this exhibition will offer a once-in-a-lifetime opportunity to see dozens of the finest items produced by the Imperial Porcelain Factory, the Tula Armouries and other Russian factories and workshops. Catherine's enormous collection of over 3000 paintings and 10,000 engraved gemstones is also well represented in the exhibition, with splendid paintings and some of her very finest cameos and intaglios.

Other exhibits will serve to remind us of the important roles that Scots played during Catherine's reign. Dr John Rogerson was the Empress's personal physician, Admiral Samuel Greig of Inverkeithing helped to win the great naval battle of Chesme in 1770 and later defended St Petersburg against the Swedes, while the architect Charles Cameron decorated and added to Catherine's favourite palace at Tsarskoye Selo. The modeller James Tassie even supplied the Empress with over 30,000 copies of cameos, which means that the Hermitage now houses the largest and most comprehensive collection of 'Tassies' in the world.

Catherine fascinated her contemporaries. Indeed, another Scot, Alexander, 10th Duke of Hamilton, was so impressed by accounts of the late Empress that he commissioned a full-length tapestry of Catherine and a bronze copy of Jean-Antoine Houdon's celebrated marble bust of her while he was British ambassador in St Petersburg in 1807.

Finally, I would like to record our grateful thanks to Baillie Gifford Investment Managers for their generous support of *Catherine the Great: An Enlightened Empress*. An exhibition on this scale is not possible without the substantial assistance and enthusiasm of many people.

THE LESSONS OF CATHERINE

Professor Dr Mikhail Piotrovsky

DIRECTOR, STATE HERMITAGE MUSEUM

Above my desk in my office, there is a portrait of Catherine the Great, founder of The Hermitage. This is a woven portrait, a specimen of the art of tapestry, the appearance of which in Russia was one of the signs of initiation of our country to the culture of Europe. Such portraits were distributed as diplomatic gifts. Thus the image of the Russian Empress was disseminated around the world.

Catherine was 'great' not only in her deeds, but also in her ability to foresee their outcome. As we know, a famous legend about 'the Potemkin villages' is a myth created by disgruntled German diplomats, though Catherine was able to theatricalize any event, even small-pox vaccination. She loved theatre, both in the theatre and in real life.

She perfectly understood that the greatness of her country was not only about a potent army and sound economy, but also about the prosperity of art and science. So she took care of that and was proud of it. Thus the Enlightenment with its aesthetics arrived in Russia via Catherine's policies. She set everything in a skilful and elegant framework of intriguing correspondence with great philosophers – her mentors. She understood how crucial it was, for the prestige of the country and for her personal self-assertion, to possess unparalleled museum collections.

And so The Hermitage was established to combine the intimacy of private receptions with unique art acquisitions, made pompously and publicly to the shock of bedazzled spectators. She knew what she wanted. She knew who could assist her in that. Diplomats and philosophers, *literati* and art dealers were amassing her collection. It is as if she left her successors a testament to spare no expense or effort on developing and expanding her museum. It is interesting to trace how this testament was fulfilled by different generations of Russian emperors.

Catherine's museum was far from resembling Peter the Great's Kunstkamera. Typologically, Catherine's museum was closer to the royal and not to the bourgeois type of collecting. However even in this case, just like in every other activity, Catherine continued Peter the Great's legacy. In fact, she made his dreams come true and completed things for which Peter the Great turned the entire country upside down: Russia became a respected and feared superpower. Well integrated with other European powers, Russia always stayed loyal to its goals, and to its own cultural peculiarities. Even though of completely German origin, Catherine may have had the strongest Russian identity in the Romanov Dynasty of the St Petersburg period of our history.

Theatricalization of Catherine's life engendered multiple legends, both positive and negative. The West surrounded her image with a plethora of anecdotes, which often overshadowed the very reason why she earned her title of 'the Great'. We are pleased that Hermitage educational activities, along with multiple comprehensive scientific and literary works of recent years, reveal Catherine's much deeper image to the world.

Nowadays, this image is very instructive. Catherine was a great 'feminist'. She openly engaged in things allowable to and even honourable for men at the time, but inadmissible for women. This applies to her love affairs, political upheavals and strong opinions. Catherine was 'infected' with ideas of the Enlightenment and was hoping to construct a smart and law-abiding state. However, the French Revolution and Russian peasant uprisings made her realize that implementation of her utopian plans could have become fatal to her country.

Catherine was both generous and reasonably economical. It was almost for nothing that she managed to acquire Gotzkowsky's renowned collection which laid the foundation of the famous Art Gallery of The Hermitage. The political effect of the purchase, which she intercepted from Frederick the Great, was enormous. Its echo is still resounding. It took Catherine a long time to pay for the Sèvres dinner service with cameos; however, when she did, she saved the porcelain factory. Political aspects of Catherine's art policy have become both theoretical and practical lessons, which could still be useful for modern rulers to draw experience from.

And now we present the audience with this multi-faceted experience, accumulated in historical and cultural monuments. Catherine founded The Hermitage. Today The Hermitage is incessantly seeking ways to ensure that not only do we preserve and multiply the memory of her, but also give everyone access to the instructive aspects of her diverse life and activities, of her mind and temperament.

CHAPTER I

Catherine
the Great

—

VYACHESLAV FEDOROV

OPPOSITE

A portrait of the Grand Duchess
Catherine Alekseyevna, *c.*1745.

Georg Christoph Grooth
(1716–49)

Voltaire was right to envy the happiness of the scholar who would be writing Catherine the Great's biography in a hundred years' time. Her complex personality is shrouded in legend and mystery, and some details of her life have still to be investigated.

To everyone's surprise, Sophie Frederica Augusta of Anhalt-Zerbst (1729–96), a princess of a small German duchy, became a Russian empress and the most powerful ruler in Europe. Although she had no right to claim the Russian throne, Catherine (as Sophie became in Russia) nevertheless governed the enormous Russian Empire for thirty-four years (1762–96); only Peter the Great's forty-three-year reign lasted longer (1682–1725). Catherine's reign can, without exaggeration, be described as the era of glory and might of Russia, and of the splendour of the Russian Imperial court. And, just like Peter I, Catherine became known as 'the Great' in her own lifetime.

Contemporary observers and later historians give contradictory descriptions and assessments of Catherine. Many memoirs about the Empress have been preserved, but it is hard to separate fact from fiction. She was adored and called a goddess, yet at the same time hated, despised and ridiculed. The French writer and philosopher Voltaire called her 'the brightest star of the North'; the French ambassador Count Ségur remarked upon her extraordinary talents, subtle mind, majesty and kindness; while the Austrian diplomat Charles-Joseph Lamoral, Prince of Ligne, wrote about the greatness of her genius.

Others with first-hand experience of Catherine were much less complimentary. The French diplomat, Baron de Corberon, observed: 'Catherine is an unparalleled hypocrite! She is sanctimonious, tender, proud, majestic, kind; however, she is true to herself at heart and pursues her personal interests exclusively, without neglecting any means to achieve them'.[1] After his private meetings with the Empress in St Petersburg, the French philosopher Denis Diderot wrote that 'she has

NOTE: Until 1918, Russia adhered to the old Julian calendar of 365.25 days and was 13 days behind the rest of Europe, which followed the later Gregorian calendar. Some dates in this book may thus reflect inconsistencies.

the soul of Brutus and the heart of Cleopatra'. The great early 19th-century Russian poet Alexander Pushkin, who was born three years after Catherine's death, likened her to playwright Molière's hypocrite and labelled her 'Tartuffe in a skirt on the throne'.

This kaleidoscope of blatant flattery, formal eulogy and malicious abuse only confirms the originality of the Empress's personality, as an outstanding stateswoman and a far-sighted and successful politician. In Russia, the grandeur of Catherine's ideas and accomplishments can only be compared with those of Peter the Great, whose direct heir she considered herself to be.

It was chance that brought Catherine to Russia. The year 1741 saw the third *coup d'état* after Peter the Great's death. His thirty-one-year-old daughter Elizabeth Petrovna received support from the Russian Guard regiments and proclaimed herself Empress. Deeply aware of the illegality of this seizure of power, Elizabeth spent the rest of her life in constant fear of being overthrown in another *coup*. She exiled the deposed regent Anna Leopoldovna and her infant son, the Emperor Ivan VI, and vowed never to sign a death sentence during her reign. After becoming Empress, the devout and superstitious Elizabeth never slept at night, was afraid of being left alone, and frequently changed her lodgings, constantly moving from palace to palace with her entire court. The Russian court was known to have switched to a nocturnal way of life during her reign.

Elizabeth did everything possible to retain the crown. Unmarried and childless, her main concern was to establish a new dynastic line of Peter the Great's direct descendants in Russia, which would guarantee her own safety. Immediately after her coronation in Moscow, Elizabeth appointed her nephew, the Duke Karl Peter Ulrich of Holstein-Gottorp, heir to the Russian throne. He was Peter the Great's grandson and the son of Elizabeth's elder sister Anna Petrovna, whom Peter the Great had married off to Duke Karl Friederich of Holstein-Gottorp, a nephew of King Charles XII of Sweden.

Elizabeth was in a hurry to carry out her plans. In 1742, just a year after the *coup*, she gave orders to have the fourteen-year-old orphan, who had recently been designated heir to the Swedish throne, secretly and quickly brought to Russia. He was obliged to renounce the Swedish crown and became known as Peter in honour of his illustrious

3

BELOW

A miniature, *c.*1752–62,
of the Grand Duke Peter,
grandson of Peter
the Great.

Jean-Françoise Samsois

CATALOGUE NO. 20

grandfather. A search for a bride began immediately, setting the secret machinery of European diplomacy into motion. After careful consideration, Elizabeth chose the almost unknown German Princess Sophie, rejecting other candidates, including daughters of English, French and Polish kings. According to the distinguished Russian historian V. O. Kliuchevsky, the entire political world of Europe was astounded by Elizabeth's choice.[2] Yet it was a perfectly logical choice, based on simple self-interest. Elizabeth believed that neither the princess herself, who came from the impoverished family of the Duke of Anhalt-Zerbst, who was in the service of the King of Prussia, nor her relatives, who had little political clout in Europe, could stake any great claim or cause any problems. The only thing required of the future Grand Duchess was to continue the dynasty.

In 1744, the future bride and her mother, Princess Johanna Elisabeth of Holstein-Gottorp, arrived in Russia. They were met at the border and were delighted with their official reception, the brilliant prospects, and with the Empress Elizabeth herself, an extremely beautiful and powerful ruler of a vast country. The young Sophie likewise pleased the Empress and Grand Duke Peter and was lavished with kindness, attention and expensive gifts from Elizabeth and her court. Sophie's mother wrote to Zerbst: 'Our daughter made a very good impression on the entire Russian court, and the Empress and the heir have tender love for her; we have made it!'[3]

On converting to Orthodoxy in 1744, Sophie broke her promise to her father not to change her faith. As part of her baptism, she took the name Catherine Alekseyevna in honour of Elizabeth's mother, the Empress Catherine I. At the end of the ceremony, the young Catherine said a few words in impeccable Russian, which moved the Empress and her courtiers to tears.

Peter and Catherine's sumptuous marriage took place in 1745. The festivities were modelled on the weddings of the French Dauphin at Versailles and the son of King Augustus III in Dresden. The various wedding ceremonies were accompanied by feasts, opulent balls, masquerades, parades and outdoor parties that lasted for five days and 'outshone all Oriental fairy-tales'.[4] The Grand Duke Peter was seventeen years old, and his wife only sixteen.

Soon after the marriage, the relationship began to sour. The couple's personalities, attitudes and interests turned out to be diametrically opposite. Count L. F. Ségur rightly noted:

This marriage was unhappy: Nature grudged the young duke her gifts, while showering Catherine with them. It seems that fate had a strange caprice to endow the duke with cowardice, inconsistency and lack of talents as a servile man, while his spouse had both the reason and firmness of a man born to reign. And, indeed, Peter only flickered on the throne, while Catherine held on to it with brilliance for a long time.[5]

Narrow-minded, infantile, often drunk, extremely passionate about playing toy soldiers and military drills, Peter not only rapidly lost Catherine's respect, but also aroused outright hatred in her. Even his virtuoso skill on the violin and love of music only served to further enrage Catherine who had no ear for music. She later wrote that after her husband's visits, she found the most boring book a pleasant diversion.

Elizabeth was also displeased with her heir. Her papers contain unflattering references – 'My nephew is an imbecile, may the devil take him!' – 'My cursed nephew has annoyed me as much as he could.'[6] Moreover, Peter neglected his marital duties, was engaged in affairs with court ladies and constantly insulted his wife. Only fear of the all-powerful Empress, and the hope of reigning in the future, compelled the couple to stay together. However, Peter was not the monster he was persistently alleged to be by Catherine and others. His tragedy lay in his weakness, immaturity and fear of his adopted country, Russia.

Catherine's first eighteen years in Russia were a nightmare. She spent them in a whirl of dangerous court intrigues, in constant fear, in the company of an unloving husband and under the watchful eye of a suspicious Elizabeth. Furthermore, the Empress separated Catherine from her long-awaited son, Paul, almost immediately after his birth in September 1754, as she had decided to bring up the little Grand Duke herself. By that time, Elizabeth had given up hope in her nephew, and was reputed to have planned to enthrone Paul, bypassing his good-for-nothing father.

To this day, it remains unclear who was the real father of the future Emperor Paul I (r.1796–1801): Catherine's husband, who was commonly thought not to be able to have children, or Catherine's first favourite, Count Sergei Saltykov, who had received the blessing of the Empress for a relationship and was sent away on a long-term diplomatic mission shortly after Paul's birth.

After bearing a son and heir, Catherine was of no further use to Elizabeth. The Empress did not talk to the young Grand Duchess for months, and Catherine was forced to consider her destiny. Peter had a life of his own – his hobbies and romances – so the couple saw each other rarely. Relations with both the Empress and her husband were becoming increasingly strained.

Although in one of her carefully crafted letters Catherine asked Elizabeth to allow her to return home, leaving Russia was not in her plans. In reality, there was no home to return to: her father had died in 1747, while her mother was travelling around Europe. These were the years that Catherine – smart, cunning and ambitious – was preparing herself for the Russian throne. She clearly understood that her husband was too inept to rule the country, and her own misfortunes spurred her on to fight for the crown.

Catherine pursued her goal with patience and resolution. She managed to find the only solution that would enable her both to survive and attain power. Later in her memoirs, she would openly and cynically admit:

> *Here … is the conclusion I arrived at when I realized that I was firmly established in Russia, and which never left my mind for a single minute: (1) please the Grand Duke; (2) please the Empress; (3) please the nation. I wanted to achieve all three goals, and if I didn't succeed, then either they were not meant to be realized, or Providence did not find them desirable, because I truly did everything possible to achieve them. I displayed servility, submissiveness, respect, tried to be liked, to act properly, to show sincere affection – everything on my part was always directed towards this from 1744 to 1761.*[7]

Indeed, Catherine made every possible effort to win over her entourage and to gain their love and affection. She was always cheerful, considerate, caring and polite to everyone: 'More than ever did I try to win over both the great and the small. I kept everyone in my mind and have made it a rule to think that I need absolutely everyone, and to gain their love in every way – in which I succeeded.' Count Stanislaw August Poniatowski, among Catherine's early favourites, described her thus:

> *Her blinding white face and bright makeup contrasted well with her black hair; she had enormous, extremely expressive blue eyes with very long black eyelashes, a delicate nose and a mouth calling for kisses, very beautiful arms and legs; she was slender, rather tall than short, her pace*

was light and full of grace, the sound of her voice exceedingly pleasant, her laughter always as cheerful as her disposition.[8]

Neglected by her husband, Catherine was left to herself. The life of the Russian court abounded with many feasts, balls and masquerades, which Catherine attended. She loved changing costumes, had fun wearing male attire, and was an eager dancer. However, the opulent life of the court, with its endless amusements and constant crowdedness, did not save the Grand Duchess from feeling completely alone.

Catherine and Peter spent every spring and summer at Oranienbaum, to the west of St Petersburg. It was here that she learned to ride and became an excellent equestrian. She walked a lot in the nearby parks and fell in love with hunting and walking along the shore. Gradually, she devoted more and more time to books, filling gaps in her education. She studied the Russian language, Russian and world history, philosophy, literature and political works. Eventually, books occupied more and more of her time, and became her favourite occupation for many years. At this time, her favourite authors included Cicero, Plato and Tacitus. Catherine was also interested in contemporary French literature and philosophy and studied the ideas of the French Enlightenment. The famous *Encyclopédie*, along with works of Montesquieu, Racine and Corneille, appeared in her library. Voltaire became her true spiritual father and she later wrote to him:

I can assure you that since 1746 when I began to dispose of my time, I am very much obliged to you. Before, I used to read only novels, but after I came across your works by chance I have never stopped reading them, and no longer wanted any other books but those written so well and from which I can benefit so much.[9]

Elizabeth's illness in the late 1750s troubled Russian society. Confusion and insecurity spread through the Russian court. The political circles and members of the Guards speculated about the future of Russia, and the Grand Duke and his spouse were frequently mentioned. Indeed, the couple provided much to talk about: the contrast between the quick-tempered, weak and foolish future Emperor and his charming wife was all too apparent and alarming. The Russian court grew increasingly distrustful and fearful of Peter.

The Empress Elizabeth suspected that the intelligent and active Catherine led a double life, that she was involved with intrigues and a possible conspiracy. Consequently, Catherine was not allowed to write letters, even to her mother, and was forbidden any involvement in political matters. Despite this, Catherine managed to keep abreast of political matters and even secretly maintained relations with many politicians and influential individuals, including Frederick the Great of Prussia and her mother, who had been sent away from Russia because of her own political intrigues and for spying on behalf of the Prussian king.

Moreover, Catherine herself became an active participant in the complex political relations between Russia and Prussia during the Seven Years War. Elizabeth took radical action when she discovered that the unjustified withdrawal of the Russian army from Prussia, just after its brilliant victory at Gross-Jägersdorf which could have led to the capitulation of Frederick II, had been initiated by Chancellor Bestuzhev-Ryumin, who had been in active communication with Catherine. Bestuzhev-Ryumin was arrested and exiled to Siberia in the spring of 1758, while Catherine was forced to endure a rather unpleasant interview with the Empress, and expend a great deal of effort to retain her position.

It was at this point, with the knowledge that she could only expect harm from the Empress, as well as her husband, that Catherine began to prepare to do battle for power.

Catherine's true friends rallied round her. In search for political and financial support, she came into contact with foreign diplomats. On 11 August 1761 she wrote to the English ambassador, Sir Charles Hanbury-Williams: 'At the moment, I am busy recruiting supporters, and preparing and making ready everything for the event that you have been looking forward to: my head is filled with a chaos of intrigues and negotiations.'[10] Peter and Catherine expected and looked forward to Elizabeth's imminent death and made their plans accordingly.

The Empress Elizabeth Petrovna died in December 1761, after twenty years on the Russian throne. The new Emperor, Peter III, was thirty-five years old. He openly rejoiced in the death of Elizabeth and, having obtained his long-awaited freedom and unlimited power, fully embraced his Holstein identity once again. Indeed, as Kliuchevsky has observed, it became even more pronounced than when he was living in the duchy itself. Weak and cowardly, Peter feared Russians and called Russia a cursed country. His actions as Emperor were the fruit of a limited mind and of political ignorance. Though now ruler of a vast state, he in effect turned himself into the loyal subject of Frederick II of Prussia. He immediately made peace and entered into an alliance with Prussia. As a result, Elizabeth's foreign policy was completely reversed, the treaties of alliance with France and Austria broken, and the successes of the Russian army in the Seven Years War entirely negated. Peter only cared about his native duchy, and tried to draw Russia into a useless war with Denmark to reclaim his inheritance rights to Schleswig, thus contravening the most basic principles of Russian foreign policy.

The Russian court had long looked upon the heir's behaviour with hostility and alarm. While still Grand Duke, Peter had never concealed his contempt for Orthodoxy, the Russian Orthodox Church and its clergy. Not trusting the Russian Guards, he surrounded himself with soldiers from Holstein, which provoked deep resentment among Russian officers who had served in the Seven Years War. Prior to his accession, Peter had publicly lamented the victories of the Russian army. After becoming Emperor of All the Russias, he openly revered Frederick II – he knelt down in front of a portrait of the Prussian king, wore a ring with his image, replaced his Russian uniform with a Prussian one, and donned the Prussian Order of the Black Eagle. The old Russian aristocracy, politicians and army were outraged by his

actions. Indeed, as if by design, he did everything he could to turn all classes of Russian society, the court and army against him.

Emperor Peter III reigned for 186 days. He was the only Russian tsar not to be crowned in Moscow (apart from the infant Ivan VI, who was deposed by Elizabeth Petrovna). Only this ancient ritual could bestow the divine right to rule Russia upon him. Naively confident of his legitimate right to the throne, Peter neither took heed of the persistent advice of his idol, King Frederick, to be crowned as quickly as possible, nor the experience of his predecessors on the Russian throne. Frederick subsequently commented, 'The Poor Emperor wanted to imitate Peter I, only he had no genius'.[11]

In contrast, the far-sighted Catherine did her best to create a favourable impression. Not only did she learn copious amounts of Russian history, but she also fully recognized the salient importance of the Russian Guards in a country where palace *coups* were carried out rapidly and successfully with the participation of the military élite. Catherine cleverly used all her husband's errors to her own advantage. She also emphasized her respect for all things Russian: she faithfully followed the traditions of the Russian court, frequently attended Russian Orthodox Church services and strictly observed its rites. Crucially, Catherine spent long hours in prayer by the coffin of Elizabeth, which earned her the sincere respect of her entourage. Unlike his wife, Peter laughed and flirted with the ladies right next to the Empress's coffin. Such disrespect would ultimately lead to his downfall.

The atmosphere at court became more tense by the day. On 9 June 1762, at a banquet celebrating the peace treaty with Prussia, Peter publicly insulted his wife, accusing her of not showing enough respect for the House of Holstein. He called her a fool and ordered her arrest. Only the intercession of his uncle, Duke Georg Ludwig of Holstein-Gottorp, saved Catherine. She and her supporters realized that the time had come to act. By this stage, Catherine's supporters had drawn up their plans for a *coup*, which was to take place before Peter's coronation in Moscow. The core conspirators were Count Kirill Razumovsky, Nikita Panin (the tutor of young Grand Duke Paul), Baron Korf, Princess Ekaterina Dashkova, and the five brothers of the Orlov family.

The chance arrest of Captain Passek on 27 June forced the conspirators' hand. Early the following morning, Catherine left her country estate of Peterhof for St Petersburg, where she was greeted with enthusiasm by the Izmailovsky Guards regiment. They were joined by the Semënovsky, Horse Guards, and Preobrazhensky regiments, with other army units. A crowded demonstration took place on Nevsky Prospekt, near Kazan Cathedral. Catherine was proclaimed sovereign Empress in her own right, and her seven-year-old son Paul, her heir. Then, at the Winter Palace, Catherine's supporters took the oath of allegiance to the new Empress, surrounded by jubilant crowds. When Catherine stepped out onto the balcony of the palace, she was greeted by an ecstatic multitude.

Tragically for himself, Peter III could not take decisive action as Catherine and her small army moved against him. On 29 June, he was arrested and forced to abdicate near Peterhof and then imprisoned on his nearby estate of Ropsha. A week later, his sudden death was reported to Catherine. He had been strangled by the officers guarding him, among whom was Count Aleksey Orlov, brother of Count Grigory Orlov, Catherine's favourite since 1760. Grigory was the father of her son Aleksey Bobrinsky, who had been born in secret on 11 April 1762, two months before the *coup*.

Unlike her late husband, Catherine was in a hurry to be crowned. A solemn ceremony was held in the Dormition Cathedral in the Kremlin in Moscow on Sunday, 22 September 1762. Eighteen years of self-education and clandestine work had produced a brilliant result. And so began the thirty-four-year-long reign of Catherine the Great, which is recognized as the Golden Age of Russia.

BELOW, LEFT

Catherine II on the balcony of the Winter Palace being acclaimed by troops and the people, 28 June 1762.

Unknown artist
(early 19th century)

CATALOGUE NO. 31

RIGHT

Count Aleksey Orlov.

By Charles Townley
(1783)

For the first time since Peter the Great, the Russian throne was occupied by an intelligent, extremely talented, well-educated and zealous ruler. Catherine possessed a variety of qualities essential for a good ruler, though rarely found in a single person: she was extraordinarily intelligent, her ambitions knew no bounds, whilst her capacity for hard work was even envied by Frederick the Great. The Prussian king repeatedly wondered whether Catherine worked harder than he did. On top of this, Catherine had a very good understanding of human psychology and the ability to use people to her advantage. It was easy for her to find and surround herself with dedicated and talented individuals and to draw them into the service of the state.

Even as a young girl, Catherine had developed a tolerance for the shortcomings of others, and an ability to get along with people. She also drew on simple worldly wisdom. The Englishman George Harley, writing to London in 1768, noted: 'It is true that the Russian Empress understands the surest way of controlling her subjects better than one would expect from a foreign princess. She is intimately familiar with their spirit and character and uses this information so well that most people believe their happiness depends on her continuing to reign.'[12]

Despite once comparing Catherine with Tartuffe, even Pushkin recognized her enormous talent for managing people: 'If to govern is to understand the weakness of the human soul and to make use of it, then in this respect Catherine deserves the acclaim of posterity. Her splendour was blinding, her affability attractive, her favours binding'.[13] Deep down, however, there was a large measure of caution. Like Elizabeth, Catherine was very suspicious, stressing that it was difficult to trust people because of the duplicity of human nature.

Catherine II always sought to understand all aspects of the Russian Empire. She had a splendid insight into politics and took a very keen interest in the sciences, culture and art, as both her Russian and foreign contemporaries fully recognized. Even Frederick the Great wrote about Catherine with undisguised respect: 'Russia needed such an Empress to complete its construction as a whole. … She includes everything in her activities, no single aspect of control escapes from her. … She serves as a rebuke to many other monarchs who are numb on their thrones with no clue about the grand things that she is putting into practice.'[14]

The very first days of Catherine's reign were marked by buzzing activity and testified to her desire to govern. She immediately took the reins of government into her own hands and became involved in all spheres of state activities. The *coup* itself and the overthrow of the lawful emperor had to be fully justified by positive, dynamic action. The new Empress's top priorities were the creation and implementation of successful foreign and domestic policies that would guarantee her security on the Russian throne. This accorded with Catherine's own notions of the monarch's mission, and she was ready to introduce large-scale reforms to reorganize the country.

Catherine's ideal hero and model statesman was Peter the Great. She constantly declared that she was continuing his work, which meant resuming his foreign and domestic strategies for creating an empire with a strong centralized government, a well-developed economy and an energetic foreign policy – goals to which Peter had devoted his entire life. Having appreciated and assimilated the fundamental principles, Catherine continued Peter's policy and largely completed what he had commenced and partly implemented.

During his short reign, Peter III had betrayed Russia's national interests. Thus Catherine's policies had to be based on reasserting the country's national interests in all areas of government. It was this pronounced nationalism in all of Catherine's undertakings that ensured her stability. As one writer has observed: 'Catherine II was the most

Russian empress in the history of Russia. Without any exaggeration, one can say that the former Princess Sophie Frederica Augusta became the first Russian nationalist'.[15]

Strangely perhaps, but like her former husband Peter III, Catherine had a personal interest in ending the war with Prussia. The young German princess had come to Russia largely through the machinations of the King of Prussia. Frederick was not called 'the Great' for nothing. He followed all the developments in Europe and tried to exploit them. He knew that the Grand Duke and heir to the Russian throne had been devoted to him from his childhood. At the same time, he also maintained secret communication with Catherine, believing that this could turn out to his advantage. Catherine never forgot her debts and settled them royally. After the *coup*, despite intense pressure from Russian politicians, she did not break Peter III's peace treaty with Prussia. Later, however, she took her revenge on Frederick, in a subtle feminine way and in the spirit of the Enlightenment. An avid collector, Frederick had practically bankrupted himself in the war with Russia and could not afford to pay for the large collection of 225 paintings assembled for him by Johann Gotzkowsky in Berlin. His ego was severely bruised when Catherine purchased the collection from Gotzkowsky, and with it began to create the famous Hermitage.

Foreign policy became the most brilliant aspect of Catherine's statesmanship. From the beginning of her reign, she controlled all areas of foreign policy, adhering to Peter the Great's three-point doctrine: (1) secure access to the Black Sea; (2) expand westwards and annex the western Slavic territories; and (3) defend the

LEFT

Carlo Bartolomeo Rastrelli, the highly-talented Florentine sculptor, moved to St Petersburg in 1715, where he spent the rest of his life. This bust of Emperor Peter I is his most famous piece. Peter the Great is represented as a great warrior. On the left is a representation of the Classical sculptor Pygmalion carving the figure of Galatea, intended to be read as Peter creating a wonderful new Russia.

Carlo Bartolomeo Rastrelli
(1675–1744)

CATALOGUE NO. 154

northern territories and, of course, St Petersburg. It was Catherine II who succeeded on all three fronts and achieved the goals that Peter the Great had set at the beginning of the century.

A series of spectacular victories in the Russian-Turkish wars of 1768–74 and 1787–92 made it possible to annex the Crimea and the Northern Caucasus to Russia. Thus the empire firmly established itself in the Black Sea region.

The 1772 and 1793 partitions of Poland, which Russia carried out with Prussia and Austria, resulted in the annexation of the West Slavonic territories to Russia and the expansion of its western borders. Catherine's former favourite, Stanislaw August Poniatowski, had already become her henchman on the Polish throne, and was crowned under the name of Stanislaw II. He did not even try to create independent policies and was a puppet in Catherine's hands. She used to jokingly refer to him as her 'wax doll'.

Finally, Russia was victorious over the Swedes, who threatened St Petersburg during the Russian-Swedish War of 1789–90.

Catherine was by nature a realist and a pragmatist. Yet her vanity and personal ambition, well known in Europe, sometimes dictated her moves. The Austrian Emperor Joseph II once wrote to Prince Kaunitz: 'We should not forget that we are dealing with a woman who cares as little about the welfare of Russia as I do: what she needs is flattery. Ambition is her idol; success and servility have spoilt her.'[16]

A consequence of her vanity were political fantasies detached from real life, such as the Greek Project, which Catherine hoped would change the map of Europe under the banner of protecting Christian nations from the oppression of the Turks. The project was conceived and developed by the Empress herself and her chancellor, Alexander Bezborodko. The main goal of the anticipated 'Christian Alliance' was the restoration of the Greek Empire, headed by the ruler of Russia. Voltaire, continually flattering his royal student, supported the Empress and told her that he had dreamt of seeing her as the 'mistress of Constantinople'. Catherine's plans were based on Russia and Austria's historically difficult relations with Turkey and their military confrontation on the shores of the Black and Caspian Seas. According to plans negotiated by the Empress and the Emperor Joseph II, Russia and Austria would establish the independent buffer state of Dacia, which would include the territories of Bessarabia, Moldavia and Wallachia, and expand their own territories by absorbing Turkish borderlands. If they were able to accomplish this, they would then go on to expel the

Turks from Constantinople and resurrect a Greek Empire, which would be completely dependent on Russia.

Catherine envisaged her second grandson, Constantine, as the head of this new empire. Born in 1779, the Grand Duke was named after the Byzantine Emperor Constantine the Great. The announcement of his birth stated that he was expected to increase the glory and power of Russia. The boy was given a Greek nanny, was taught Greek, and a medal in his honour was produced showing Hagia Sophia in Constantinople and the Black Sea. Catherine wrote in one of her letters to Joseph II: 'These proposals may appear formidable and overly bold … but given the close alliance between our two countries, almost anything can be accomplished'.[17]

Although the disagreements between Catherine and the Austrian Emperor prevented the realization of the project, Catherine never abandoned her dream. In her will, drawn up in 1792, she once again reiterated her intention to put the Grand Duke Constantine Pavlovich on the throne of the 'Greek Empire of the East'.

According to Charles Masson, towards the end of her life Catherine liked to repeat: 'I came to Russia poor, but settled my accounts with the state: Tauride [the Crimea] and Poland is the dowry I am leaving it with.'[18] Despite the fact that her foreign policy was overtly expansionist, it certainly helped to raise Russia's prestige in the international arena.

At the start of her reign, Catherine did not entirely understand the true state of affairs in Russia, but she nonetheless planned radically to reform virtually all areas of state and public life, following the example of Peter the Great and inspired by the ideas of the Enlightenment. However, the domestic problems turned out to be much more complex than she expected.

In her manifesto, dated 6 July 1762, the new Empress promised her subjects the rule of law in public life and the elimination of the arbitrariness that characterized the reign of Peter III. She acted boldly in announcing the creation of a new Code of Laws of the Russian Empire. This was meant to embody the idea of the supremacy of law in the spirit of the French Enlightenment. A Commission of elected delegates from all classes of Russian society was set up to draft it. For the Commission's first meeting in July 1767, Catherine wrote her 'Nakaz' ('Instruction') to guide the delegates. The Empress had spent two years compiling this document, drawing on Montesquieu's famous *L'Esprit des lois* and works by other figures of the Enlightenment.

The main thrust of the 'Instruction' was the need for laws that would support autocratic rule and embrace all areas of life. However, the main articles of the Empress's treatise regarding changing the existing order, abolishing serfdom in Russia, creating an autocratic state based on the rule of law and ensuring the equality of all citizens under the law, were ahead of their time and took insufficient account of the reality of 18th-century Russia. The nobility strongly resisted these tenets, and the delegates were unable to compromise on a single issue. Appreciating the discontent of the nobility and the very real danger of alienating them, Catherine quickly terminated the activities of the Commission, disbanded it in 1768, and withdrew her 'Nakaz' from circulation. Despite the failure of the reform, many articles in the 'Instruction' played a truly prominent role in the history of Russian social thinking.

Catherine's later domestic policies were directed at strengthening absolutism, expanding the privileges of the nobility and reinforcing serfdom. It was during her reign that 800,000 free peasants were put into bondage, which directly contradicted one of the principal statements of the 'Nakaz', regarding the abolition of serfdom in Russia, and all the ideals of the Enlightenment. In her domestic policies, Catherine completely abandoned the essentially idealistic theories of the French philosophers, and became much more realistic and pragmatic. Visiting St Petersburg in 1773, Diderot asked why the Empress was in no hurry to put his recommendations into practice and received the reply:

> *Your elevated good ideas are good for filling books with, but bad for carrying them out. When drafting various plans of reforms, you forget the difference between our situations. You work on paper, which can suffer anything, while I, poor empress, toil for mere mortals who are extremely sensitive and volatile.*[19]

Catherine II's firm and consistent domestic policies generated truly brilliant results. Despite internal disturbances, such as those associated with the Cossack rebellion of 1773–74 led by Yemelyan Pugachëv, who claimed to be the miraculously resurrected Emperor Peter III, Catherine's thirty-four-year reign was a unique period of political stability in Russian Imperial history. Even Catherine's most vehement critics agree on this point. That said, stability did not mean stagnation.

Catherine II was possibly 'the most successful Russian reformer'.[20] It is daunting even to try to list her principal legislative initiatives and reforms. However, her key reforms include the statutes of 1785, the Charter (or Decree) of the Nobility and the Charter of Cities. The Charter of the Nobility recognized all the rights and privileges of the nobility as a ruling class and exempted them from compulsory military service. But it also called on them to unite into so-called assemblies of the nobility and urged them to promote the development of provinces, which had been the subject of other legislation on the new territorial division of the country. As one would expect, no mention was made of the hugely problematic issue of serfdom.

The Charter of Cities granted city residents a new social status as members of the middle class, thereby distinguishing them from the peasantry. This encouraged the development of the country's economy and culture, as well as the rapid growth of its cities.

Not only did Catherine's legislative activities prove effective, but also durable. For instance, she introduced a new structure for local government, which lasted for a hundred years, while the new administrative-territorial division of the country remained unchanged until the collapse of the Russian Empire in 1917. Conversely, compared to general trends in European countries at the time, Catherine II's political activities were clearly conservative, and quite at odds with the ideology of the Enlightenment.

The cult of Peter the Great prevailed in 18th-century Russia. Catherine began fully to understand the true significance of Peter I for Russia at the court of the Empress Elizabeth, and each new emperor swore to protect Russia's national interests and to continue the policies of Peter I. It had been sufficient for Elizabeth to be the daughter of the great colossus to carry out her successful *coup d'état*. Catherine II naturally expressed her admiration and veneration of Peter; worshipping the wrong hero had, after all, cost her husband both his crown and his life. But Catherine had every right to consider herself Peter's heir and successor, as she deliberately continued and completed his policies of increasing Russia's influence, promoting economic growth and advancing the arts and sciences. Peter the Great was her icon and role model. According to the Prince of Ligne, Catherine always wore a ring with Peter's portrait and had a snuff-box with his image, in order to maintain his constant presence.[21]

Peter I and Catherine II considered themselves to be servants of the state and, unlike other Russian rulers of the 18th century, pursued a dynamic state policy of reform and transformation, rather than simply enjoying the benefits of their privileged positions. Neither settled for short-term advantages, but focused on political and patriotic programmes which would lead to very major gains for Russia over decades and generations. For both rulers, the success of their reforms was directly linked to the need to develop the sciences and arts, improve the educational system, and promote social programmes and trade. Peter addressed these issues through his well-known 'Europeanization' of Russia, while Catherine was guided by contemporary theories of the Enlightenment.

Both Peter and Catherine took it upon themselves to teach their subjects, and were looked up to as role models. They both regarded the chief source of misfortune and evil as idleness and were extremely hard workers. Legend has it that Peter only slept a few hours a night, and considered his lathe shop the best form of relaxation. His personal interests were truly encyclopaedic, with active interest in the sciences, shipbuilding, medicine, architecture. He studied drawing and engraving, wrote a history of the Great Northern War, engaged in collecting, and founded the first Russian museum. For breadth of interest and exceptional daily productivity, only Catherine II can be compared with Peter the Great.

The best expression of the invisible but strong ties between the two great monarchs is the bronze equestrian monument to Peter I, which was commissioned by Catherine and finally unveiled in St Petersburg in 1782. The French sculptor Etienne-Maurice Falconet spent almost ten years completing the famous 'Bronze Horseman'. On the sides of the enormous granite pedestal is the remarkable, short inscription, 'To Peter I from Catherine II', in both Russian and Latin.

In a letter to her correspondent in Paris, Baron Friedrich Melchior Grimm, Catherine wrote that she worked like a horse. Her secretary, Adrian Gribovsky, described her daily schedule when she was sixty-six years old: she would get up at seven o'clock in the morning, drink strong coffee, and then proceed to write in her office until nine. From nine until noon she would listen to reports; at two she would have lunch, then sort out her correspondence and read. Receptions at the Hermitage would start at six and last until about ten; occasionally guests were invited to the Empress's private rooms. Attendance at court theatre was one of the evening rituals, but Catherine would generally retire to bed around eleven.

Catherine had various interests. As she considered herself a disciple of the French Enlightenment, she devoted a lot of attention to developing the arts, sciences and culture, and was patron to many architects, artists, sculptors, poets, writers and scientists. The authoritarian nature of her power allowed her to employ various art forms and architecture to demonstrate her power and glorify her reign. Part of her policy was to patronize the arts and project the image of herself as an 'enlightened monarch'. In 1766, early in her reign, Catherine explained her intentions: 'I am building, I will build, and will encourage others to build, I will promote the sciences and will have theatre performances …'.[22]

The same year, 1766, saw the first public performances in St Petersburg, during Catherine's reign, of the so-called 'carousels', which continued the tradition of the public masquerade festivals of the reigns of Peter the Great and the Empress Elizabeth. Similar carousels were organized in Germany and France in the 17th and 18th centuries. In June and July 1766, carousels and masquerade contests in the spirit of medieval jousting were held in the square in front of the Winter Palace, where a wooden amphitheatre with lodges for spectators was constructed. The carousel included four teams – Slavic, Roman, Turkish and Indian. Catherine headed the Slavic team, whilst Aleksey and Grigory Orlov headed the Turkish and the Indian teams respectively. Each team had more than a hundred cavalry and infantry participants: knights on horseback, ladies in chariots, musicians and retinue. Gentlemen competed in horse fights, ladies and gentlemen hurled spears at cardboard targets of tigers and bears, while galloping knights beheaded dummies representing Moors. The programme included a costume competition of bejewelled participants wearing stylized historical dresses studded with precious stones. The competitions culminated in an awards ceremony, at which winners received gold medals and jewels. These were followed by a masquerade in the Summer Palace.

Catherine's carousels were extremely successful. Crowds of people came to witness the cavalcades marching towards the amphitheatre, with curious spectators thronging onto the rooftops. Such festivals were carefully prepared and helped to divert attention from the recent *coup*.

* * *

Catherine loved and understood architecture. She closely followed the work of contemporary European

architects, and collected architectural drawings, books and albums about architecture. The most distinguished European architects would send their portfolios to Russia and many received an invitation to St Petersburg. Building took up a significant portion of Catherine's time. She compared her hobby to a fever, often saying 'the more I build, the more I want to build'. The scale of construction was enormous, particularly in St Petersburg and the royal residences surrounding the capital.

In order to streamline and centralize urban construction in Russia, Catherine established the Commission for Stone Construction of St Petersburg and Moscow, which supervised more than 300 architectural and planning projects in the capital and elsewhere in Russia. All were examined and approved by the Empress herself. Under Catherine II, the rich and sumptuous Baroque was replaced by Classicism, with its noble simplicity and quiet grandeur inspired by Antiquity. The buildings and planned areas by Giacomo Quarenghi, Charles Cameron, Antonio Rinaldi, Yury Velten and Ivan Starov largely determined the appearance of modern St Petersburg.

Catherine's passion for books and her daily literary activities led to the creation of a huge private library of around 40,000 books by Russian and foreign authors. Catherine paid particular attention to collecting ancient Russian chronicles and manuscripts, which were delivered to the Winter Palace from all parts of Russia. This was invaluable material for studying Russian history: it enabled the Empress to learn more, and also underlined her deep commitment to Russia. It is interesting to note that Catherine herself assembled libraries for specific purposes, such as for ships setting out to travel round the world. She loved to work a lathe, and to engrave cameos and bone. Collecting cameos was the Empress's passion, which, like her architecture, she likened to a 'fever' or 'sickness'.

Catherine II was one of those European monarchs for whom creative writing was not just a fashionable pastime, but a pleasure and necessity. She often said that she could not behold a pen and a blank piece of paper without feeling an urge to write. It would have been as difficult for Catherine to do without a pen and a book as for Peter the Great to renounce his axe and lathe.[23] In letters to her correspondents, Catherine referred to her creative writing as a diversion. Although written by an amateur, some of her works merit attention. She wrote about thirty plays, as well as a series of articles, pamphlets and short stories. The exact number of Catherine's literary writings is unknown because she wrote in both Russian and French, and some of her writings were published abroad. In addition, the Empress's literary works were always anonymous or published under a pseudonym, often that of a man. Although Catherine called her works 'trifles' and did not attach much importance to them, she followed the reactions of her readers like a hawk. She often entered into polemics with her opponents, who were aware that she was the author of the anonymous publications.

The start of the Empress's literary activities is associated with several journals that she founded, but she soon became bored with journalism. Just like Peter I, this enlightened monarch undertook the mission of educating her subjects, this time in the spirit of the Enlightenment. Several of Catherine's works developed Enlightenment ideas about education, such as the fairy-tales *The Tale of Tsarevich Khlor* (1781) and *The Tale of Tsarevich Fevey* (1782). She wrote these tales and her *Notes on Russian History* for her grandsons, Alexander and Constantine, in whose education she took a personal interest and for whom she collected an entire school library.

Among Catherine's most successful literary works are the historical plays about the first Russian princes: *From the History of Rurik* and *The Beginning of Oleg's Rule*, which has the subtitle *A Pastiche of Shakespeare*. Her literary activities display a remarkable range and a breadth of subject matter. They reflect not only her thorough knowledge of world history, but also her familiarity with the literature of the past and of contemporary authors. Despite many of Catherine's writings being imitative and often interpreting the works of ancient and European authors, they are certainly engaging and clever. Her language is simple and close to the spoken idiom, intentionally avoiding contemporary 'elevated style'. This simplicity is particularly evident in the Empress's writings about Russian history. She often used Russian proverbs, sayings, legends, lore and fairy-tales, combining them with information drawn from chronicles and works by contemporary historians.

Theatrical plays and comedies were Catherine's favourite forms of literary expression and were usually written in the style of contemporary French drama, with which she was well acquainted. As a rule, her plays have a didactic character and expose the morals and evils of Russian society – such as bigotry, superstition, the lure of fashion, ignorance, and the like. Catherine also incorporated political satire and ridiculed Russia's hapless enemies. Her most successful comedy was *The Misfortunate Hero*, where the main anti-hero was represented as the Swedish King Gustav III, whom Catherine openly mocked in real life and in her letters.

Catherine devoted three comedies – *The Impostor*, *The Siberian Shaman* and *Seduced* – to deriding Freemasonry. She had always rejected Freemasonry, which was becoming increasingly widespread in Russia, and members of secret societies were the subject of her constant mockery. The Empress was familiar with Masonic literature, and declared the doctrines to be complete quackery and folly.

Many of Catherine's works were staged at the court theatre, where the actors were often her courtiers and favourites.

Catherine II's literary works have been praised by historians. For example, Kliuchevsky has written: 'German by birth, French through her beloved language and education, she occupies a prominent place among Russian writers of the 18th century.'[24] It is hard to think of any other monarch with so many publications to his or her credit.

To disseminate the progressive ideas of her mentors in the Enlightenment, Catherine set up a programme to translate the principal works of the French writers into Russian. This work involved teachers and students of Moscow University. Thus, Rousseau, Voltaire and Montesquieu were rendered into Russian, and the translation of the *Encyclopédie*, along with other works, was begun.

Catherine's role in the development and study of the Russian language cannot be overestimated. Here, too, the Empress continued the endeavours of Peter I, who had instituted reforms in grammar and spelling. From the earliest years of her life in Russia, Catherine spent much time and effort learning the Russian language. Although she never eliminated her German accent and made mistakes when writing, Catherine spoke good colloquial Russian. She often used Russian proverbs and sayings in both her conversation and writings. In 1783, the Russian Academy was founded in St Petersburg and became a hub for the study of the Russian language. Among its members were the most prominent writers of the time, such as the poet Gavriil Derzhavin and the playwright Denis Fonvizin. Princess Ekaterina Romanovna Dashkova, an active participant in the *coup* of 1762, was appointed President, and between 1789 and 1794 the Academy compiled and published the first dictionary of the Russian language.

Catherine kept a close eye on many educational institutions, and recognized the particular importance of the Academy of Sciences and the Academy of Arts in the development of national culture. It was during her reign that the national school of painting and sculpture emerged and the decorative arts flourished. An

A miniature of Princess Ekaterina Romanovna Dashkova from a notebook, made in Paris by goldsmith Jean-Jacques Prevost, *c.*1765. The miniature was painted in Britain in 1770.

Miniature by Ozias Humphry (1742–1810)

CATALOGUE NO. 48

important aspect of the Empress's activities was collecting works of art and creating the Hermitage. The Empress's artistic agents, including Count Ivan Shuvalov, Prince Golitsyn, Baron Grimm, Denis Diderot and Johann Friedrich Reiffenstein, acquired not only individual works of art but also entire collections of paintings, drawings and engraved gemstones. The enormous scale of these acquisitions – and the vast amounts of money spent on them – astonished her contemporaries.

In addition to art, Catherine acquired manuscripts and the entire libraries of the greatest philosophers and scientists of Europe and Russia. Her most famous acquisitions include the libraries of the French philosophers Diderot and Voltaire. When purchasing Diderot's library, Catherine allowed him free use of it during his life, appointed him her librarian, and paid him a salary. After Voltaire's death, the Empress added his library to the Imperial collection. She also planned to build an exact replica of Voltaire's home, the château of Ferney in Switzerland, on her great country estate at Tsarskoye Selo, but this unique project was never carried out.

During Catherine's reign, the Russian court was transformed into one of the most impressive in Europe. It was elegant, intellectual and known for its European refinement. However, the fashionable ideas of the Enlightenment co-existed with unprecedented luxury and extravagance. The English traveller, Reverend William Coxe, wrote in 1778:

> *The Russian court retains many traces of its Asiatic pomp, blended with European refinement. An immense retinue of courtiers always preceded and followed the empress; the costliness of their apparel and a profusion of precious stones, created a splendour, of which the magnificence of other courts can give us only a faint idea.*[25]

Card games, masquerades, music and theatrical performances were popular pastimes.

Catherine took a special interest in the court theatre and devoted much time developing the theatrical arts in Russia. It was during her reign that the Bolshoi Theatre was constructed in St Petersburg, and the Theatre School was founded. The Winter Palace Theatre and later the Hermitage Theatre, built for Catherine by Giacomo Quarenghi, staged operas, ballets, tragedies and comedies, and hosted performances of the best European musicians, as well as theatre troupes from England, Germany, Italy and France. Although Catherine was not fond of French drama, it was plays by Molière, Beaumarchais and Marivaux that enjoyed the greatest success in St Petersburg. The Russian troupe of the court theatre staged works by Russian writers and playwrights, such as Sumarokov, Fonvizin and Kheraskov.

Opera occupied a special place in the repertoire of the court theatre and Russian theatres in general. Preference was given to Italian works; Cimarosa, Sarti and Paisiello were the most popular composers, but operas by Mozart and Gluck were also performed.

Chamber concerts, operas and ballet were an obligatory part of court life, even though Catherine herself did not like music and had to be given a sign when to applaud. Her contemporaries often noted this peculiarity. Charles Masson writes:

> *Catherine did not like either poetry or music, and often talked about this. During interludes she could not stand hearing the musicians play and usually ordered them to remain quiet. This lack of sensitivity in a woman so richly endowed in other respects seems a surprising shortcoming. It helps explain why Catherine, who possessed such intelligence and had such a range of interests, could also be dispassionate and cruel.*[26]

Catherine II's personal life has drawn most of the fire of her contemporaries and subsequent generations. All her life, she was surrounded by favourites, who played a much greater role in her life and politics than her son and heir, the Grand Duke Paul. Catherine displayed little affection for her son and even regarded him with apprehension – possibly his character and interests reminded her too much of her unloved husband. Barred from public affairs, Paul in turn had no love for his mother, and feared her. The birth of her grandsons, Alexander in 1777 and Constantine in 1779, delighted Catherine. Just like the Empress Elizabeth, she took the boys away from their parents, and raised and educated them herself, proclaiming that a brilliant future lay ahead of them.

Favouritism, for which Catherine has so often been criticized, was certainly not limited to the Russian court and, in this respect, she merely embodied the spirit of her time. In her *Sincere Confession*, she confided: 'I have no inclination for libertinism, and if fate had given me a husband I could have loved, I would have been forever loyal to him.'[27] In relationships with her favourites she always knew how to draw on both their strengths and their weaknesses, successfully avoiding embarrassing situations. The most troublesome problem for the Empress was Count Grigory Orlov's insistent demand that she marry him in gratitude for his key role in the 1762 palace *coup*. Manoeuvring between political factions, Catherine brilliantly responded to this by passing the decision to the State Council. Count Nikita Panin assisted her by declaring: 'The Empress is free to do as she pleases, but Mrs Orlova will never be the Empress of Russia.'[28] The Council agreed with Panin, which helped Catherine put an end to the claims of the powerful Orlov brothers.

In 1774, Catherine secretly married Count Grigory Potemkin, whom she had always liked and respected. Compared to the Empress's other favourites, Potemkin was an outstanding statesman and was involved in practically all the Empress's major projects. As a talented military leader and strategist, Potemkin was one of the few figures in Catherine's entourage whom she could not only trust, but also receive very substantial support. In 1791, Catherine was prostrated by his sudden death and tearfully admitted that 'now all the burdens of rule rest on me alone'.[29]

In the 1790s, Catherine's health deteriorated. She put on weight, had difficulty breathing, and walked with difficulty. However, she continued working. Catherine usually spent her summers at her beloved Tsarskoye Selo. She strolled around the palace park with her favourite dogs. She dressed simply and preferred spacious, comfortable clothing, resembling the Russian sarafan, which concealed her obesity. The French painter Élisabeth Louis Vigée Le Brun recalled the Empress a year before her death:

> *I was struck by how short she was, I had imagined her as grand as her glory. She was very full-bodied, but still had a beautiful face, which her lifted white hair admirably framed. The mark of genius prevailed on her broad and rather high brow, her eyes were tender and penetrating, her nose truly Greek, her complexion extremely lively, and the overall expression of her face very animated.*[30]

Catherine II died in 1796 at the age of sixty-seven. In the playful epitaph she composed on the eve of her fiftieth birthday, she summed up her life's journey and character thus:

> *Here lies Catherine II, born in Stettin on April 21, 1729. She came to Russia in 1744 to marry Peter III. At the age of fourteen, she conceived a threefold resolution to please her husband, Elizabeth, and the nation. She neglected nothing in trying to achieve this. Eighteen years of boredom*

and loneliness gave her the opportunity to read many books. When she came to the Russian throne, she wished to do what was good for her country and tried to bring happiness, freedom, and prosperity to her subjects. She forgave easily and hated no one. She was merciful, courteous, cheerful by nature, she had a republican spirit, kind heart, and friends. Work came to her with ease, she loved arts and enjoyed being sociable.[31]

NOTES

1. Russian Archive, 1911, vol. 2, no. 5, pp. 4–6.
2. V. O. Kliuchevsky, *Historical Portraits* (Moscow, 1990), p. 258.
3. E. Donnert, *Catherine the Great. Her Personality and Epoch* (St Petersburg, 2003), p. 58.
4. Kliuchevsky, p. 260.
5. L. F. Ségur, 'Notes about a Stay in Russia during Catherine II's Reign', in *Eighteenth-century Russia through the Eyes of Foreigners* (Leningrad, 1989), pp. 317–18.
6. V. P. Naumov, 'Elizabeth Petrovna', *Problems in History*, 1993, no. 5, p. 59.
7. *The Memoirs of Empress Catherine II* (St Petersburg, 1907), p. 58.
8. Donnert, p. 73.
9. G. Brikner, *The History of Catherine II* (Moscow, 1998), p. 64.
10. E. V. Anisimov, *Russia in the Mid-Eighteenth Century. The Battle for the Legacy of Peter I* (Moscow, 1986), p. 219.
11. S. Mylnikov, *Tempted by a Miracle: 'The Russian Prince', His Prototypes and Doubles or Impostors* (Leningrad, 1991), pp. 90–91.
12. *Collection of the Russian Imperial Historical Society*, vol. 12, 1873, p. 334.
13. A. S. Pushkin, *Diaries. Autobiographical Prose* (Moscow, 1989), p. 85.
14. Russian Archives, 1906, vol. 2, p. 113.
15. E. V. Anisimov, *Women on the Russian Throne* (St Petersburg, 1997), p. 358.
16. E. N. Guslyarov, *Catherine II in Person* (Moscow, 2004), p. 269.
17. Brikner, p. 402.
18. C. Masson, *Secret Notes about Russia* (Moscow, 1996), p. 33.
19. *Catherine II and G. A. Potemkin. Personal Correspondence, 1769–91* (Moscow, 1997), p. 478.
20. A. Kamensky, *In Catherine's Shadow* (St Petersburg, 1992), p. 430.
21. C. J. de Ligne, 'Portrait of Catherine II', in *Catherine II as Remembered by Her Contemporaries and Judged by Historians* (Moscow, 1998), p. 261.
22. *Collection of the Russian Historical Society*, vol. 12, 1873, p. 334.
23. Kliuchevsky, p. 279.
24. Ibid.
25. 'Russia One Hundred Years Ago: The Journey of William Coxe', *Old Times in Russia*, vol. 19, 1877, p. 30.
26. Masson, p. 52.
27. Ibid: *Catherine II and G. A. Potemkin. Personal Correspondence, 1769–91*, p. 478.
28. Guslyarov, p. 222.
29. Russian Archives, 1787, vol. 3, p. 199.
30. 'Madame Vigée-Lebrun in Russia. Excerpts from Her Memoirs', *Old and New Russia*, 1876, no. 10, p. 189.
31. *Collection of the Russian Historical Society*, vol. 23, 1873, p. 77.

CHAPTER II

'The Glory of Russia is my Glory'

YURY EFIMOV

OPPOSITE

Rokotov's portrait is a version of the large portrait of Catherine by the Swedish artist Alexander Roslin. Catherine's gesture with the sceptre towards the bust of Peter the Great, with an inscription stating that she was 'completing that which was begun', drove home the message that Catherine was continuing the work of Peter the Great.

Fedor Stepanovich Rokotov (1732/35–1808)

CATALOGUE NO. 93

I desire and wish only good for this country, where the Lord has brought me; He is my witness in this. The glory of the country creates my glory. Here is my rule: I will be happy if my 'Thoughts' encourage this …

So wrote Princess Sophie Frederica Augusta of Anhalt-Zerbst in her *Thoughts from a Special Book*. Fate destined her to rule the largest country in the world for thirty-four years, and she became known as Catherine the Great.

It is not easy to list all the things Catherine did for the benefit and prosperity of Russia. She commenced her reign with a noble attempt to improve living standards in the country, and established a home for foundlings where they would be brought up to become independent citizens able to benefit their homeland. Over the course of her long reign, she would play a crucial central role in the improvement of industry and agriculture, the establishment and reform of state institutions, the development of new army and navy policies, health care, education and law, and the advancement of science, literature and art.

Posterity evaluates the activities of any ruler by two criteria – their domestic policies and the political weight and influence of the country in the international arena. The interests of the state were the cornerstone of Catherine II's policy. She appreciated the achievements and policies of her mighty predecessor of the early 18th century, Peter the Great, and was keen to continue and complete his work.

Times had changed, however, and Catherine was dealing with another generation of people, while Russia was facing a new epoch with different political accents. However, the Empress's main political aims were those laid down by Peter the Great, and that is why, by the end of her reign, Russia had become one of the most powerful European states, whose opinion was taken notice of world-wide.

Catherine came to power in a troubled country, just as Peter the Great had done. After the devastating Seven Years War (1756–63), the country's finances were depleted, the army went unpaid, the fleet had become dilapidated, trade was in decline, 'justice was sold and laws observed only when they were in favour of those in power', and the public sector was disorganized. Catherine realized it was necessary to reform the country, and she believed that it should be reformed in the modern spirit of liberalism and the Enlightenment.

The new Empress thought of herself as a disciple of the French Enlightenment philosophers. She corresponded with Denis Diderot and Voltaire, and aspired to put some of their ideas into practice and correlate them with Russian reality. She did everything to become an 'enlightened' monarch in whom the figures of the Enlightenment could put their trust. At the same time, Catherine sought to maintain her unlimited autocratic rule, believing that it could assist her in transforming Russia in accordance with the spirit of the Enlightenment. While historians may interpret the results of Catherine II's domestic policies as being somewhat ambiguous, her foreign policies constitute some of the most brilliant pages in the history of her reign.

From the very beginning, Catherine II was actively involved in guiding foreign policies, and focused on the key issues herself. After the unexpected decision of Russia to withdraw its troops from Prussia in the Seven Years War, her priority was to resuscitate and strengthen the international prestige of her country. This task engendered a new direction of policy aimed at establishing a separate and independent role for Russia in Europe. Catherine never attempted merely to imitate any of her predecessors or contemporaries. Her achievement was the ability to understand the long-standing issues of Russia's foreign policy. Thus she became a direct successor to Peter the Great, and successfully continued and completed his goal of establishing the Russian Empire as a world power by the end of her reign.

But these were very different days and Catherine acted in the spirit of her times. While Peter the Great travelled Europe-wide to meet the heads of European states and scientists, Catherine invited them to visit her in Russia, which she would not leave. King Gustav III of Sweden, Emperor Joseph II of Austria, King Stanislaw Poniatowski of Poland, Diderot and many other distinguished individuals, all came to visit her in Russia.

Like Peter, however, Catherine recognized three main facets of Russia's foreign policy. The first involved its dealings with the North, with Sweden and Scandinavia and access out into the North Sea. The Swedes were constantly attempting to reclaim the land they had lost during Peter the Great's reign. Swedish power, however, had declined during the reign of their king, Charles XII. After the Great Northern War (1700–21), the country had lost its domination of the Baltic Sea and could not recover its economic and human resources to the level that it could wage a successful war against Russia. Nevertheless, there were those in Stockholm who were determined to pursue these aspirations. In 1741, under preassure from France and England, Sweden confronted Russia in an attempt to reclaim its lost territories. Although a treaty was concluded in 1743, the situation did not change. Despite improved relations, the Swedes continued to contemplate revenge and the return of the territories lost during the Great Northern War.

In 1788, Gustav III of Sweden, having received the promise of Turkish subsidies and diplomatic support from England and Prussia, committed a violation of the peace treaty concluded with Russia in 1743 and began military operations in the Baltic and Finland. However, the Swedish army was not fully mobilized, nor was its combat capability on a par with that of the troops of Charles XII eighty years earlier. Furthermore, Gustav's leadership left much to be desired. Despite some successes, the Swedes failed to achieve their goal and signed the Treaty of Varala, agreeing to the status quo. Catherine the Great had managed to retain the territories that Peter the Great had conquered and, importantly, Russia's access to the Baltic and North Seas.

In the south of Russia, access to the Black Sea was deemed vital for Russia's economy and defence, and was thus a long-standing dream of the Russian rulers. Peter the Great started the Russian-Turkish War, having captured the fortress of Azov in 1696. However, expansion in the south was not his priority. The unsuccessful Prut Campaign of 1711 against the Ottoman Empire in Moldavia did not affect the overall direction of Russian foreign policy.

By the beginning of Catherine's reign, the Ottoman Empire had fallen into decline, and many European powers were keeping a watchful eye on its territories. Russia was prospering and its army and navy were among the strongest in Europe. As fear of the Ottoman Empire dwindled, cautious defensive tactics were replaced by large-scale offensive operations, and people were confident of a speedy victory over the once-formidable enemy. When Catherine came to power and continued Peter the Great's policy, she prioritized Russia's southern expansion. In 1768, pushed by France, Turkey declared war on Russia. However, it was the Russian army that was victorious. In the spring of 1769, Russian troops occupied Azov and Taganrog and later overcame two large Turkish regiments near Khotin. On 24–26 June 1770, the Russian navy, under the command of Count Aleksey Orlov and Admiral Grigory Spiridov, won a tremendous victory over a Turkish fleet twice its size at the battle of Chesme, between mainland Turkey and the island of Chios. A month later, General Pyotr Rumyantsev defeated a Turkish army of 150,000 men by the Kagul River. Between July and October, the fortresses of Ismail, Kiliya, Akkerman and Bender were captured. The following year, forces under General Vasily Dolgorukov occupied the Crimea.

Despite such favourable developments, the war was still a heavy burden for Russia, and as early as 1770 the government was contemplating ways of concluding a treaty. In 1774, Russia and Turkey signed the Treaty of Kuchuk Kainardzhi, obliging Turkey to grant autonomy to Wallachia and Moldavia (which still remained under its control) and to pay St Petersburg a large sum. Russia gained the ports of Kerch and Enikale, and the right of free passage through the Dardanelles and Bosphorus – of key importance to the country's development. Turkey also recognized the independence of the Crimea, which facilitated its annexation to Russia in the future.

If it had not been for the Cossack rebellion headed by Yemelyan Pugachëv, which forced the Empress to sign the peace treaty as soon as possible, the treaty conditions could have been arranged even more advantageously for Russia. Pugachëv's rebellion broke out in 1773–74 and spread over the vast areas of southern and central Russia, down to the Ural Mountains and Western Siberia, frightening Catherine so much that considerable military forces led by top leaders, including Alexander Suvorov, were gathered to suppress it. Twenty infantry and cavalry regiments were withdrawn from the army operating against the Turks, and in 1775 the rebellion was completely suppressed.

The subsequent strengthening of Catherine II's power contributed to the development of a new foreign policy doctrine embodied in the so-called 'Greek Project', which was undoubtedly one of the most ambitious ideas ever put forward by the Empress. In spite of the fact that it remained largely unrealized, the Greek Project continued to play a crucial role in Russian cultural and intellectual life for several decades. Its goal was to restore the Byzantine empire, to liberate Constantinople (Istanbul) and the Orthodox peoples from Turkish domination and to re-establish the Greek Empire. Tsar Aleksey Mikhailovich (reigned 1645–76), Peter the Great (1682–1725), and the Empresses Anna Ivanovna (1730–40) and Elizabeth Petrovna (1741–61), all dreamed of releasing Christian nations subjugated by Turkey, seizing Constantinople and reviving the Greek Empire. During Catherine's reign this idea was becoming more than a mere dream; it was a very real possibility. However, even though Russian troops operated successfully on land and at sea, taking Constantinople was impossible without allies.

For this reason, Catherine initiated a rapprochement with Austria, and an informal meeting between her and Joseph II took place in Mogilev, Belorussia, in 1780 to lay the foundation for a future alliance between the two powers. The project seemed so real that Voltaire wrote to Catherine: 'I beg your Majesty's permission to come and spend a few days at Your court as soon as it is transferred to Constantinople, and I sincerely believe that if the Turks are ever to be banished from Europe, this will be done by the Russians.'

Implementation of the Greek Project – the partition of Turkey and the formation of the Greek Empire – would have ensured the hegemony of the Russian fleet in the Mediterranean, while the liberation of the Greeks and significant weakening of the Ottoman Empire would have made Russia the most powerful nation in the Middle East and Eastern Europe. Prince Grigory Potemkin was an advocate of the Project, and ideas that he developed during the First Russian-Turkish War of 1768–74 complemented Catherine's strategic plans.

Catherine's second grandson, Constantine Pavlovich, became a symbol of the Greek Project. The Grand Duke, born in April 1779, even received his name after the Roman Emperor Constantine, who converted to Christianity and founded Constantinople, in accordance with his grandmother's ambitious plan. Greek poetry was read at his birthday celebrations, and a medal was minted with an image of the former cathedral of Hagia Sophia in Constantinople, which had been turned into a mosque, with a cross instead of a crescent. Later on, Constantine was taught the Greek language, and Greek motifs became fashionable in art.

Catherine desired to turn Constantinople into the centre of a new Greek Empire, with Constantine Pavlovich as its ruler, on condition that he and his descendants would forever give up their claims to the Russian crown. The two neighbouring powers would thus be united by fraternal friendship under the sceptres of the 'Star of the North' and 'Star of the East' (that is, her grandsons, Alexander and Constantine). Needless to say, Russia would retain its role as the 'older brother' in this alliance. During the early 1780s, Catherine embarked on this plan, beginning with the annexation of the Crimea and Kuban in 1783.

The Crimea was important in its own right, as well as for the Greek Project, so Catherine travelled there in 1787. Her retinue comprised some 3000 people, amongst whom were the ambassadors of Britain,

France and Austria, and more than thirty senior Russian officials. During this journey the Empress also had a meeting with Stanisław Poniatowski of Poland and conducted negotiations with Joseph II of Austria.

In 1783, Turkey appeared to be staring at defeat and had signed an agreement with Russia which came close to declaring her consent to the annexation of the Crimea. But the balance of power changed when Russia's relations with Britain soured, and Turkey found itself in a position to acquire a new strong ally. Another war between Russia and Turkey broke out in July 1787, and the Russian ambassador Yakov Bulgakov found himself imprisoned in the Castle of the Seven Towers in Constantinople for two years.

In October 1787, the Turkish navy blockaded the mouth of the Dnieper River and landed 6000 troops on the Kinburn Spit, where they were destroyed by Russian troops under the command of General Suvorov. The main Russian forces, led by Potemkin, besieged the fortress of Ochakov, which fell in December 1788. Another Russian army, commanded by General Rumyantsev, crossed the Dniester River and entered Moldavia.

The following year saw Suvorov's rout of a much larger Turkish force at the battle of Fokshany in Moldavia, and the victory by the Rymnik River two months later. Russia's spectacular successes – the most outstanding of which were Suvorov's capture of the fortress of Ismail in 1790 and Fedor Ushakov's defeat of the Turkish navy off

BELOW

Assault on the Ismail Fortress by the Russian Army in December 1790.

Artist unknown (late 18th century)

CATALOGUE NO. 153

Cape Kaliakra in 1791 – forced the Turks to enter negotiations. A peace treaty was signed at Jassy, the capital of Moldavia, in December 1791. Turkey finally recognized the annexation of the Crimea to Russia, and a new border was established along the Dniester River. Turkey also abandoned its claims to Georgia. Thus, the Treaty of Jassy put an end to the 18th-century confrontation between Russia and Turkey. Although the war ended successfully for Russia, the Greek Project was never implemented.

The third facet of Catherine's foreign policy reflected the age-old aspiration to annex all the territories inhabited by closely-related Slavonic people – the Ukrainians and Belarusians – to the Russian Empire. Poland was going through turbulent times in the 18th century. Whilst its neighbours were developing their industry and trade, and establishing powerful armed forces and strong absolutist regimes, Poland could not overcome the inability of its magnates to sort out the country's political chaos and it fell easy prey to its neighbours, Prussia, Austria and Russia.

Poland became a toy in Catherine's hands when her protégé and former favourite, Stanislaw Poniatowski, was enthroned in Poland in 1764. However, Austria and Prussia were also keen to acquire Polish lands. Russian troops were therefore dispatched to Poland, and in a series of campaigns between 1768 and 1772 defeated Polish armies that had been formed with Austrian and Prussian support. On the suggestion of Austria and Prussia, who feared a Russian invasion of Poland, the First Partition of Poland took place in February 1772, which resulted in the country losing some of its strategically important border territories. Parts of the Baltic and Belorussia, with a population of 1,300,000 people, were annexed to Russia.

The events of 1768–72 led to the growth of patriotic sentiment in Polish society, which intensified after the outbreak of the French Revolution in 1789. The party of 'patriots' led by T. Kościuszko won victory in the Polish *Sejm* (parliament) over the pro-Russian party. Catherine II, occupied with the war with the

36

Ottoman Empire, could not provide any effective help to her supporters in Poland. On 3 May 1791, the *Sejm* approved the new constitution supported by Prussia, Sweden and Britain (that is, countries interested in deterring the further expansion of Russia).

The Second Russian-Turkish war being over, Catherine issued a protest on 18 May 1792 against the new Polish constitution and called on Poles to engage in civil disobedience. Russian troops subsequently entered Poland, defeated its militia and occupied Warsaw. Supporters of Russia declared all decrees of the *Sejm* null and void, after which the Prussian government entered into negotiations with Russia on a new partition of Poland. On 13 January 1793, Russia and Prussia signed a secret agreement on the Second Partition of Poland, according to which Russia received Belorussia, Eastern Polesia and the Right-Bank Ukraine, involving approximately 250,000 square kilometres. Russian garrisons were established in Warsaw and a few other Polish cities. As a consequence of the Second Partition, Poland's territory was reduced by half and the country became a Russian dependency.

In March 1794, a revolt headed by the Generals Kościuszko and Madalinski broke out in south-western Poland. The inhabitants of Warsaw and Vilna expelled Russian garrisons. However, the forces were unequal, and Prussian and then Austrian troops entered Poland in May. Until the summer of 1794, the rebels managed successfully to deter the interventionists, but in September, when the now Field Marshal Suvorov became head of the Russian army, the situation changed dramatically. Suvorov forced Warsaw to surrender and the Polish uprising was crushed.

In 1795, Russia, Austria and Prussia proceeded to the Third Partition of Poland. By this, Russia annexed Courland (a part of modern Latvia), as well as Lithuanian, Belarusian and Ukrainian lands east of the Bug River, with an entire area of 120,000 square kilometres and a population of about 1,200,000. For a long time, the Polish state ceased to exist, and Russia could consider the Polish issue resolved – at least for the short or medium term.

This brief review of the major historical events does not give a complete picture of the wide range of developments in Russia during Catherine's reign. However, it is clear that a brilliant period in the history of the Russian Empire had dawned. By the end of Catherine's reign, Russia had solved the major geo-political problems inherited from the time of Peter the Great. It had gained access to the Baltic Sea and the Black Sea, strengthened itself in the West, and regained the

lost Ukrainian and Belarusian lands. Never before in its history had Russia achieved such power and influence in its international relations. The chancellor of the Russian Empire, Alexander Bezborodko, remarked that not a single cannon in Europe dared shoot without the permission of Russia. Catherine the Great should be credited for these colossal changes.

That said, Catherine's reign would not have been so glorious without the constant support of her entourage and officials. One of the Empress's greatest talents was being able to find talented, energetic and loyal administrators, statesmen, military commanders and diplomats, who became her devoted supporters. By the efforts of such people, Russia was transformed into a powerful empire.

One should mention some of the most famous personalities, amongst whom Grigory Potemkin (1739–91) occupies a special place. Potemkin proved himself a gifted administrator and organizer of the army and navy, and played a key role in strengthening the Absolutist State. He was also actively involved in Russian economic life and the improvement of international relations. Another prominent figure was Count Nikita Panin (1718–83), who was in charge of foreign policy from 1762 until 1783. The Russian army's glorious victories during Catherine's time were due to Generals (later Field Marshals) Pyotr Rumyantsev (1725–96) and Alexander Suvorov (1730–1800), while the young Russian navy was led by a talented team that included Admiral Fedor Ushakov (1745–1817), Count Aleksey Orlov (1734–1808) and Admiral Grigory Spiridov (1713–90), who were all highly successful.

As mentioned above, Catherine sincerely believed herself to be a disciple of the French Enlightenment philosophers, and paid great attention to the development of arts. She was a patron of numerous architects, artists, sculptors, poets and craftsmen, whose work reflected Russia's foreign policies and the Empress's belief that she was continuing the policies she had inherited from Peter the Great. The artists did not simply glorify Catherine's reign, but created potent images of an enlightened monarch and the ruler of one of the strongest countries in Europe. Russian art of this period is dominated by images of Catherine as the extremely successful follower of Peter the Great and a very wise and benevolent ruler.

The most significant work of art is possibly the bronze equestrian monument to Peter the Great by the French sculptor Etienne-Maurice Falconet, which was unveiled in St Petersburg in 1782. The Empress ordered that the inscription, 'To Peter I from Catherine II year 1782', should be placed on one side of the pedestal, and 'PETRO primo CATHARINA secunda MDCCLXXXII' on the other. This demonstrated Catherine's recognition of Peter's achievements and her own adherence to his policies, whilst at the same time reminding people of her own successes and importance. The representation of this remarkable monument can be found in or on many works of art, including a gold snuff-box made in Switzerland.

The portrait of an allegorical image of the Empress was often combined with a representation of Peter the Great. Heinrich Buchholtz's *Allegory of the Victory of the Russian Fleet in the First Turkish War* (see page 40) shows Peter the Great seated in the clouds above St Petersburg, with the figure of Fame holding a portrait of Catherine II and a map of the Crimea and the Black Sea. Below, Russian soldiers, with trophies and Turkish prisoners, march triumphantly across a pontoon bridge. Turkish flags are lowered as they pass Falconet's statue of Peter. The artist hammers home the message that Peter's legacy and Russia are safe in the hands of the Empress.

The large full-length portrait (see page 28) of Catherine II by the famous Russian artist Fedor Stepanovich Rokotov depicts the Empress standing before a throne and the Imperial regalia, pointing with the sceptre to a bust of Peter the Great. A nearby inscription reads 'Completing that which was begun', and underlines what is already obvious in the composition – that Catherine was continuing Peter's policies.

The most significant works of art at the time were those ordered by the Empress. A great example is the series of twelve large paintings by the German artist Jacob Philipp Hackert (see page 132), surrounded by stuccowork representing the spoils of war in the state room in Peterhof Palace, which was named in honour of the famous naval battle of Chesme. Arranged in two tiers, Hackert's paintings record events during the Russian naval campaign in the Aegean Sea and the great victory at the battle of Chesme. The State Hermitage Museum has a version of one of these paintings, which is included in this exhibition. It shows the 100-gun Turkish flagship blowing up, with *The Three Bishops,* the 66-gun ship of Aleksey Orlov, the Russian commander-in-chief, in the foreground. As one would expect, the battle of Chesme was a very popular subject and was represented on fans and household items, as well as on paintings and prints.

The victory at Chesme was so dear to Catherine that she had it

OPPOSITE

Catherine's son, Emperor Paul I, ordered a statue to be erected to Russia's greatest general, Alexander Suvorov, during his lifetime. Paul approved Kozlovsky's model in January 1800, and the statue of Suvorov as Mars, the Roman god of war, was unveiled in May 1801 – a year after Suvorov's death.

Mikhail Ivanovich Kozlovsky (1753–1802)

CATALOGUE NO. 143

ABOVE

The *Allegory of the Victory of the Russian Fleet in the First Turkish War*, dated 1777, is set overlooking the River Neva and St Petersburg. To the left is Peter the Great, founder of the Russian navy.

Heinrich Buchholtz
(1735–80)

CATALOGUE NO. 155

celebrated and commemorated in several monuments at her palaces around St Petersburg. In 1794 the artist Vladimir Lukich Borovikovsky (1757–1825) painted a portrait of the Empress walking in the park at Tsarskoye Selo, with the Chesme Column in the background (see page 75). Another Hermitage painting relating to this subject is *Catherine II laying the Trophies of the Battle of Chesme on the Tomb of Peter the Great* by the German artist Andreas Caspar Hühne (see page 72), who moved to Russia at the invitation of the Empress. Naturally the Empress is depicted at the centre – with Aleksey Orlov, the conqueror of the Turks, nearby – once more underlining the key 'message' that Catherine was continuing Peter's foreign policy of strengthening and expanding the empire and was, very clearly, his worthy and extremely successful successor.

Catherine was repeatedly painted in the guise of Minerva, the goddess of wisdom and war in Roman mythology, to emphasize the great scale of her achievements. An example of this is an sketch in oils of *The Apotheosis of the Reign of Catherine II* by Gregorio Guglielmi (1767), created for a proposed ceiling painting in the Great Palace at Tsarskoye Selo. In the centre, the Empress is represented as Minerva with the royal regalia and the sash of the Order of St Andrew. She is surrounded by figures representing Fertility, Mercury (the patron of trade and crafts) with a cornucopia full of coins, and different nationalities showing Russia flourishing under Catherine's rule.

Sculptural portraits of Catherine as Minerva were also common. One of the best is a gilt-bronze bust by French bronze-maker Pierre-Marie-Louis Agi, dated 1781, which showed the Empress wearing magnificent armour and a helmet surmounted with an owl, the symbol of wisdom. Such portraits of Catherine as Minerva appeared shortly after her coronation, and included a gold snuff-box by Jean-Pierre Ador. This was designed as a gift to participants in the palace *coup* of 1762, and archival documents record that thirty snuff-boxes of this kind were produced. Even Catherine's daughter-in-law, Grand Duchess Maria Fedorovna, engraved a small glass medallion with a portrait of the Empress as Minerva for Catherine's sixtieth birthday in April 1789.

Other porcelain, bronze and glass items celebrated and commemorated the great deeds of the Empress and the history of her reign. From the 1770s, the Imperial Porcelain Factory focused on the production of 'Greek style' vases – a stylized variation of the classic amphora and a clear allusion to Catherine's Greek Project. The Greek Project also forms the subject of a painting of the Grand Duke Alexander and Grand Duke Constantine by the English artist Richard Brompton, of 1781, and a miniature copy by Heyde. They show an allegory (a narrative describing one subject under the guise of another) of Catherine II's Greek Project and the future of her grandchildren. The Grand Duke Alexander was destined to become the future Russian Emperor, while Grand Duke Constantine would become the Emperor of the new Greek Empire. Four-year-old Alexander, likened to Alexander the Great, cuts the Gordian knot, thereby resolving the issue of a quick and definitive Russian victory over Turkey; while two-year-old Constantine holds the *labarum* – an emblem of Christianity and the state banner of the Imperial Rome introduced by Constantine the Great – to indicate that he will rebuild a new Christian empire on the ruins of the Byzantine and Ottoman Empires (see page 42).

One of the best works by Austrian artist Johann Baptist Lampi the Elder – the portrait of Grand Dukes Alexander and Constantine (1795) is devoted to the same subject. The picture abounds with Antique motifs. The young men are represented against a Classical colonnade, with a statue of Minerva (Athena) on the right, the goddess of wisdom being a traditional representation of the Empress. Below the statue, an incense-burner sends up sweet-smelling smoke to honour the goddess and the Empress. The inscription in Greek (a quotation

This painting of the *Grand
Dukes Alexander and
Constantine as Children*
is based on Richard
Brompton's painting
*Alexander breaking the
Gordian Knot* (early 1780s).
Alexander and Constantine
are represented as successors
to the Roman emperors
and great Christian warriors
who will establish a new
Greek Empire.

Heyde (1790)

CATALOGUE NO. 207

from the ancient Greek poet Pindar (522–448 BC) reads: 'The Owl-
Eyed One [as the Greeks referred to Athena] gave them the best valour
and skill, which exceeds that of all mortals.' This was inscribed in gold
letters on the temple of Athena at Lindos.

A significant number of works of art are also associated with the
conquest of the Crimea and the famous Crimean journey of the
Empress in 1787, which formed part of the Greek Project. A superb
gilt-bronze inkwell by Agi, made in St Petersburg in 1794 for the
College of War, commemorates the victory over the Turks. It shows
two Eastern warriors genuflecting before an altar on which stands
the Russian eagle. An impressive, partly gilt silver tray that Moscow
merchants presented to the Empress's son Paul in 1775 is engraved
with a map of the Black Sea, together with the Crimea and the wind

rose, symbolizing Russia's new territorial acquisitions. Echoes of the Greek Project can also be found much later. A large silver dish based on an engraving after Ferdinand de Mey's painting of *The Triumph of Catherine* of 1787, which showed an allegorical representation of Catherine's visit to the Crimea earlier that year, seems to have been made in St Petersburg during the 1870s. Inscribed 'Catherine II born 1729, crowned 1762, died 1796', it appears to be connected with Russia's successes in the later Russian-Turkish War of 1877–78 and the 150th anniversary of Catherine's birth in 1879.

Porcelain was also used to promote the Empress Catherine and her successes. In 1776, Francis Gardner's private porcelain factory near Moscow started producing the so-called 'Order Services' – services made for the ceremonial banquets of the Knights of the four highest Russian military Orders (Saints George, Alexander Nevsky, Andrew and Vladimir). The decoration was based on the stars, chains and sashes of the Orders.

No less splendid were the Classical allegorical motifs and compositions decorating the finest weapons produced during Catherine's reign. The decisive victories of the Russian army during the second half of the 18th century could not have been achieved without a highly developed weapons industry. Tula, a town south of Moscow, was the main centre of the weapons industry. It produced swords and guns for both the army and navy. High-quality rifles, pistols and various types of sword were manufactured by first-class master gunsmiths at the Tula Arms Factory founded by Peter the Great. To ensure a constant supply of efficient weapons for the Russian armed forces, the Empress and her courtiers often visited Tula to inspect the factory. We know that on returning from the Crimea in 1787, Catherine and her entourage stopped to view the factory. The armourers presented the Imperial visitors with the best of their products.

Richly-decorated weapons were also commissioned by and for the Imperial court. The best were used for royal hunting or given as presents to members of the Imperial family, Russian officials, and foreign diplomats and visitors. Like many other products of this period, weapons were decorated with military attributes, such as figures of warriors clad in antique armour and helmets, eagles, laurel wreaths and other Classical motifs. Their decoration underlined the successes of the Russian army and navy during the Golden Age of Catherine the Great.

CHAPTER III

Two Pastimes of Catherine II: Collecting and Building

SERGEI ANDROSOV

Catherine the Great's tastes in art and architecture have been discussed frequently, with writers often simplifying matters and failing to take into consideration the Empress's multifarious and often contradictory activities. Any proper assessment has to take into account the evolution of Catherine's tastes, her astonishing ability to evaluate and understand the people around her, and the development of her personality following certain events.

Princess Sophie Frederica Augusta of Anhalt-Zerbst arrived in Russia in February 1744, when she was only fourteen years old, and remained there for the rest of her life. She converted to Orthodoxy and in 1745 married the Grand Duke Peter Fyodorovich, heir to the Russian throne. However, she did not have any real power until the death of the Empress Elizabeth in 1761. During these early years in Russia, Catherine had a great deal of free time and read profusely, preferring the Classical authors and philosophers of the Enlightenment. Over the course of these years, she was able to enter deeply into the spirit of the Russian people – something that her distant husband so flagrantly rejected. Her innate intelligence and powers of observation allowed her to win the hearts not only of those close to the throne, but also of the clergy and even the ordinary people. It is likely that this combination of a European education and her deep respect for Russian traditions laid the foundation for the long and successful reign of the future Catherine the Great.

It is difficult to understand where the young Catherine acquired the strict and refined tastes which characterized her activities during her reign. Even Count Fyodor Golovkin, a close acquaintance, and renowned for his sharp tongue, expressed his surprise tinged with admiration:

It would be hard to explain how a woman, brought at such a young age from a small Prussian garrison town into court circles, and being half German, was able to acquire such impeccable tastes quite naturally, which would have been more readily found in a young woman brought up in the best Parisian society rather than in someone who was to rule all of Russia.[1]

Golovkin tried to find an explanation in Catherine's friendship with the famous Prince Stanislaw August Poniatowski (later King of Poland), who was 'the most impeccable person in all of Europe with regard to his good manners and the excellent tone of his courtesy and speech'.[2] Another memoirist, Countess Varvara Golovina, points to Ernst Münnich, son of Field Marshal Münnich and author of the first manuscript catalogue of the Hermitage paintings, as the person responsible for the education of the Grand Duchess:

[Ernst] *Münnich, a man of understanding, was the first to guess at Catherine's abilities. He pressed her to improve herself – a proposal that she welcomed. He gave her to read first of all* [Pierre] *Bayle's dictionary, a poisonous, dangerous and seductive work, especially for one who never had any notion of divine truth.*

To support her views, the Countess noted: 'I have all these details from my uncle, M. de Chouvalov [Shuvalov], to whom the empress recounted them herself.'[3] However, Münnich could only have influenced Catherine after 1762, since before this he was exiled in Vologda. Thus, regardless of who influenced Catherine in her youth, it was her own innate qualities of moderation, good judgment, common sense and the ability to sum people up, which made her into not only a clever and charming woman, but also a true Empress and admired ruler.

Once Catherine had ascended the throne after the *coup d'état* of 1762 and become Autocrat of All the Russias, she could devote herself seriously to both construction projects and collecting works of art. It can be argued that her first purchase, the acquisition of paintings from the Berlin dealer Johann Ernst Gotzkowsky, which took place in late 1763 or early 1764 and laid the foundations of the Hermitage, was motivated more by political than aesthetic reasons. These pictures had been intended for Frederick the Great of Prussia, and their acquisition made it possible both to strike a blow at Frederick's pride and show the state of the Russian Treasury in a favourable light.[4]

It appears that this successful transaction stimulated further purchases of both old and contemporary works of art – and even entire collections – at sales in Western Europe. Over the next six years, the Empress bought paintings from the collections of Jean de Julienne (1767), Johann Philipp von Coblenz and the Prince de Ligne (1768), Heinrich von Brühl (1769) and François Tronchin (1770). In 1771, pictures from the collection of Gerrit Braamcamp were bought but

BELOW

A bust of François-Marie
Arouet de Voltaire
(1694–1778), philosopher,
writer, journalist, historian
and orator of the French
Enlightenment.

*Workshop of
Jean-Antoine Houdon*
(1741–1828)

CATALOGUE NO. 40

sadly lost at sea, in a shipwreck off Finland. A year later, the famous gallery of Baron Louis Antoine Crozat, Baron de Thiers, was secured. It was followed by eleven paintings from the collection of the Duc de Choiseul in 1773. This was undoubtedly Catherine's most active period of collecting paintings, and allowed her to establish the Hermitage as the most outstanding picture gallery in Russia and one of the most prominent in Europe. On 30 January 1772, the Empress wrote to Voltaire: 'You are surprised by my purchase of paintings; I would do well perhaps to buy less at the moment, but lost opportunities are never recovered.'[5]

Catherine's personal involvement in selecting these paintings and collections is not entirely clear. Usually she made her decision by correspondence, taking the views of her diplomatic or art agents into consideration. She rarely expressed her opinion about works of art in her letters, but some of her thinking and priorities can be gleaned from regular exchanges with Baron Friedrich Melchior Grimm, who was based in Paris. On 14 July 1779, for example, she declared (and with reference to the Prussian art agent, Johann Friedrich von Reiffenstein): 'For the Reiffensteinian purchase of works by Correge, Raphael, Leonardo da Vinci, Carrache, Palma, Scarsellino and Poussin, who the devil could resist these great names.'[6]

Another 'great name' which appealed to the Empress was that of Anton Raphael Mengs. On 19 November 1778, she asked Grimm to 'find out if you will at the same time, with all suitable discretion, of any works by Mengs. Will the day finally come when I can say: I have seen work by Mengs.'[7]

Sometimes it is unclear whether Catherine was attracted to an artist or to the subject matter of the picture. In the same letter to Grimm, she mentions the painter and architect Giovanni Paolo Panini, but it appears that her interest was aroused by the fact that his paintings depicted the interiors of major Roman churches: 'I heard tell in the past few days that Panini, painter in Rome, was selling paintings of the interiors of as many basilicas as possible. I asked M. de Schouvalof to write to the divine Reiffenstein to purchase them on my behalf.'[8] After such effusive remarks, it will come as no surprise to learn that a number of paintings by Mengs and Panini entered the Hermitage during the Empress's lifetime.

In November 1762, Dmitry Mikhailovich Golitsyn, the Russian ambassador in Vienna, received the following instructions: 'I wish that the painter called Liotard, now working in Vienna and formerly most of the time in Constantinople should by your persuasions come here to Us.'[9] Unfortunately, Liotard had moved to Geneva and Catherine was unable to recruit him.

There can be no doubt that one of Catherine's great gifts was the ability to find people who were able to carry out her most daring ideas, assimilate their advice and act upon it. During the busy period in the Parisian art market in the 1760s and early '70s, the Empress's agents were Prince Dmitry Alekseyevech Golitsyn, ambassador first in France and then in Holland,[10] the French philosopher Denis Diderot and the sculptor Etienne-Maurice Falconet. This combination achieved an outstanding series of major acquisitions. Indeed, it is significant that the activity of Russian representatives in the European, primarily Parisian, art markets declined rapidly after Diderot lost some of Catherine's respect during his six-month visit to St Petersburg in 1773. And the cooling of relations between the Empress and Falconet, due to the problematic completion of the equestrian monument to Peter the Great, also affected activity.

The well-established circle of experts in St Petersburg, with whom Catherine could discuss her most recent acquisitions, included Count Ernst Münnich, president of the College of Commerce; Ivan Betskoy,

BELOW

The unveiling of Etienne-Maurice Falconet's monument to Peter the Great in Senate Square, St Petersburg, in 1782.

Engraving by Alexander Melkinov after A. P. Davidov

president of the Academy of Arts (in charge of the Buildings Department and a collector and patron of the arts in his own right); and later Ivan Shuvalov, the original founder of the Academy of Arts and its first curator. Catherine also paid attention to such experts as the sculptor Falconet (from 1766), and to other professionals like Hermann Lucas Conrad Pfandzelt (1716–86), a restorer and keeper of the Hermitage collections, and the Venetian Giuseppe Antonio Martinelli, who took over from him in 1775.[11] Talking to these enlightened amateurs and professionals, Catherine was able to develop and refine her taste, learn how to distinguish between copies and original works, and judiciously select further works for the Hermitage.

Two examples demonstrate Catherine's increasing discrimination. In 1767, the Marquis Pano Maruzzi, a Venetian of Greek origin who later became the Russian consul in Venice, sent thirty-seven paintings by Italian artists to St Petersburg. Apparently Maruzzi himself was aware that these pictures were not masterpieces (in the list only eight of them were valued at more than 1000 ducats), but he underestimated the high standards set by the Empress. Almost all of the paintings were given away by the Hermitage as gifts to Grigory Orlov and others.[12]

Catherine also rejected works which had been acquired in Rome by the agent Reiffenstein. On 27 September 1781 she wrote to Grimm:

One of the first things I did was to go and see what Admiral Borissof had brought me from Italy. To my great surprise, apart from the Mengs and a few other things, not very much. Everything else, apart from Raphael's Loggia, is nasty coarse paintings: I have ordered Martinelli, the painter who looks after my gallery, to make a selection and send them to auction in aid of the town's poor-house. Zounds! It's extraordinary that the divine one [Reiffenstein] managed to be duped on this occasion. Please tell him expressly not to purchase anything more from Mr. Jenkins. It's scandalous passing off such sorry things as the work of such and such a painter. My people at the Hermitage were embarrassed to let anyone else see them before I had, and the consternation these coarse paintings has occasioned has been great.[13]

In Reiffenstein's defence, however, it should be noted that it is still not clear which paintings caused such a negative reaction.

Catherine's passion for contemporary art deserves special mention. In Paris this interest was constantly supported by Diderot, with whose help Golitsyn commissioned Chardin's *Still Life with the Attributes of*

OPPOSITE

Antinous was the favourite youth of the Emperor Hadrian and a popular subject of Classical sculpture. This head was found in Hadrian's villa, at Tivoli, in 1769, and acquired by Count Ivan Shuvalov, one of Catherine's art agents, in Rome in 1777. It was displayed in the Grotto of the Imperial residence at Tsarskoye Selo.

Unknown sculptor
(Roman, second quarter of 2nd century AD)

CATALOGUE NO. 232

the Arts and acquired Jean Baptiste Greuze's *The Paralytic*. Acting for the Empress in Rome were Ivan Shuvalov (from 1763) and then the man that he recommended, the aforementioned Prussian agent Reiffenstein, who in 1771 became an honorary member and subsequently a commissioner of the Academy of Arts. During these years, Rome was once again becoming a progressive artistic centre and setting the pace for the development of the Neo-Classical style. In some ways, it is surprising that Count Shuvalov became one of the proponents of this new taste in Russia because the architect Savva Chevakinsky had recently built him a palace in the exuberant Baroque style that Catherine criticized.[14] Shuvalov, however, was a man with a deep respect for Greco-Roman culture.

In 1769 Shuvalov sent the Academy of Arts a collection of plaster casts of famous Ancient statues and group sculptures, and several works by contemporary masters. The latter were mostly examples of Neo-Classical sculpture and included a bust of Peter the Great, a statue of Catherine the Great by Carlo Albacini, a statue of the philosopher Xenon by Gioacchino Falcioni, and busts of Socrates and Homer signed by Bartolomeo Cavaceppi.[15] A little earlier, and at Catherine's request, Shuvalov had commissioned two large paintings on Classical subjects from Pompeo Batoni: *The Continence of Scipio* and *Thetis taking Achilles from the Centaur Chiron* (both now in the Hermitage).[16]

Documents in the State Archive in Rome record the export of many works of art by 'General Shovalov' between 1769 and 1773.[17] As far as one can judge from the short entries, these were mainly mass-produced works by Roman workshops – marble tables, vases and columns, and copies of ancient statues and busts in bronze. But there were also several original Antique pieces. Few of these works can be identified today, but they undoubtedly helped form general taste in St Petersburg, especially as they were not intended solely for the Empress Catherine.

Acquisitions continued to be made after Shuvalov left Rome, although, as we have seen, these were not always successful. None-theless, in the early 1780s Reiffenstein and the Russian consul Gaspar Santini purchased paintings and drawings by Mengs which were in his workshop after his death.[18] On Catherine's instructions they also organized the copying of Raphael's Loggia, an undertaking that took several years.

During the 1780s, many orders were placed for pictures by other popular painters working in Rome, notably Angelica Kauffmann,

Jacob Philipp Hackert and Johann Heinrich Wilhelm Tischbien. However, the role of intermediary during this period was taken more often than not by Prince Nikolai Yusupov (1751–1831), a passionate collector and the Russian envoy in Turin from 1783 until 1789.

From about the end of the 1770s, Catherine became increasingly attracted to collecting engraved gems, both ancient and modern, which she ordered from leading engravers throughout Europe. This enthusiasm may have arisen because she had largely satiated her passion for paintings: by 1774 there were already about 2080 pictures in the Hermitage and her last major purchase was a large part of Sir Horace Walpole's collection in 1778–79.[19] But it also seems that Catherine's obsession was fuelled by the influence of her new favourites, Ivan Korsakov and especially Alexander Lanskoy. In her letters to Grimm, Catherine sketches out a slightly eccentric picture of Lanskoy as a passionate collector, seriously 'infected' by 'cameo disease'. 'Had it not been for Lanskoy, perhaps Catherine would not have become such a passionate lover of carved gems,' as M. I. Maksimova observed.[20]

After Lanskoy's sudden death in 1784, his successor, Alexander Dmitriev-Mamonov, turned out to be equally passionate about cameos and intaglios. It was as a result of pressure from him that in 1787 the famous collection of the Duc d'Orléans was bought for 40,000 roubles, after negotiations lasting two years. The Orléans collection contained around 1500 gems and was considered one of the finest in the world.[21] In addition, by 1786 gems were regularly purchased from the London engravers William and Charles Brown, resulting in a large and unique assemblage of their work.[22] By 1794, Catherine's massive collection contained more than 10,000 carved gemstones.

It is possible that Catherine developed an interest in Classical sculpture as a result of her fascination with Classical gemstones. At the same time, it is equally possible that she was inspired by the acquisition of Antique sculpture by Count Shuvalov in Rome, and by other factors. At any rate, in 1785 she managed to secure the very large collection of John Lyde Brown, a director of the Bank of England, who had been buying Antique sculpture from Italy for over forty years.[23] The story of how this collection was acquired by the Empress is rather hazy, however, and the documentation is limited to payments to the merchant and banker Stender in 1783 and 1785.

The acquisition of Lyde Brown's collection, which contained many portraits of emperors, military commanders and philosophers, led to greatly increased activity in the foundry workshop attached to the Academy of Arts, which engaged in casting copies of ancient statues and busts in bronze. It was here that the Russian founder Vasily Mozhalov cast the colossal statues Farnese Hercules (in 1784–85) and Flora Farnese (in 1787), which were both the same size as the originals.[24]

From 1790, the list of works coming out of the foundry was dominated by busts of ancient gods and public figures, with many based on pieces from Lyde Brown's collection. Just like the huge statues of Hercules and Flora, these were intended for Tsarskoye Selo, and more specifically, for the Cameron Gallery, built by Charles Cameron between 1783 and 1786. Bronze busts of famous people from Antiquity were placed along the perimeter of the upper gallery between Ionic columns and supplemented with bronze busts of contemporaries, including the Russian scholar Mikhail Lomonosov and the English Whig politician Charles James Fox. Together they awaited the Empress on her frequent strolls and no doubt inspired many thoughts and reflections.

This cameo of *Catherine II as Minerva* was carved and engraved by Alexander Dmitriev-Mamonov (1758–1803).

CATALOGUE NO 273

This highly-rated cameo of *Perseus and Andromeda* was acquired from the collection of the German painter Anton Raphael Mengs in Rome in 1780.

CATALOGUE NO 250

Acquired with the Duc d'Orléans' collection of gemstones in 1787, this cameo is of Livia Drusilla, the third wife of the Emperor Augustus and mother of Emperor Tiberius.

CATALOGUE NO 251

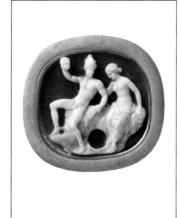

One gets the impression that Catherine regarded the Hermitage as a picture gallery and did not think of it at all as a sculpture museum. Thus in 1784 she gave the order that ten works of sculpture (including six bas-reliefs) should be taken from the Hermitage to the Academy of Arts.[25] Most of the statues and busts acquired from the John Lyde Brown collection ended up not in the St Peterburg Hermitage, as might have been expected, but in Tsarskoye Selo, in the Grotto or Morning Room. According to the 1791 inventory, the *Voltaire Seated* and *Diana* by Jean-Antoine Houdon were kept here, and the marble portrait bust of Charles James Fox by Joseph Nollekens.[26] Following the death of Catherine II, most of these works were moved to the Emperor Paul I's Mikhailovsky Palace, and then to the Tauride Palace, before finally occupying their rightful places in the New Hermitage after it opened in 1852.

In general, sculpture seems to have been the art form that was least attractive to Catherine. Even the bronze busts in the Cameron Gallery at Tsarkoye Selo did not appeal to her artistic sensibilities so much as embody history. It was typical of the Empress to have an already completed bronze bust, which was considered a representation of Brutus, melted down for the simple reason that 'he is now the idol of the Jacobins'.[27] And writing to Falconet about the recently commissioned equestrian statue of Peter the Great in 1767, the Empress confessed, not without a certain degree of coquetry, '… but how can you rely on my taste. I cannot draw. It will perhaps be the first good statue I see in my life. How can you be satisfied with such insignificant support? The merest schoolboy knows more of Your art than I do.'[28] Indeed her views on sculpture appeared to change very little in later years. Falconet remained in her memory not as the creator of the magnificent 'Bronze Horseman', but as an artist 'somewhere high above in the clouds'.

Architecture, however, was another matter. Catherine paid special attention to this discipline throughout her reign, building palaces, cathedrals and state buildings, not only in St Petersburg but in Moscow, old Russian towns, and in the newly-acquired territories.

Catherine caught 'building fever' as soon as she became Grand Duchess and found herself able to construct something on the piece of land at Oranienbaum that belonged to her: 'I set about drawing my plans and laying out the garden, and since this was the first time I had worked with plans and buildings, all I did turned out huge and rather clumsy.'[29] Despite this, she persevered, regularly consulting books on architecture and studying engravings. Eventually she acquired enough knowledge to express her demands clearly and accurately, and actively to engage and collaborate with architects.

The Empress's experience and character made her highly receptive to the leading ideas of the times and the 'new taste' in architecture. In her memoirs, Catherine frequently recalls the sufferings she endured because of bad living conditions. In even the grandest palaces of the mid-18th century, only the official, ceremonial apartments were richly decorated. The living quarters were often disagreeable due to their wretched decoration, lack of furnishings and total absence of comfort. Moreover, the court of the restless Empress Elizabeth was always on the move, journeying from town to town and palace to palace. Some of the palaces were decrepit, others unfinished, while others had been built very quickly without observing rules and good building practices. Catherine herself was almost asphyxiated by a fire that burned an old wooden building to the ground. Another time, she miraculously escaped from the ruins of a palace that collapsed because it had been built too hastily and had no proper foundations. It is not surprising, therefore, that she accepted the wisdom of Vitruvius, the immensely influential Roman writer on architecture. Her rational and balanced mind, which had a fine sense of proportion and loved regularity and order, found itself in perfect harmony with notions of true beauty, graceful simplicity, noble austerity and symmetry based on the accurately calibrated proportions of the Classical orders of architecture.

Building became for Catherine one of the most important aspects of her state activity. A few months after her rule began, she issued a decree establishing a Commission for Stone Construction in St Petersburg and Moscow. In 1765 a competition was announced to find the best plan for St Petersburg with the aim of 'bringing St Petersburg to such an excellent condition and giving it such greatness as befits the capital city of an ever-expanding state'.[30]

Two years later, a plan which was designed under the leadership of the architect Kvasov was completed. It consolidated and supplemented the existing well-defined layout of the city and laid down the basic principles for the construction of buildings. In the centre it was forbidden to build wooden structures, and residential properties could only have four or five storeys so that their size would be in keeping with the new directives for government buildings. Houses had to be built with a complete or solid façade, not leaving spaces between them,

OPPOSITE

Acquired from the collection of John Lyde Brown, this head of Athena is one of the best examples of Greek art of the Classical period in the Hermitage Museum. It was found in 1764 near Rome. The contemporary art historian Johann Winckelmann described it as 'the most perfect of all beauties found upon this earth'.

Unknown sculptor (Roman, first half of 1st century AD)

CATALOGUE NO. 228

The English Embank-
ment in St Petersburg, built
between 1763 and 1767.

Edward Gaertner
(1801–77)

and not being set back from the building line. No less significant were
the proposals for the creation of granite embankments on the River
Neva, 'small' rivers and canals, bridges, and squares to break up the
monotony of the streets.

Catherine's intention to rebuild and beautify St Petersburg anew
generated an ardent response from Russian society and was perceived
as a far-reaching decision for the capital and for Russia as a whole. In
'The Opening of the Imperial Academy of the Arts in St Petersburg',
the poet Alexander Sumarokov declared:

*Our descendants will see you, Petropolis, in a new guise – you will be
the Rome of the North. My prediction will come about, if the throne of
the Monarchs is not removed from you, and it may be that this will not
come about if your wealth multiplies, if your marshlands dry up and
your channels be adorned with splendid buildings. Then you will become
the eternal gates of the Russian Empire and the eternal home of the most
honourable sons of Russia and a timeless monument to Peter the First
and Catherine the Second. Your architecture will serve a most useful
purpose, for it will give a glorious example to other cities.*

Behind Sumarokov's statement was a half-century-long polemic about the historical future of Russia, which was naturally linked to the future of St Petersburg. If Peter the Great's opponents had foreseen a swift demise of the city, then his supporters took the very name of the city as a symbol and a pledge of immortality. In their view, this newest of European capitals should be like the most ancient capital of the world. It should become the second eternal city and, like Rome, reproduce the history of the empire and the actions of its leaders in the impressive beauty of its architecture, statues and monuments. Thus, the turning to Classicism, and through it to Antiquity, acquired very profound meaning. St Petersburg had to become the visual symbol of immortality and historical continuity, and its external appearance had to embrace everlasting aesthetic values.

These plans began to take shape and were largely carried out during Catherine's reign of over thirty years. The transformation of St Petersburg took place with an extraordinary swiftness that was only possible in Russia. While not squandering money, Catherine allocated vast resources for building in St Petersburg and in Tsarskoye Selo, considering that these investments were fully justified. Following the Empress's example, those close to her also began to acquire houses and palaces, often throwing caution to the wind. In a letter to Baron Grimm of 23 August 1779, Catherine made a significant confession: 'As you know, the building frenzy is as powerful as ever with us, and hardly any earthquake can have knocked down as many buildings as we are putting up.' Later, French words could not express her feelings well enough and she switched to her native German to observe, '… building is a devilish thing: it devours money, and the more you build, the more you want to build; it is a sickness, like drinking, or else it's a sort of habit.'[31]

It should be noted that this was said before the construction of Charles Cameron's complex at Tsarskoye Selo and before Giacomo Quarenghi's arrival in Russia.

The initial phase of the reconstruction of St Petersburg involved architects who were already in Imperial service by 1762 – Antonio Rinaldi, Jean-Baptist-Michel Vallin de la Mothe and Yury Velten. Judging by the number of important commissions they received, their work fully satisfied the Empress. Rinaldi's activities only came to an end as a result of old age, Vallin de la Mothe's because of illness, while Velten became increasingly occupied with administration and teaching at the Academy of Arts. At the same time, by the early 1770s Catherine had already begun to look for other architects whose interests and work were more consistently based on Antiquity. At first, she pinned her hopes on the extraordinarily gifted Vasily Bazhenov and the profound knowledge of Charles-Louis Clérisseau. She commissioned Bazhenov to reconstruct the Moscow Kremlin and gave Clérisseau the project of the House of Antiquity for Tsarskoye Selo. However, both proposals had to be abandoned because of their huge scale and incredible costs.

In the end, the Scottish architect Cameron and Italian Giacomo Quarenghi were invited to work in Russia. In the eyes of the Empress, their work reflected an ideal expression of Classicism. Both Cameron and Quarenghi adhered to a rigorous Palladian Neo-Classicism and made full use of their knowledge of Ancient Roman architecture and applied arts. They were both extraordinarily hard-working and were able to respond to all their enlightened employer's requests. In Russia,

they were granted exceptionally favourable conditions to realize their numerous projects and to turn their designs into actual palaces and churches.

Among the Russian architects Catherine particularly favoured were Ivan Starov and Nikolai L'vov, who also belonged to this new trend. Several projects for the building of a cathedral in the city of Mogilev (now in Belorussia) were apparently submitted to her, but the one she chose was in the Palladian style and designed by a man with no formal education in architecture, Nikolai L'vov. The cousin of the architect, Fedor L'vov, later wrote eloquently: '[The Empress] ordered him to present himself, she gazed with her regal, compassionate look on this unusual creature! … But his project was carried out and the church was built.'[32]

The changes that occurred during Catherine's reign are reflected in the accounts of three Italians who visited Russia at different times. The St Petersburg that Giacomo Casanova encountered in 1765 was only the 'embryo' of what he learned about in the last years of his life. Arriving in 1780, Quarenghi noted: '[This] city is immense, full of gigantic buildings, public and private, many of which do not in any way reflect Palladian taste.'[33] Finally, in 1792, the stage designer and architect Pietro Gonzaga, who had just started working for the state, informed Francesco Fontanesi: 'The city is big and beautiful: construction continues hurriedly, despite all the wars, and the buildings grow like mushrooms … most of the buildings are in good taste, and among the best are those of our Quarenghi.'[34] Even from this brief sampling, one can appreciate that St Petersburg changed very dramatically in less than three decades.

Although the capital was replete with new buildings of a type never seen in Russia and reminiscent of Roman architecture, it did not resemble Rome. The city retained its own personality and it remained the creation of Peter the Great. Those living after Catherine and the fleeting reign of her son, Paul I, considered the palaces on the outskirts of St Petersburg the real monuments to Classicism. They understandably focused on Tsarskoye Selo, Catherine's own personal ancient world, with the Agate Rooms and Cameron Gallery, and the Alexander Palace built by Quarenghi after the Empress's death, and also the unique architectural and park complex of Pavlovsk, which was begun by Cameron for the Grand Duke Paul and completed by Vincenzo Brenna, Pietro Gonzaga and Andrey Voronikhin.

St Petersburg itself, which had long since bade farewell to most of the insubstantial buildings of the Petrine era and replaced the exuberant Baroque with the restrained grandeur of the Classical style, became, if one may put it thus, even more St Petersburg than before. The Neo-Classical architects had managed to understand at a fundamental level the artistic concept of the city, which had been defined by the founder himself. They were struck by the city's outstanding individuality and shared a sense of common purpose and respect for their predecessors. According to tradition, architects such as Quarenghi would always remove his hat when they passed Smolny Cathedral, Francesco Bartolomeo Rastrelli's masterpiece. The late 18th-century architects never lost the sense of the colossal scale and rhythm which nature itself had given the city and which had been exploited by the first builders of the city, beginning with Domenico Trezzini.

The process of the rebuilding of St Petersburg did not necessitate its total demolition: a few features of the city were changed, but the main ones were given greater prominence. The sketch gradually developed into a finished painting of the city. And although the definitive version of St Peterburg was only completed during the first half of the 19th century, the foundations for it were unquestionably laid during Catherine the Great's enlightened reign.

NOTES

1. Quoted in N. Shilder, 'Two Characteristics', *Russian Olden Times* (1896), vol. 88, p. 372.

2. Ibid.

3. *Souvenirs de la comtesse Golovine née princesse Galitzine, 1766–1821* (Paris, 1910), p. 38.

4. V. F. Levinson-Lessing, *History of the Hermitage Painting Gallery 1764–1917* (Leningrad, 1986), p. 53.

5. SIRIO, *Collection of the Imperial Russian Society*, vol. 13 (St Petersburg, 1874), p. 214.

6. SIRIO, vol. 23 (St Petersburg, 1878), p. 154.

7. Ibid., p. 110.

8. Ibid.

9. Foreign Policies Archive of the Russian Empire, collection N. 32, op. 1, d. 22, p. 1, 2.

10. About his activities in particular, see G. K. Tsverava, *Dmitry Alekseyevich Golitsyn* (Leningrad, 1985); A. M. Schenker, *The Bronze Horseman. Falconet's Monument to Peter the Great* (New Haven and London), p. 79.

11. For more about Martinelli, see O. G. Dintser, 'Martinelli, the first Curator of the Hermitage', *The Sciences and Culture in Eighteenth-century Russia* (Leningrad, 1984), p. 178.

12. For more about this, see SIRIO, vol. 10 (St Petersburg, 1872), p. 252; V. Antonov, 'Un acquisto enigmatico per l'Ermitage', *Antichità viva* (1975), XIV, no. 4, p. 33; V. Antonov, 'Dipinti da Venezia per l'Ermitage', *Arte Veneta* (1980), 34, p. 220; S. Androsov, 'I collezionisti dell'arte italiana in Russia', *Pietroburgo e Italia 1750–1850. Il genio italiano in Russia*, exhibition catalogue (Milan, 2003), p. 102.

13. SIRIO, vol. 23, p. 221.

14. *Memoirs of Empress Catherine II* (Moscow 1990), p. 210.

15. S. O. Androsov, 'Catherine II, the Hermitage and the Sculpture Collection', *The History of the Hermitage and its Collections* (Leningrad, 1989), p. 38.

16. T. B. Bushmina, 'Towards a History of Two Paintings Forming a Pair by Pompeo Batoni for Catherine II', *Trudi Gosudarstvennogo Ermitaga* (2000), vol. 29, p. 76.

17. Rome, Archivio di Stato, Camerale II, Antichità e Belle Arti, busta 12.

18. C. Frank, '"Plus il en aura mieux ce sera", Caterina II di Russia e Anton Raphael Mengs. Sul ruolo degli agenti "cesàrei" Grimm e Reiffenstein', in Mengs, *La scoperta del Neoclassico*, exhibition catalogue (Venice, 2001), p. 92.

19. L. Dukelskaya, A. Moore, *A Capital Collection, Houghton Hall and the Hermitage* (New Haven and London, 2002).

20. M. I. Maksimova, 'Empress Catherine II and the Hermitage's Collection of Engraved Gems', *Gosudarstvenniy Ermitage*, fasc. 1 (St Peterburg, 1920), p. 58.

21. J. Kagan, O. Neverov, *Splendeurs des collections de Catherine II de Russie, Le Cabinet de pierre gravées du Duc d'Orléans*, exhibition catalogue (Paris, 2000).

22. J. Kagan, *The Engraved Gems of William and Charles Brown*, exhibition catalogue (Leningrad, 1976).

23. X. Gorbunova, 'Classical Sculpture from the Lyde Browne Collection', in *Apollo* (December 1974), p. 460; O. Neverov, 'The Lyde Browne Collection and the History of Ancient Sculpture in the Hermitage Museum,' in *American Journal of Archaeology* (1984), vol. 88, no. 1, p. 33.

24. M. I. Androsova, '"Hercules" and "Flora" of Tsarskoe Selo at Mikhailovsky Palace', *Towards a History of Bronze Copies of Classical Sculpture at the Saint Petersburg Academy of Arts* (St Petersburg, 1999), p. 66.

25. Androsov, 1989, p. 40, *Dvortsi Russkogo museya*.

26. State Archives of Russian History, fonds 487, inv. 21, dossier 178, sheets 6, 7v, 8v.

27. O. Y. Neverov, 'Sculpture Portraits in the Collection of Catherine II at Tsarskoye Selo', *Skulptura v musee* (Leningrad, 1984), p. 94.

28. SIRIO, 1876, vol. 15 (St Petersburg), p. 15.

29. *Memoirs of Empress Catherine II* (Moscow, 1990), p. 171.

30. N. A. Yevsina, *Russian Architecture in the Time of Catherine II* (Moscow, 1994), p. 36.

31. SIRIO, vol. 23, p. 157. This quotation is generally rendered in Russian translation, which slightly diminishes its expressive, even eccentric nature, which also appears in the blend of both languages.

32. N. A. L'vov, *Selected Works*, (ed.) K. O. Lappo-Danilevsky (Cologne, 1992), p. 368.

33. Letter to Pier Serrassi, 1 May 1780. (*Giacomo Quarenghi Architetto e Pietroburgo. Lettere e altri scritti* [ed.] V. Zanella, [Venice, 1988], p. 22.)

34. G. Pavanello, 'Al servizio della Corte di Moscovia', in *Capolavori nascosti dell'Ermitage Dipinti veneti del Sei e Settecento da Pietroburgo*, exhibition catalogue, I. Artemieva, G. Bergamini, G. Pavanello (eds) (1998), p. 65.

CHAPTER IV

Painting and Sculpture during the Reign of Catherine the Great

YURI GUDIMENKO

OPPOSITE

This is one of the copies of the portrait of
Catherine which Mikhail Shibanov painted in
Kiev in April 1787, during the Empress's visit
to the south of Russia. Entitled *Catherine II in
Travelling Costume*, it was rare for Catherine
to accept graciously such an unflattering
portrait, showing her as an old woman.

Unknown artist after Mikhail Shibanov
(dated after 1787)

CATALOGUE NO. 158

The reign of Catherine the Great saw the completion of the cultural 'Europeanization' of Russia, an important part of Peter the Great's plan for reforming the country. During the first half of the 18th century, many works of art by European artists had been acquired by the Imperial court and by Russian aristocrats, and European art styles and types of work had replaced the Russian Orthodox Church's traditional iconography, architecture and decorative arts. Catherine II was completely committed to this transition and quickly began to develop art education, commission European art in quantity, and establish a national school of Russian art.

Professional art education had been introduced during the reign of Peter the Great. The study of painting, sculpture and architecture took place at the Armoury Chamber in Moscow, and at the Admiralty and later at the Academy of Sciences, which Peter founded in St Petersburg in 1724/5. However, his immediate successors did little to advance the artistic life of Russia. Only the Empress Elizabeth continued her father's active policy in the field of art. Together with Ivan Shuvalov, Elizabeth founded 'The Academy of the Three Noblest Arts' – painting, sculpture and architecture – in 1757. Established at Moscow University, the Academy produced such important representatives of Russian art as the painters Fedor Stepanovich Rokotov and Anton Losenko, sculptor Fedot Shubin, and the architects Vasily Bazhenov and Ivan Starov.

The beginning of Catherine's reign was marked by dramatic developments. The Elizabethan Baroque gave way to a Classicism that proclaimed the aspirations of the new Empress. Moreover, in November 1764, Catherine granted a new status to the Academy of Arts by renaming it the Imperial Academy of Arts, with herself as its founder and patron. The new Imperial Academy of Arts was established as an institution independent of Moscow University. As part of the system of Imperial institutions, the Academy expressed the ideology and artistic tastes of the court and the Empress herself, and it was the Academy that really instituted major state-funded, professional art training and triggered the birth of the Russian national school of art.

In accordance with the French Enlightenment ideas fashionable in

Europe at the time, the new President of the Imperial Academy of Arts, Ivan Betskoy, included a wide range of subjects and specialized courses of art in the curriculum, which favourably distinguished it from similar institutions in other European countries. The Academy began to recruit boys of five to six years of age, who would first complete a programme of general studies in the Education School of the Academy, and then proceed to specialized art classes. Training lasted for about fifteen years. The most talented graduates were given an opportunity to continue their education in Italy, France or Germany. In France, the philosopher Denis Diderot looked after the Academy fellows, in obedience to Catherine's instructions. By the end of the 18th century, the Imperial Academy of Arts was one of the largest art institutions in Europe, and as an institution of the Imperial state, it influenced the development of Russian culture in general.

However, it is important to note that Russian artistic life was not completely monopolized by the Academy. The most famous Russian portrait painter of the second half of 18th century, Dmitry Levitsky, was not one of its graduates. Nevertheless, he was pulled into its orbit, eventually becoming an academician, and the head of a portrait class there.

Throughout the 18th century, Russian art developed through close contact with West European artists. European painters were employed on court commissions and also trained local craftsmen. Prior to coming to Russia, many of these artists had been employed at other courts. They greatly influenced the artistic tastes of Russian artists and customers, and produced first-rate work during Catherine's time. Although many came to Russia to work temporarily, some chose to stay there for good.

The German portrait-painter Georg Christoph Grooth worked in Moscow and St Petersburg from 1740 until his death in 1749. He began his Russian career preparing designs for the coronation of the Empress Elizabeth, and then became a court painter and custodian of art galleries. Grooth created many portraits of Elizabeth, the Grand Duke Peter, and the young Catherine during her first years in Russia. His pairs of small equestrian portraits of the Grand Duke Peter and Catherine are of particular interest in Catherine II's early iconography. Grooth also had Russian students, among whom was the famous Russian painter Ivan Argunov.

Grooth's brother, animal painter Johann Friedrich Grooth, also stayed in Russia until the end of his life. He benefited from the fact that animal painting was not popular with Russian artists. His work was much sought after, and he was in charge of an animal painting class at the Academy of Arts from 1763–75.

Italian artists had long been present in Russia. Since the beginning of the 18th century, it was the Italians who had made major contributions to the construction of St Petersburg and the training of Russian painters and sculptors. Pietro Antonio Rotari gained fame and popularity in Russia, mainly as a portraitist, during his brief stay from 1756 until his death in 1762. Even though his elegant portraits in the Rococo style often lacked psychological depth, they were valued for their stunning resemblance to the sitters. Rotari had a private studio in St Petersburg, where the well-known painter Aleksey Antropov worked alongside other painters. Creative interests united Rotari with the famous Russian portrait painter, Rokotov.

Another Italian, Catherine's court painter Stefano Torelli, was appointed professor of the Academy of Arts. From 1762 until his death in 1780, he worked in St Petersburg as a portraitist and a painter of decorative and allegorical compositions. Torelli created numerous decorative murals and painted ceilings in the Imperial palaces, as well as portraits of the Empress. His 1763 coronation portrait of Catherine II became one of the most successful official portraits, and the Empress made a gift of it to the Senate. Russian artists repeatedly copied and imitated this portrait.

Ivan Betskoy commissioned Torelli to paint a typical composition of Catherine II's reign: an allegorical portrait of Catherine as *Minerva, Patroness of the Arts* (1770). Torelli was the last great Baroque painter in Russia and enjoyed enduring popularity at the Imperial court. The only work by Torelli that Catherine did not like was his equestrian portrait of her.

Almost all the Russian and foreign painters produced portraits. During Catherine's reign, a special type of formal portrait emerged in Russia – portraits with complex allegorical and symbolical subject-matter, which was passed on from one painter to another. Catherine's own portraits are full of symbolism. The Empress was keenly aware of the influence of art as a means of showing the legitimacy of her authority and promoting herself and her ideas. Thus, she was very careful about the portraits of herself.

Vigilius Eriksen, Alexander Roslin and Johann Baptist Lampi the Elder were among the most important creators of Catherine's allegorical portraits and projected potent images of her as an Enlightened

Empress. The Danish painter Eriksen (1722–82) worked in St Petersburg between 1757 and 1772 and is known in history as Catherine's court painter. In a letter to Baron Friedrich Melchior Grimm in Paris, the Empress mentioned a number of portraits Eriksen had created for her. He was given the very important commission of a huge portrait of the new Empress shortly after the *coup d'état* of 1762. Ericksen portrayed Catherine in officer's uniform with a sword in her hand, riding her horse, Brilliant, in a masculine or military manner. The painting was commissioned for the Audience Hall of the Grand Palace at Peterhof, from where Catherine had made her way to St Petersburg to seize power and to which she returned to receive her husband's surrender and abdication. The portrait was a great success and Eriksen was ordered to produce several copies in different sizes. It became a monument to the *coup d'état* and a personification of Catherine's triumph.

LEFT

A small version of Vigilius Eriksen's *Equestrian Portrait of Catherine II*, dated after 1762, was undertaken for the Grand Palace at Peterhof. Catherine is depicted in Horse-Guard's uniform on her stallion, Brilliant.

Vigilius Eriksen
(1722–82)

CATALOGUE NO. 32

Eriksen became Catherine's favourite portraitist and was entrusted with the most important commissions, including an order to paint her official coronation portrait in 1762. Despite the fact that many other artists also created coronation portraits, only Eriksen's pleased the Empress – so much so that she had it repeatedly copied and used as diplomatic gifts. The original portrait was kept in the ceremonial portrait gallery of the Romanov dynasty in the Winter Palace. Not exhibited for a long time, the painting has been restored especially for this exhibition. Eriksen also created one of the most original portraits of the Empress – *Catherine II in front of a Mirror* (1762–64). In this rare 'double portrait', Eriksen combined a reflected profile of the Empress on the left with the 'real portrait' on the right.

The Swedish painter and member of the *Académie française* Alexander Roslin (1718–93) worked in Paris for a long time, and spent the years 1775 to 1777 in Russia. He enjoyed great popularity with his patrons and customers, but his work had little impact on Russian artists. Roslin's work includes formal portraits of Catherine II, her son, Grand Duke Paul, and his wife, Maria Fedorovna, along with a few portraits of Russian court nobility. Roslin's Russian sitters appreciated his crisp and clear imagery, his accurate depiction of detail and texture of the materials, and his simple representation of his subjects devoid of concerns.

Nearly all official portraits of the period incorporated some ideological message expressed through allegory. In 1776–77, Roslin painted the Empress before a throne, with an Imperial crown and an orb close by, pointing to a bust of Peter the Great with her sceptre. An inscription reads 'Completes what was commenced', thus revealing the message of this portrait: Catherine was completing the reforms of Peter the Great. The Empress did not like her face in the portrait, and in a letter to Grimm complained that Roslin had painted her with a 'vulgar face, like that of a Swedish cook'. She ordered that copies of Roslin's portrait should have her head taken from a portrait by Rokotov.

The work of Austrian painter Johann Baptist Lampi the Elder (1751–1830) is of special importance and interest. Lampi was a master of miniature portraits, as well as of historical, allegorical and mythological paintings. He was a member of the Verona Academy of Arts and a professor at the Vienna Academy of Fine Arts. In 1791, Lampi accepted Prince Grigory Potemkin's invitation and moved to St Petersburg, where he worked until Catherine's death in 1796. Lampi created a number of portraits of the Empress, Grand Duke Paul and

Grand Duchess Maria, Catherine's grandsons Alexander and Constantine, Potemkin himself, and Catherine's last favourite, Platon
Zubov, as well as numerous portraits of Russian nobility. The portrait
of Potemkin became iconic even in the artist's lifetime and is now considered one of Lampi's greatest works. In accordance with the artistic
ideals of Classicism, Lampi depicted Catherine's mighty favourite as
an 'ideal commander', clad in armour. An expressive movement of his
gloved left hand and Potemkin's smooth facial features are contrasted
with the hard armour. Colour and tonal solutions introduce a note of
sentimentalism into this portrait.

Of particular interest are the portraits of Catherine that Lampi
created during the last years of her life. He continued his work in the
tradition of the 'allegorical' portraits of the Russian Minerva, which
traditionally depicted Catherine as an arbiter of justice, patron of
the arts and sciences, goddess of wisdom, and so forth. Lampi had to
cope with his royal client's tough 'censorship' – more than once, he was
obliged to alter Catherine's face in his portraits.

Lampi's last portrait of Catherine, painted during her lifetime, was
completed in 1793. It represents her as an Enlightened sovereign and
tone who continued the reforms of Peter the Great, with her left hand
pointing to a table with law books and a bas-
relief portrait of the former Emperor.

Lampi was employed at the Academy of
Arts and was in close contact with his Russian
colleagues. The great Russian artist Vladimir
Borovikovsky was among his students and
Lampi left him his studio when he returned
to Vienna.

The 1790s witnessed an even larger in-
flux of foreign artists to Russia. At the time,
portraits and miniatures by French painter
Élisabeth Louise Vigée Le Brun (1755-1842)
were extremely fashionable all over Europe.
She was the most brilliant representative of
European Sentimentalism, which was becoming increasingly prevalent in Russia.
During her stay in Russia (1795–1801),
Vigée Le Brun brought themes of affection
and love into Russian art, mainly through her
portraits of women. Most of her diverse

BELOW

Prince Grigory Potemkin
is represented here as the
'ideal military leader', a
heroic and freedom-loving
character, c.1790.

*Johann Baptist Lampi
the Elder*
(1751–1830)

CATALOGUE NO. 139

portrait themes served the main goal of revealing the 'life of the heart' and included figures of mothers and Madonnas who were hugging their children, young women at rest, and others standing next to vases of flowers. Many of these themes were not present in Russian painting before Vigée Le Brun's arrival.

In Russia, her works were found to be innovative and unusual, as is revealed by the story of the portrait of Catherine's granddaughters, Alexandra and Elena, in 1796. This was painted in the tradition of French Sentimentalism – the two embracing girls symbolize love for each other and for their grandmother, whose portrait one of them holds in her hand. Originally the sisters were represented as bacchantes, with grapes in their hair. However, Catherine disapproved of this quite innocent treatment and had the portrait redone: the grapes were replaced with wreaths of flowers, while the girls' arms, originally bare up to the shoulders, were concealed under their dresses. At the end of her life, Catherine would accept neither the emerging Sentimentalism nor Romanticism, just as she decisively rejected the Baroque style as being out of date at the commencement of her reign.

As well as bringing their best work to Russia, foreign artists also imported long-standing traditions of their national schools. This was

RIGHT

Vigée Le Brun's painting of the *Daughters of the Emperor Paul I, the Grand Princesses Alexandra and Elena Pavlovna* (1796), did not receive the blessing of the Empress. She thought her grand-daughters looked like 'pug dogs' or 'repulsive little French peasant girls'.

*Élisabeth Louise
Vigée Le Brun*
(1755–1842)

CATALOGUE NO. 204

when Russian artistic culture was under the powerful influence of the Enlightenment, with its cult of reason and the liberation of human beings. The Russian academic school became the hub for the dissemination of Classicism, which contemporaries called 'the enlightened style', and was based on the idea of serving one's Motherland. Art was assigned the honourable role of nurturing civic virtues. The political situation during the first decade of Catherine the Great's reign, when most contemporaries regarded her as the iconic 'Enlightened' monarch, contributed to the dissemination of ideas of Classicism. Devotion to citizenly values replaced military prowess and leadership talents as the greatest virtue.

In accordance with the doctrine of Classicism, historical paintings – including historical mythological, allegorical and religious subjects – were at the top of the hierarchy of genres of painting at the Academy of Arts, and were successfully undertaken by Anton Losenko, Ivan Akimov, Grigory Ugryumov and other Russian artists.

The first picture about national history in Russian painting is thought to be *Vladimir and Rogneda* (1770) by Anton Pavlovich Losenko (1737–73), a graduate and later director of the Academy of Arts. His most famous painting was repeatedly copied and became a model for numerous interpretations, including tapestries woven at the Imperial Tapestry Factory in St Petersburg.

Russian art also assigned a special place to the depiction of current events, typically government commissions that celebrated and commemorated military victories, portraits of the Empress with historical and allegorical references, or portraits of the main military commanders. These pictures generally abound with symbols and allegories.

Scenes of contemporary history were mostly represented by foreign painters. Amongst the most remarkable examples are the twelve large paintings of the highly successful Russian naval operation in the Mediterranean during the First Russian-Turkish War, by the German artist Jacob Philipp Hackert (1737–1807), which decorate one room of the Grand Palace at Peterhof. Traditionally, multiple copies of such paintings were produced, and the Hermitage's *The Destruction of the Turkish Fleet at the Battle of Chesme* in this exhibition is one of the copies that Hackert himself painted (see page 132).

Allegories, symbols and historical associations constituted the very art language of the triumphal compositions, repeatedly commissioned by the state and designed to further its interests. As a rule, war allegories contained an idealized or mythologized image of the monarch, and were intended to justify the legality, necessity and major benefits of state policy. Heinrich Buchholtz's *Allegory of the Victory of the Russian Fleet in the First Turkish War* (1777) (see page 40), and Andreas Caspar Hühne's *Catherine II laying the Trophies of Chesme on the Tomb of Peter the Great* (1791), represent typical examples of allegorical painting of the second half of the 18th century.

The greatest achievements of Russian painters of the second half of the 18th century are related to portraiture, the most widespread genre in Russian art at this time. Researchers attribute its vigour to the growth of national and personal identity in a period that began with Peter the Great's reforms and ended with the spread of the Enlightenment under Catherine II. In this sense, apart from its artistic value, portraiture acquired increasing social and historical significance in Russian art.

The work of the Russian-Ukranian painter Dmitry Levitsky (1735–1822) reflects the peak of Russian portraiture during Catherine's reign. Levitsky's artistic skills made him equal to the greatest foreign masters of the time. Most importantly, his work possesses a strong personality and his portraits are distinguished by their extraordinary emotional

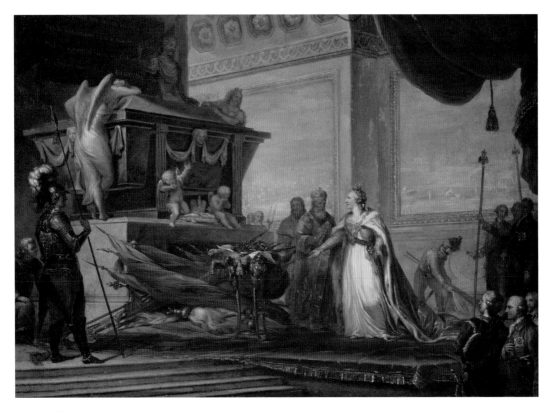

expressiveness, which reveal the finest shades of human feelings. Like that of any great master, Levitsky's work exceeds the confines of Classicism, and modern scholars find features of romantic elation and realistic psychology in his portraits.

Levitsky's largest undertaking of the 1770s was a 'suite' of portraits of the students of the Smolny Institute for Noble Maidens (all now in the Russian Museum, St Petersburg). It is possible that Catherine commissioned these portraits herself, to perpetuate the 'new breed of people' in art. As well as being the patron of the Smolny Institute, she was directly involved in the issue of women's education and training. The Smolny portraits later became known as a 'suite', although Levitsky did not conceive them as a set and worked upon them separately from 1772 until 1776.

Levitsky was a frequent painter of portraits of Catherine. His most famous work, *Catherine II as Lawmaker in the Temple of Justice*, was completed in 1783. It represents the Empress as 'the first citizen of the Motherland', and the servant of the law whom contemporaries regarded as an Enlightened monarch, destined to govern the state wisely. Catherine points to an altar with smouldering poppies that symbolize sleep. Just like these poppies, she burns herself on the altar of service to the Motherland. A statue of Justice is above her, and an eagle symbolizing wisdom and divine power is at her feet, while a distant ship symbolizes maritime power. The allegorical language of this portrait is a tribute to Classicism. However, the majority of Levitsky's portraits reveal him as an artist capable of creating multi-faceted and psychologically rich images of his contemporaries. In 1774, he painted a portrait of Denis Diderot, who came to Russia to visit Catherine. This portrait of Diderot, in his *robe-de-chambre* and without a wig, became one of Levitsky's first intimate portraits.

Fedor Stepanovich Rokotov (1732/35–1808) was another prominent portraitist of the time. He is renowned for his virtuosity, exceptional understanding of the emotional nature of light and colour, and the poetic and spiritual nature of his portraits. Rokotov was among the founders of a special kind of intimate portrait – usually a small-size, shoulder-length image without sophisticated attributes. His characters are always multi-faceted, and his brushstrokes create the impression of a glimmering and moving colourful layer, of transparent haze, and a particular airiness of the portrait space.

Catherine valued Rokotov's portraits of herself, possibly due to his skill in conveying identity and spirituality without idealizing his model. One of Catherine's most famous portraits by Rokotov, which she considered an iconic image of herself, can be found on page 28. A number of 'head and shoulders' portraits are known to have been copied from this full-length ceremonial portrait, and it became a model for many tapestry portraits woven at the Imperial Tapestry Factory as diplomatic gifts. It was also reproduced in miniatures and on porcelain. Levitsky himself copied the head of Catherine in Rokotov's portrait as he was unable to paint the Empress from life. Rokotov's paintings are exquisite and are on par with the greatest works of European painters.

While Dmitry Levitsky's body of work launched a brilliant epoch of Russian portraiture, the paintings of his student Vladimir Lukich Borovikovsky (1757–1825) completed it. Although Borovikovsky lived under the rule of Emperor Alexander I for quarter of a century, his imagery continued to reflect the dissemination of Sentimentalism and other features of the 1790s.

Catherine came across Borovikovsky's work during her journey to the Crimea in 1787. One of the Imperial palaces she stayed in contained two portraits by him: Catherine in a traditional allegorical composition as Minerva surrounded by Greek philosophers, and Catherine sowing the land ploughed by Peter the Great. As Lampi's student, Borovikovsky picked up some of his techniques, colour palette and tonal solutions, and was consistently developing the subjects and style of the Austrian painter.

Lampi and Borovikovsky brought sentimental sensitivity into their paintings. It is especially apparent in Borovikovsky's female portraits, whose characters he succeeds in conveying due to his ability to capture the finest of feelings, elegance of movements, and vivid naturalness. Like Jane Austen's characters, a beholder of such portraits was meant to exclaim: 'What a pretty face and figure! What graceful movements! What a heart of gold!' Both Lampi and Borovikovsky created decorative portraits, subtle in mood, where every movement and every line were well thought out and meaningful. The movements of Borovikovsky's characters are graceful, light and airy. Endowing a portrait with a particular mood was of paramount importance at the time. During the 1790s, this trend was linked to the obligatory introduction of a landscape background into the portrait. These landscape backgrounds are generally unconnected with the people in the portrait, but were intended to express the attitude of the time and the most general philosophical views, such as 'the powerful and passionate love of nature, which turns the entire world into paradise' (Goethe).

Sentimentalist aesthetics affected the portrait of *Catherine walking in the park in Tsarskoye Selo* of 1794 – the Empress is portrayed as a private individual, in her morning gown and with no hint of her Imperial status. The Chesme Column in the backgound was included in many paintings. Symbolizing valour and victory, it often made reference to Count Aleksey Orlov, hero of the battle of Chesme. However, in this portrait the column is solely used to identify the location. Borovikovsky's portrait was frequently copied in graphics and painting.

In addition to the historical genre, the Imperial Academy of Arts also developed landscape painting, the genre of 'domestic scenes', and animal and flower painting. Even though these genres were peripheral to Russian art of the second half of the 18th century, the achievements of Russian painters were remarkable and greatly influenced Russian painting of the following century.

Mikhail Shibanov (active 1770s–80s) was the most talented painter of genre scenes during Catherine's reign, and the creator of famous 'costume-ethnographic' compositions such as *Peasants' Lunch* (1774) and *The Feast of the Wedding Contract* (1777). It is interesting that the former serf never got to study at the Academy of Arts, and possibly received private art education from Levitsky and Kozlov, as researchers have suggested. By chance, Catherine's powerful favourite, Grigory Potemkin, discovered Shibanov. During her journey to the Crimea in 1787, Shibanov was in Potemkin's retinue, employed as a painter. It was during this journey that he created one of the most original portraits of the Empress, *Catherine II in Travelling Costume* (see page 62), a copy of which is included in this exhibition. Shibanov's work is representative of Russian art, where academic traditions are entwined with traditions of private tutoring, both often involving painters of different genres.

Landscape painting was for a long time confined to the limitations of the past. Since Peter the Great, the *raison d'être* of such painting had been to capture the precise image of an area or architectural

ABOVE

This is a copy of a picture by Vladimir Borovikovsky of 1794, now in the State Tretyakov Gallery, Moscow. It shows Catherine walking in the parkland at Tsarskoye Selo. The original was commissioned by the court administration, but was not purchased by the Empress due to its very informal nature.

*Unknown artist
after Vladimir Borovikovsky*
(late 18th/early 19th century)

CATALOGUE NO. 102

landmarks. Engraved views of cities were the only available urban landscapes.

Semyon Shchedrin (1745–1804) was the founder of Russian landscape painting. After graduating from the Academy of Arts, the young painter continued his studies in Paris and Rome, where he was influenced by Hubert Robert. On returning to Russia, Shchedrin's skills were recognized and he was appointed head of the landscape painting class at the Academy. Although committed to Classicism and imaginary landscape compositions, court commissions obliged Shchedrin to paint specific views of Imperial parks and gardens. He had to draw from nature and record the landscapes of Pavlovsk, Tsarskoye Selo, Peterhof and Gatchina. For many years, his pictures were used as iconic models for copying at the Academy.

The career of the Russian landscape painter Fedor Matveev (1758–1826) took a very different course. After graduating from the Academy, he was sent to Rome to continue his studies, and remained in Italy for good. Views of Italy and monuments of ancient Rome were his main themes. Matveev's works were eagerly acquired by the Russian aristocracy and are regarded as the greatest achievements of landscape painting during the age of Classicism. In 1813, the artist was elected Fellow of the Academy of Saint Luke in Rome.

Architectural landscape painting occupies a special place in Russian art of the second half of the 18th century. Up to this time, urban landscapes were mainly represented by engravings, and were largely influenced by German and Dutch masters, and later by Venetian *vedute* or views. During the second half of the century, the urban landscape emerged as an independent genre and much of the credit for this belongs to Fedor Alekseev (1753–1824). Like many other talented graduates of the Academy, Alekseev perfected his art in Italy. Upon returning to Russia, he often copied the work of Canaletto, Bellotto and Robert's paintings on the orders of the Empress Catherine. In obedience to her instructions, Alekseev undertook a long trip south along the route of Catherine's journey to the Crimea in 1787, to paint picturesque views of places she had visited. In addition, his urban landscapes of St Petersburg also brought him fame. Despite the influence of the great examples of Venetian *vedute*, these views of St Petersburg are far more than imitations. Alekseev's particular colour palette, introduction of staffage (figures), and individuality, enabled him to create a series of lyrical portraits of St Petersburg.

The last decades of the 18th century inaugurated a new period in the development of Russian landscape painting, which was filled with emotional content that became more lyrical and responsive to the new trends in Russian culture associated with Sentimentality. Of great importance for the development of landscape painting was the work of such foreign artists as Gérard de la Barthe (active 1787–1810), John Augustus Atkinson (active 1784–1801), Benjamin Paterssen (active 1787–1815) and Johann Georg De Meyr (active 1778–1816). Meyr's *View of the Palace Embankment, St Petersburg, from Vasilyevsky Island* (1796), is a typical example of urban landscape painting. Apart from the magnificent, majestic capital of Russia, we can also see everyday urban life with all its hustle and bustle, strolling townspeople and merchants going about their business. Alekseev and Meyr succeeded in creating such a convincing and attractive image of the northern capital in their series of paintings of St Petersburg that even today we tend to look at the city largely through their eyes.

One of the most significant achievements of Russian art of the second half of the 18th century was the foundation of a national school of sculpture. Unlike Europe, whose centuries-old history of portraiture and sculpture was based on Ancient prototypes, Russia did not possess its own traditions. The art of the Russian Orthodox Church limited the role of sculpture chiefly to the decoration of buildings and interiors with carved wood and stone. Three-dimensional wooden sculpture was known

CATHERINE
THE GREAT

BELOW

This view of the Palace Embankment, St Petersburg from Vasilyevsky Island was one of a series of views of the capital completed between 1796 and 1803. It has been suggested that the series was carried out to mark the centenary of the foundation of St Petersburg.

Johann Georg De Meyr
(1760–1816)

CATALOGUE NO. 58

only in some northern areas of the country. Ancient Greek and Roman sculpture only began to be collected during Peter the Great's time.

After the foundation of St Petersburg in 1703, Italian, German and French sculptors were invited to the new capital to work and to train local craftsmen. It is they who created a foundation for the rapid development of secular sculpture in Russia during the second half of the 18th century.

The Empress, while deeply enthusiastic about architecture, carved gems and art collecting, did not profess any particular interest in sculpture. Her acquisition of ancient sculptural monuments and works of European masters was rather dictated by her passion for architecture and was of a 'subordinate' character. Catherine regarded sculpture as an accompaniment to architecture – as decoration for interiors, art galleries, and so on. Nevertheless, her passion for building numerous architectural complexes and monuments in St Petersburg and her suburban residences of Peterhof, Tsarskoye Selo and Pavlovsk, did necessitate some sculptural decoration. Thus her urban and architectural projects resulted in the development of sculpture as well.

An invaluable role in the creation of the national school of sculpture is attributed to the teaching activities of the French sculptor Nicolas-François Gillet (1709–91), who was in charge of the sculpture class of the Academy of Arts for twenty years after its foundation. All the leading Russian sculptors were trained by him, including Fedor Gordeev, Mikhail Kozlovsky, Ivan Prokofiev, Theodosius Shchedrin, Fedot Shubin and Ivan Martos.

Russian sculpture of the second half of the 18th century has a special place in the artistic life of Catherine's reign, and demonstrates the ideals of Classicism and the skills of local craftsmen even more than painting. It is sculpture that most clearly reveals the change of artistic styles: from the exuberant Baroque to the strict balance of Classicism. However, the images of ancient mythology so widely exploited by Baroque masters were no less organically incorporated into Classicism in order to express civic and moral ideals of the Enlightenment. Unlike painting, sculpture was more inclined to profess abstract ideas of the Enlightenment and was actively introduced into architecture in the form of reliefs and statues. During this period, close attention was paid to the perfection of artistic forms, which was supposed to be inseparable from the new content, and to the manifestation of citizenship, heroism and virtue.

The most remarkable achievements are associated with Fedot

Shubin (1740–1805). After graduating from the Academy, he had an opportunity to continue his studies in France, England and Italy. Shubin created a gallery of sculptural portraits of the Russian aristocracy, court, figures in the sciences and the arts, and famous military commanders. His greatest works include portraits of Grigory Potemkin, Alexander Suvorov, Alexander Bezborodko, Ivan Betskoy and the Emperor Paul I. Shubin's style is distinguished by his virtuoso carving in marble, which he often used for his busts. It was marble that gave the sculptor the opportunity to develop very intricate sculptural surfaces. Due to his keen interest in the human mind, the modelling of the faces in his works merits close attention. The spectrum of moods in Shubin's sculptural portraits is tremendous; his characters are endowed with a sense of harmonious existence and life, with painful thoughts, romantic dreams, and sometimes with an almost exaggerated honesty. His later works reveal a growing desire for serenity and simplicity, and his treatments become more integral and convincing.

As in the past, sculpture of the second half of the 18th century adorned public and administrative buildings, as well as palatial buildings, though on a smaller scale when compared to the Baroque palaces of the Empress Elizabeth. A much greater ideological significance was attached to sculpture during Catherine's reign. The practice of erecting commemorative obelisks, columns and sculptures in suburban gardens and parks was becoming widespread. Such sculptural ensembles were part of many sculptors' work in the second half of the 18th century.

The city of St Petersburg required sculptural monuments with a clear patriotic message. The introduction of sculpture into urban spaces began with the erection of Etienne-Maurice Falconet's monument to Peter the Great in Senate Square, St Petersburg. It was Diderot who recommended the Parisian sculptor Falconet to Catherine II. According to Falconet himself, he aspired to create an image of Peter the Great as a creator, legislator and reformer. However, Falconet's imagery turned out to be much more multi-faceted. The 'Bronze Horseman' embodied the perception of Peter the Great as a hero, military commander and triumphant victor. In an attempt to avoid multiple allegories, Falconet only included a snake trampled by the rampant horse. The snake as a symbol of hostility and evil was of both symbolic and compositional value (see page 49).

Not only did this image echo the major Classical concepts of the time, but it was also directly related to the monument's commissioner,

Catherine II, who positioned herself as Peter the Great's successor on the throne and in politics, as well as the heiress to his glory. It is no accident that the monument's inscription (made by a student of Falconet', Marie-Anne Collot) reads in Russian and Latin: 'To Peter I from Catherine II.' Falconet's talented assistant was also entrusted with modelling the head of Peter the Great for this famous monument.

Collot's work enjoyed great success in St Petersburg, and although Jean-Antoine Houdon was the most popular sculptor in Russia at the time, with his works present in many palaces in the capital, Collot was able to withstand the competition of her brilliant compatriot and received numerous commissions for portraits in marble. In 1769, she made a bust of Catherine II, which the Empress liked so much that she decided to give it to Voltaire. Like Houdon, Collot created several busts of French philosophers who were Catherine's friends. Particularly successful were the portrait busts of her teacher, Falconet, and their mutual friend, Diderot.

The dominant feature of the Field of Mars ensemble in St Petersburg was a monument to Field Marshal Alexander Suvorov by the sculptor Mikhail Ivanovich Kozlovsky (1753–1802), in which we can trace a constant struggle between Baroque and Classicism. This also applies to other monumental works by Kozlovsky, as well as to his sculpture and portraiture in which expressive movement and form characteristic of Baroque are subjugated to the massive monumentality of the image.

Kozlovsky's body of work is a splendid demonstration of Russian Classicism. The success of the Suvorov monument lies in the finesse and expressiveness of austere forms, the integrity of compositional solutions and the genuine monumentality of Classicism. Kozlovsky idealized Suvorov and represented him as Mars, God of War. The commission successfully integrated monumental sculpture into an urban architectural ensemble and inspired other architects, sculptors and projects.

For the prominent Russian sculptor Ivan Petrovich Martos (1754–1835), the last decades of the 18th century were just the beginning of an artistic journey that led to the most important works he completed during the reign of Emperor Alexander I, including the monument to Minin and Pozharsky in Moscow. The monument to Potemkin is an example of Martos's early work, revealing his talent as a monumental sculptor committed to the elevated ideals of Classicism.

The historical genre dominated sculpture classes at the Imperial Academy of Arts. As a rule, subjects and themes were tackled in multi-figured compositions in relief. Decorative and allegorical sculpture was popular with nearly all the sculptors involved in state commissions, including those for public institutions. For instance, the sculptor Ivan Prokofiev (1758–1828) created a large allegorical group for Catherine's home for foundlings in 1791. Catherine, the patroness of the orphans, is represented as Terra, the goddess Mother Earth.

The construction of obelisks to mark victories or to honour military commanders was common not only in cities, but also on Catherine's country estates and residences. Tsarskoye Selo, her favourite summer residence, had obelisks and columns honouring the victories of Field Marshal Pyotr Rumyantsev, the battle of Chesme, the battle of Kagul, and other successes. This powerful 'propaganda through monuments' was continued after Catherine's death by her grandson, Alexander I, under different historical conditions.

Catherine II's epoch is justly known as the Golden Age of Russian art. It was during this period that the Russian national school of fine arts emerged, as many talented artists and sculptors appeared in the country. However, the most important outcome of this period was that Russian art finally became a fully-fledged and dynamic part of the European or Western mainstream.

RIGHT

Martos was one of the leading Russian sculptors of the time and was appointed senior professor at the Academy of Arts in 1794. This sculpture of Grigory Potemkin is dated *c.*1794–95.

Ivan Petrovich Martos (1754–1835)

CATALOGUE NO. 141

Catherine the Great's Collection of Paintings: The Purchase of Old Masters and the Acquisition of Contemporary Works of Art

MARIA GARLOVA

OPPOSITE

The Apotheosis of James I, 1632–33,
is a sketch for the central painting of Rubens's
famous ceiling in the Banqueting Hall of
Whitehall Palace, London, commissioned by
King Charles I. It shows Charles's father,
James VI of Scotland and I of England,
being crowned with a laurel wreath by figures
personifying Religion, Faith, Justice, Victory
and Minerva, on his way up to heaven.

Sir Peter Paul Rubens (1577–1640)

CATALOGUE NO. 223

BELOW

Wealthy Count Alexander
Sergeievich Stroganov
(1733–1811) lived in
Paris from 1771 to 1778
and became a friend and
patron of the sculptor
Jean-Antoine Houdon and
the painters Hubert Robert,
Jean Baptist Greuze and
Élisabeth Louise
Vigée Le Brun.

Attributed to *Nicolas Soret*
(1759–1830)

CATALOGUE NO. 303

In 1764, when Catherine the Great was thirty-five and in her second year as the absolute ruler of Russia, there appeared at her court the first important group of paintings which would lay the foundation for the collection of paintings in the State Hermitage Museum. This was the collection which had been assembled by the Berlin businessman Johann Ernst Gotzkowsky, who was the commissioner for the Prussian King Frederick the Great of Prussia, one of the most important art collectors in Europe.

Because of the Seven Years War, Frederick had stopped purchasing and Gotzkowsky had suffered huge losses. Having large debts to the Russian Military Departments, Gotzkowsky suggested to the Russian ambassador, V. S. Dolgorukov, that part of these might be met with paintings. Catherine was only too happy to strike a blow to the pride of Frederick the Great, her enemy in the Seven Years War. She bought the collection, which was made up of over 200 canvases, including some works of very high artistic quality – three works by Rembrandt van Rijn, *Family Portrait* by Jacob Jordaens, *Allegory of Peace, Art and Abundance* by Hans von Aachen, and *Portrait of a Young Man with a Glove* by Frans Hals.

In Catherine's memoirs there is no mention of her love for, or even her interest in, art during her childhood and youth, although she devoted a lot of time to self-improvement and self-education. Prior to her reign, the Russian court had already acquired some paintings. The Emperor Peter the Great, who had travelled widely and had seen great collections of art at various European courts, used to buy pictures through his agents in Italy, France and The Netherlands. Peter considered the task of 'the protection of art and antiquities to be a matter of state importance'.[1] His daughter, the Empress Elizabeth, who had excellent taste, would make lists of the artists who decorated her palace. She loved painting, dabbled in it, and collected it for her own pleasure. Indeed, many of her courtiers followed this fashion. In their foreign travels, they became acquainted with the leading works of previous eras and also with modern artists. Some courtiers, such as Alexander Sergeievich Stroganov and Ivan

Shuvalov, were passionately interested in collecting and they knew the thriving art market in Europe very well.

However, it was only in Catherine's reign that a definite policy of large-scale purchases of works of art and of radically increasing the collections of European masters began. The decision was also made to create the Hermitage. Catherine, who, especially in the first years of her reign, feared the accusation of having usurped the throne, declared to everyone that she was continuing the work initiated by Peter the Great. 'That which was begun will be completed,' reads the inscription on her portrait by Alexander Roslin, in which she points to the bust of the first Russian Emperor.[2]

The collecting of art was one of the many things which had been started by Peter. It occupied an important place in Catherine's programme of measures when she came to the throne. She had announced her adherence to the ideas of the French Enlightenment, and thus had to show herself before European society as an 'enlightened' monarch, and one who stimulated the development of the arts and the sciences in her own country. Diplomatically and politically, this was one of the most important ways of raising the prestige of Russia in Europe.

Here, as in virtually all her undertakings, the Empress made use of the advice and abilities of experts, people with whom, through her truly remarkable 'hunches' and a surprising sense of circumspection, she surrounded herself with. She relied on her experienced advisers and agents. Prince Dmitry Alekseyevech Golitsyn played the most active role, starting in 1765 as ambassador in Paris and thereafter at The Hague from 1768. Golitsyn was a friend of Diderot and Etienne-Maurice Falconet, and through a friend of Voltaire, the Genevan collector François Tronchin, he was able to make contact with Swiss agents for acquiring art. He was also in touch with Baron Friedrich Melchior Grimm, Catherine's correspondent in Paris for many years. Catherine's agent in Rome was Johann Friedrich von Reiffenstein, an admirer of the theorist of Classicism, Johann Joachim Winckelmann, who had devoted his life to the study of antiquity.

After the successful acquisition of Gotzkowsky's collection, Catherine commissioned work from artists favoured by Diderot – the Venetian Francesco Casanova and the Frenchmen Joseph-Marie Vien and Louis-Michel van Loo. Golitsyn also conducted discussions about bringing Jean-Baptiste Greuze and van Loo to Russia, but nothing came of these plans.

Catherine's collection grew with incredible speed. In order to house the works not too far from the Winter Palace, the Small Hermitage was built (1764–75, by the architect Yury Velten, based on designs by Jean-Baptist Vallin de la Mothe) and the Large Hermitage, which is now called the Old Hermitage (1771–87, by Velten).

Catherine had acquired a taste for collecting, knew her pictures well, could work through catalogues, and often called her new interest 'gluttony', just as Prince Elector Lothar Franz von Schönborn used to call his obsession and insatiability for collecting, 'Malereiwurm' ('painting worm') and 'Bilderappetit' ('appetite for pictures').[3] However, unlike real art lovers, the Empress did not show any special preferences in her search for really outstanding discoveries, as did Frederick the Great, who collected Flemish Baroque art with passion. Frederick also collected Italian artists of the 17th and 18th centuries and decorated the walls of his castle Sanssouci with paintings by Jean Antoine Watteau. Frederick would not consider exhibiting the modern Italians, and, as for the Germans, he used to say that they were too coarse to go in for painting and it was not even worth trying to teach them.[4] It was only rarely that Catherine expressed her opinion about art as openly as her Prussian relative.[5]

The start of Catherine's reign coincided with a change in artistic style. It is well known that she did not like the Baroque, preferring the noble simplicity of Classicism, which at that time was still, in many works of art, strongly imbued with the Rococo, or had a 'veneer' of sentimentalism. Catherine would simply 'exile' some of the items she did not like to the palaces on the outskirts of St Petersburg. Vien's picture *Minerva*, for example, was given to the Academy of Arts. Works by Charles-André van Loo, from the collection of Louis-Michel van Loo, were also sent there. Sometimes it would happen the other way round. Although Jean-Baptiste-Siméon Chardin's *Still Life with the Attributes of the Arts* had been bought especially by Golitsyn for the Academy of Arts, Catherine kept it for herself in the Hermitage. She devoted much time and effort to the picture gallery there, and even helped the restorer clean off mould from damp objects with her own hands.[6] Her astonished contemporaries considered that she had taken on too many things at once and that she loved to start, direct and revise projects at one and the same time. She showed great zeal in all her endeavours and made her ministers work without stop. Frederick the Great was amazed at this boundless energy.[7]

The agents of the tireless Empress of Russia tried not to miss a single opportunity to make a significant acquisition, be it in Paris or at the auctions in The Hague, Amsterdam or Dresden. Purchases of Old Masters alternated with acquisitions of, and commissions for, paintings by contemporary artists.

In 1766, Golitsyn managed to buy some French and Dutch paintings at a sale of the collection of the king's painter and member of the French Académie, Jacques-André-Joseph Aved (1702–66). A year later, he bought a series of paintings of Dutch and Flemish masters, including Nicolaes Berchem, at an auction of the collection of Jean de Jullienne (1686–1767), a patron of the arts, collector, and director of the Gobelins Factory.

In the summer of 1768, Diderot tried to acquire the fine collection of Gaignat, the deceased former secretary of Louis XV. However, he only managed to acquire two *Bathing Girls* and one *Bathing Boy* by Gerrit Dou and Bartolomé Esteban Murillo's *Rest on the Flight into Egypt*. Here Diderot 'let slip' Rembrandt's *The Carpenter's Family*, which ended up in the Louvre. In contrast, Golitsyn had a wonderful piece of luck. He acquired from the Duc d'Ancezune the most valuable of all the Rembrandts in the Hermitage, *The Prodigal Son*. This came from the collection of the Archbishop of Cologne, Clement August von Bayern, which was sold after his death in Bonn in 1764 and brought to Paris for sale.[8] *The Prodigal Son* was one of the unsold works at the auction and cost the Hermitage less than a whole series of works by Teniers, Wouverman and Adriaen van Ostade.

In 1769, a collection arrived at the Hermitage that greatly enriched its Dutch and Flemish holdings. This was the famous gallery of Count Georg Brühl, minister of Augustus III of Saxony, who emulated his king in his passion for collecting. In 1754 the works in this magnificent collection had been reproduced in a splendid engraved edition.[9] They included Rembrandt's *Portrait of a Scholar*, *Portrait of an Old Man in Red* and *Old Lady*, five landscapes by Jacob van Ruisdael, and *The Messenger* by Gerard ter Borch. The most valuable Flemish School paintings were Peter Paul Rubens's *Perseus and Andromeda* and *Landscape with a Rainbow*, along with several works by Teniers. This acquisition also brought to the Hermitage two of Watteau's paintings, *An Embarrassing Proposal* and *The Holy Family*. Among the Italian paintings were Albani's *The Abduction of Europa*, Guido Reni's *Noah's Ark*, and Crespi's *Death of Joseph* and *Holy Family*.

The next collection acquired for the Hermitage through the efforts of Golitsyn, and with Diderot's help, was that of the aforementioned

François Tronchin, who had lived in Paris since 1762. If not as significant as the previous acquisitions, it nevertheless consisted of a hundred paintings by Dutch, Flemish and Italian masters. Unfortunately, Golitsyn did not manage to deliver all the works he had acquired at the sale of the famous collection of Gerrit Braamkamp in Amsterdam in 1771. These valuable canvases were lost in a shipwreck on their way to St Petersburg. Only one painting – Bon Boullogne's *The Return of Jephtha* – arrived safely; it had been sent on another ship.

In the 1770s, the Paris market continued to be the main source for the expansion of the Hermitage. Two paintings by Carle van Loo, *The Spanish Concert* and *Spanish Readings*, which had been commissioned in 1754 by Marie-Thérèse Geoffrin (1699–1777), hostess of a famous Parisian Literary Salon popular with the *Encyclopédistes* (contributors to Diderot and Jean le Rond d'Alembert's French encyclopedia), were purchased for Catherine, with Diderot as the intermediary. In 1771, on the recommendation of the sculptor Falconet, Claude Lorrain's canvas *Landscape with Christ on the Road to Emmaus* was acquired from an unknown Parisian dealer.

The most important acquisition for the Hermitage was also made in Paris. This was the purchase in 1772, on the initiative of Tronchin and with the active help of both Diderot and Golitsyn, of the outstanding Crozat collection. The Parisian home of Pierre Crozat (1665–1749), a genuine and profound connoisseur of art, as well as a financier and adviser to Louis XV, was a centre of cultural life in Paris. The *Encyclopédistes* used to gather in Crozat's treasure-filled mansion, and Watteau, Charles de La Fosse and Rosalba Carriera all lived and worked there at various times. The house was open to all lovers of art and artists. After Crozat's death, his collection of paintings was left to his heirs – first to his nephew, the Marquis du Châtel, and then to Baron de Thiers. The smaller part of the collection went to du Châtel's daughter, who married the Duc d'Choiseul, the former foreign secretary and minister for war and the navy. After the death of Baron de Thiers, his heirs sold the collection as quickly as possible.

After some eighteen months of negotiations, Tronchin, Grimm and Golitsyn managed to buy the entire collection for 460,000 *livres*. This caused a real sensation. Europe was amazed that Catherine had bought Thiers's collection at the same time as Russia was at war. The Italian part of the Crozat collection was especially strong and included Raphael's *Holy Family*, Giorgione's *Judith*, Titian's *Danae* (then thought to be by Raphael), Paulo Veronese's *Deposition from the Cross*,

Capriolo's *Portrait of a Man*, Lambert Sustris's *Jupiter and Io*, and Domenico Fetti's *Portrait of an Actor*. The Flemish portion contained such masterpieces as Rubens's *Portrait of a Lady-in-Waiting*, *Bacchus* and *The Banishment of Hagar*, as well as some of his sketches, and seven works by Antony Van Dyck including his *Self Portrait*. Among the Dutch canvases were seven paintings by Rembrandt, whose *Danae* and *Holy Family* became the pride of the Hermitage. French painting was represented by works by Pierre Mignard, Nicolas de Largillière, Watteau, Nicolas Lancret, Chardin and Pierre Subleyras.

Diderot managed to acquire eleven works from the group of Crozat's paintings which had gone to Choiseul and were sold at auction after the fall of that powerful minister. Among these were works by Murillo and Teniers. Catherine was delighted that her collection was increasing. This demonstrated the economic and political power of Russia. The country had found the means, in spite of the lengthy war with Turkey, to make very expensive purchases not only of individual works of art, but of entire outstanding, magnificent collections which contained real pearls, so desirable for any collector.

Soon after the Choiseul auction, Diderot was able to buy two

ABOVE

Landscape with Christ on the Road to Emmaus, 1660. The French painter Lorrain worked in Rome and produced beautifully composed and painted ideal landscapes. These were greatly prized by collectors and had a huge influence on contemporary and later artists.

Claude Lorrain (1602–82)

CATALOGUE NO. 225

wonderful paintings by Nicolas Poussin from the impoverished Marquis de Conflans. From Conflans also came Jean Lemaire's *Square of an Ancient City*, which was then thought to be the work of Gaspard Dughet.

Comparable in significance to the acquisition of the Crozat collection was the purchase in 1779 of a large part of the British collection assembled by Sir Robert Walpole, the 1st Earl of Orford (1676–1745) and prime minister during the reigns of King George I and George II.

RIGHT

The painting *Darius opens the Tomb of Nitocris* (*c.*1649) was acquired from the Crozat collection in 1772. According to the ancient historian Herodotus, the Babylonian queen Nitocris had a message put on her tomb informing people that it contained riches. After the Persians conquered Babylonia, King Darius had it opened. All that he found were the decayed remains of Nitocris and an inscription reproaching him for his great greed.

Eustache Le Sueur
(1616–55)

CATALOGUE NO. 221

It was housed at Walpole's country seat, Houghton Hall, in Norfolk. The Russian ambassador in England, Aleksei Semenovich Musin-Pushkin (1732–1817), led the negotiations with George Walpole, 3rd Earl of Orford (1730–91), the great-nephew of Sir Robert Walpole. The Hermitage acquired almost 200 treasures, including such notable Dutch and Flemish works as Rembrandt's *Sacrifice of Abraham* and Van Dyck's family portraits and *Madonna with Partridges*. There were also paintings by Rubens, Snyders, Jordaens and by Van der Werff. Among the Italian paintings were Salvator Rosa's *Prodigal Son*, Guido Reni's *Fathers of the Church Disputing the Dogma of the Immaculate Conception*, and Lucas Giordano's *Young Bacchus Sleeping* and *Vulcan's Forge*.

Walpole's French and Spanish pictures included Sébastien Bourdon's *Massacre of the Innocents* and *Jacob burying Laban's Images*, canvases by Lorrain and Poussin, and four paintings by Murillo.

Quite recently, and thanks to the careful research of a member of the Hermitage staff, Irina Artemieva, it was discovered that another collection arrived on the same ship as the Walpole collection. This was an important batch of paintings that had come from Venice.[10] They had been acquired by the Empress from the English consul and art

dealer in Venice, John Udny (1727–1800), who hailed from Aberdeen. Udny had become the right-hand man of the ageing British consul in Venice, Joseph Smith, who recommended that the young Scot should fill his position after his retirement in 1760. It is now known from documents that Udny was in St Petersburg in 1768. The following year, he managed to gain an audience with the Empress and was able to persuade her to buy a group of paintings. Udny received payment for them in the same year, 1769.

Udny took a risk, daring to propose these paintings personally to the Empress. Artemieva suggests that he was encouraged to do this by the example of the Marquis Pano Maruzzi who, shortly before, had supplied thirty-seven paintings to the St Petersburg court from Venice.

The delivery of Udny's pictures from Venice turned out to be a lengthy process. In order to avoid paying customs duties, and because the Doge of Venice had not given him permission to transport them via land, Udny sent the consignment to the Tuscan port of Livorno, where it was loaded onto an English ship and taken to England. There his elder brother, Robert Udny, was waiting to receive it. A decade later, the crates were put on board the same vessel as the Walpole collection and finally entered the Hermitage. Twenty-one of Udny's sixty paintings can be identified. The Italian Schools are represented by Tintoretto, Salvator Rosa and Antonio Bellucci; and among the works

RIGHT
AND OPPOSITE

The paintings
*St Sebastian tended
by St Irene* and a *Group
of Female Musicians*
were both acquired from
John Udny in 1779.

(RIGHT) *Antonio Bellucci*
(1654–1726)
CATALOGUE NO. 227

(OPPOSITE)
*Attributed to the Master of
Female Half Lengths*
(Second quarter of 16th century)
CATALOGUE NO. 222

by northern artists is the 16th-century panel painting of a *Group of Female Musicians*, which was thought to be by Hans Holbein but is now attributed to the Master of Female Half-Lengths.

The last important input to the Hermitage collection during Catherine's reign was Count Baudouin's collection, acquired on the recommendation of Baron Grimm in 1783 after four years of negotiations. Grimm was certain that it was one of the best collections in Paris, and he was right. There were 119 paintings, including nine by Rembrandt, six portraits by Van Dyck, four works by Ostade, three by Ruisdael and six by Teniers. There were also several Italian and French pictures of the 17th century.

A distinctive feature of Catherine's collecting is that she did not restrict herself to gathering famous and well-known Old Masters. She also bought contemporary works or works which she herself commissioned, and thus succeeded in outstripping rival major collectors.

This was the case with the collecting of English works, which were still largely unknown on the Continent and missing from the best European collections. In 1773, Catherine bought her first English painting, *The Iron Forge Viewed from Outside* by the almost unknown English artist, Joseph Wright of Derby. Six years later, she acquired another two of Wright's works – *Firework Display at the Castel San Angelo in Rome (La Girandola)* and *The Eruption of Vesuvius*. In 1785, the Earl of Carysfort, who, thanks to his friendship with the British ambassador, moved in the highest circles of the Russian Imperial court, was able to persuade Catherine that her collection would be incomplete without works by Sir Joshua Reynolds.[11] Very soon, two pictures were commissioned from the president of the Royal Academy, on subjects of his own choosing: one was for the Empress and the other for Prince Grigory Potemkin. For Catherine, Reynolds created the huge allegorical composition *The Infant Hercules Strangling the Serpents*, where the powerful infant Hercules symbolizes Russia and the serpents he is strangling are her enemies.

Since her youth, Catherine had showed an interest in English literature. She began to study English in 1750, and read Henry Fielding, Laurence Sterne, R. B. Sheridan, Samuel Richardson and Alexander Pope (mostly in French). It comes as no surprise that, between 1785 and 1797, she acquired paintings by Angelica Kauffmann (one of only two women in the Royal Academy) illustrating Pope's *Abelard and Héloïse* (*The Farewell of Abelard and Héloïse*) and Laurence Sterne's *A Sentimental Journey* (*The Insane Maria* and *The Monk of Calais*).

It had been Princess Dashkova, on her return from her travels abroad, who had acquainted the Empress with the work of Angelica Kauffmann. Dashkova had given the Empress a painting of a Greek beauty to honour the Russian victory over the Turks. The hint of sentimentalism in Kauffmann's early Classical works suited the sentimental mood of Russian society at that time. Indeed, many Russians visited Kauffmann's studio after she moved to Rome, including Catherine's son, Paul, and his wife, Maria Fedorovna, who called on the artist during their tour of Europe in 1782. Prince Nikolai Yusupov was also a great admirer and purchased her works.

Unlike Frederick the Great, Catherine paid artists generously, and she did not overlook the colony of German Classical painters in Rome. Catherine had long wanted to possess works by Anton Raphael Mengs, the leading representative of this group. With Reiffenstein as intermediary, she bought up, from Mengs's heirs, everything that remained in the artist's studio after his death. Her acquisitions included his *Judgement of Paris*, which had been commissioned by Frederick the Great but not paid for, and also *St John the Baptist Preaching in the Desert* and the *Self Portrait*. For the Empress, Grimm also managed to acquire the famous large canvas *Perseus and Andromeda*, which Mengs had painted shortly before his death.

In 1778, having been impressed by the engravings of Volpato, Catherine decided to commission a full-size copy of the so-called Raphael Loggia in the Vatican for the Hermitage. Johann Reiffenstein engaged Meng's friend and assistant, Christopher Unterberger, to produce this. Unterberger created life-size cartoons and the painters Giovanni Angeloni and his son Vincenzo transferred them to canvas. They finished in 1782; three years later, the Italian architect Giacomo Quarenghi completed the construction of a special building in the Hermitage to display the replicas.

Thanks to Catherine, Jacob Philipp Hackert, who had arrived in Rome and was the pioneer of the heroic Classical landscape in Germany in the second half of the 18th century, gained the attention of all Europe. In 1771, he completed a commission for the Empress of a painting of the great naval victory of the Russian fleet over the Turks at the battle of Chesme (see page 132). In order to gain greater authenticity, Hackert was allowed to blow up an old Russian ship off the port of Livorno. The explosion attracted a huge number of spectators, and the picture itself caused such a sensation in the European press that Hackert became an overnight success. After this he gained work and

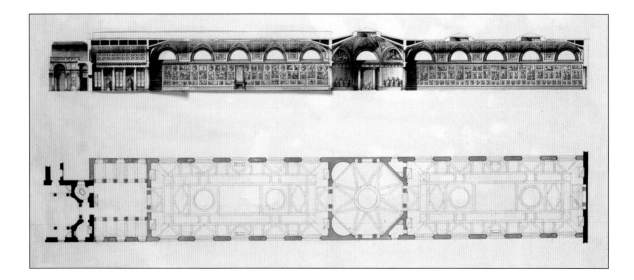

renown at the court of the King of Naples, and the Prussian King began
to give him commissions, while the Queen of Greece was envious of
those monarchs who had already managed to acquire his works.

Thus, wittingly or unwittingly, Catherine played a role in the fate
of many contemporary European artists. Many of them were made
most welcome at the court of St Petersburg and worked there for several
years. The portrait painters are worth special attention. Among these
were the talented Dane, Vigilius Eriksen, the Englishman Richard
Brompton, the Austrian Johann Baptist Lampi the Elder, and the
French portrait painter Élisabeth Louise Vigée Le Brun.

The collections of Catherine the Great had a huge and decisive
significance in the great task of creating the Hermitage. Goals were set,
and these determined the future development of the picture gallery.
At the end of her reign, the Empress did not buy large collections or
groups of paintings. However, her interest never waned and the successful activities of other European monarchs gave her no respite. In 1796,
the year of her death, she commissioned from the Saxon artist Anton
Graff, who was working in Dresden, same-size copies of all the best
paintings which were being shown in the Dresden Gallery. Thanks to
the intervention of the Russian ambassador, permission for this was
granted as a special exception.

In the end, it was only death that put a stop to the ambitious
activities of Catherine the Great.[12]

1. V. F. Levinson-Lessing, *History of the Painting Gallery of the Hermitage (1764–1917)* (Moscow, 1985), p. 42.

2. In the State Hermitage Museum, inv. no. GE–1316.

3. W. Boll, 'Zur Geshichte der Kunst Bestrebungen des Kürfusten von Mainz, Lothar Franz von Schönborn. Archivalische Beiträge zur Kunst- und Sammeltätigkeit eines rheinischen Zeitgenossen Johann Wilhelms von der Pfalz', *Archiv für Geschichte der Stadt Heidelberg und der Kurpfalz* 13, 1928, pp. 168–248.

4. *Ein Potsdamer Maler in Rom. Briefe des Batoni-Schülers Johann Gottlieb Puhlmann aus den Jahren 1774 bis 1787*, Hrsg. und kommentiert von Gotz Eckhardt (Berlin, 1979), p. 8.

5. In a letter to the sculptor Falconet, dated 16 July 1762, Catherine II ridiculed the painting by Anna-Dorothea Lisiewska-Therbusch of *Jupiter admiring the sleeping Antiopa*: 'Mme Therbusch's painting is terrible, in my opinion, never has so much been spent on the colour red: apparently she's heard much too much about a rose-coloured imagination' (Trofimoff, 'Studies on Gatchina Paintings', *Old Times*, St Petersburg, June to September 1916, p. 99). She reacted particularly harshly to Vigée Le Brun's portrait of her granddaughters Alexandra Pavlovna and Elena Pavlovna: 'two little monkeys sitting side by side', 'little pug dogs basking themselves in the sun', 'dishevelled little Bacchic revellers', and 'little girls pulling faces'.

6. Jacob Shtaehlin's *Notes on the Fine Arts in Russia* (Moscow, 1990), vol. II, p. 373; *The History of Paintings in Russia*, pp. 353–90.

7. 'P. I. Sumarokov says that her silk dresses and sheets sometimes emitted electrical sparks and once, when Perekusikhina touched her naked body, she felt a strong jolt in her hand so great was Catherine II's life force': M. I. Pyl'ayev, *Old Petersburg: Accounts of the History of Life in the Capital* (St Petersburg, 1889), p. 191.

8. I. A. Sokolova, 'Rembrandt's "Return of the Prodigal Son" Revisited', *The Hermitage Readings in Memory of V. F. Levinson-Lessing* (St Petersburg, 1999), pp. 6–9.

9. *Recueil d'estampes d'après les Tableaux de la Galerie et du Cabinet de S. E. Monsieur le comte de Bruhl* (Dresden, 1754).

10. I. Artemieva, 'Alla nascita della pinacoteca dell'Ermitage: L'acquisto della collezione del console Udney', in *Il collezionismo d'arte a venezia. Il Settecento* (Venice, 2009).

11. Martin Postle, 'Sir Joshua Reynolds and the Court of Catherine the Great', in *British Art Treasures from the Russian Imperial Collection in the Hermitage*, ed. B. Allan and L. Dukelskaya (New Haven and London, 1986), pp. 56–67.

12. Ekhart Berckenhagen, *Anton Graff. Leben und Werk* (Berlin, 1967), p. 36.

Landscape with the Finding of Moses,
acquired from the collection of Prince
Grigory Potemkin in 1792.
The artist has arranged his composition
in compliance with the rules of Roger
de Piles, French artist and art critic,
which stated that buildings in a landscape should be 'stately edifices' –
Classical-style temples, monuments,
tombs, pyramids and altars.

Etienne Allegrain
(1644–1736)

CATALOGUE NO. 224

CHAPTER VI

'Flourishing Industries' during the Reign of Catherine II

NATALYA GUSEVA

During the reign of Catherine the Great, Russia, which now occupied a secure place in the international arena, was one of the centres of the Enlightenment where science, art and trades had flourished and gone from strength to strength.

From the start of her reign, a new style, that of Classicism, actively began to be developed. The rapid change of artistic tendencies, which were now directed towards the Ancient Classical world, had been determined by a whole series of objective and subjective reasons. The marked growth of the economic potential of the country, the putting of scientific achievements into practice, the development of trade, brought about a reorientation of architecture from the building of churches and palaces to the creation of city ensembles with administrative, educational and social centres.

All of this could not have been done within the scope of the Baroque which demanded, with its language of extravagant splendour, huge financial expenditure for the construction of a single palace. Even at the start of the 1760s, to regularize the building of towns throughout Russia, a Commission for Stone Construction was set up by an Imperial decree or edict of the Empress, to engage in the introduction of 'model' buildings and to work out principles of regular planning.

Having been freed from compulsory military service by the Freedom of the Nobility decree of 1762, many courtiers who had returned to their estates had started to design and construct buildings for their own use. The aesthetic principles of the new-born Classicism, both laconic and rational in its artistic resources, were more suited to the economic possibilities of the 'small town' courtiers. The personal correspondence of the young Empress with leading French philosophers and members of the Enlightenment, whose views were turned towards the 'Golden Age' of humanity, to Antiquity, became the ideological basis for the active development of Classicism in Russia.

Craftsmen received new directions for their creative inspiration, while working under the 'watchful eye' of the leading court architects. In the place of Francesco Bartolomeo Rastrelli, who had been the basic founder of the previous Empress's 'Elizabethan Baroque', there arrived the likes of Jean-Baptist-Michel Vallin de la Mothe, Alexander Filippovich Kokorinov, Yury Velten and Antonio Rinaldi, all of whom were representatives of 'early Classicism'. As leading architects in St Petersburg during the 1760s–70s, they played an active role in the creation of fashionable architectural projects in the city. The basis for their creative work was 'a new and as yet unused taste', which 'in its great simplicity contained beauty, calm and usefulness' – and beauty and usefulness were indivisible both in 'the outer embellishments and in the inner adornment'.[1]

However, in the provincial towns and estates of Russia, where such fashionable stylistic tendencies arrived somewhat later, items of great extravagance, still in the Baroque style, continued to be ordered and purchased right up to the end of the 1770s.

Catherine herself understood the importance of the 'respected arts' in the creation of an image of an enlightened ruler who cared for the well-being and flourishing of the state entrusted to her. Thus she considered the reorganization of the Academy of Arts to be a high priority. From 1763, Vallin de la Mothe and Kokorinov were engaged in a project to create a new building for the Academy. This building, which was surmounted by a sculpture of Catherine II, took until the late 1780s to complete.

The increase in both civic and private construction, especially after the 1762 decree, stimulated the growth of many industries connected with the decoration of interiors. The need for qualified craftsmen who knew how to produce fashionable ornamentation, and who understood the complex allegorical 'language' of Classicism, led to proposals for the organization of special schools attached to the important state departments of the capital. It was thus suggested that the overall leadership for this process should be given to the Academy of Arts. In connection with this, by a decree of Catherine in March 1764, the 'institution of skills' and a 'class of various skills' were set up. And as the activities of the Academy of Sciences became more vigorous, so too did those of the Imperial Porcelain and Glass Factories, while attempts were made to improve the output of the State Bronze Factory and to increase the manufacture of tapestries.

A year earlier, Catherine had turned her gaze to the output of the Imperial Tapestry Factory, instituted by Peter the Great in 1718. The main production was given over to 'the care of' Count Nikita Panin, and in 1764 a decree was issued to determine the staff, requirements and material base of the factory. Each year 19,010 roubles, a vast sum of money, would be allocated to the operation, creating orders exclusively

BELOW

Count Nikita Ivanovich
Panin (1718–83), the
governor of Catherine's
son, Paul, was in charge of
Russian foreign affairs
during the first twenty years
of Catherine's rule. He also
supervised the Imperial
Tapestry Factory from
1763 to 1783, which
produced this tapestry
portrait of him.

Imperial Tapestry Factory
(second half of 18th century)

CATALOGUE NO. 92

for the court (this sum did not include 5000 roubles for the purchase
of materials). At a time when the tapestry industry in Europe was
experiencing a period of decline, Russia was busy weaving enormous
tapestries with portraits, historical scenes and allegorical compositions.

The widespread introduction of coloured stone into the decoration
of architectural interiors merits a special page in the annals of Russian
applied arts. This stimulated an active search throughout the vast landscape of Russia, beginning in the 1750s, for new sources of natural
minerals.

Decorative and precious stones for the embellishment of the
interiors of the capital were transported from the stores of the Peterhof
Lapidary Factory, located near St Petersburg. Founded by a decree of
Peter the Great in 1723, initially for glass-engraving and later for cut-
ting coloured stone, this factory worked with raw materials brought
from various places in Russia. The engravers specialized in the creation
of small 'decorative' items, in particular the making of small vases and
snuff-boxes.

As the Neo-Classicist style developed, the natural beauty of stone
became especially attractive to architects, and the need arose for a reorientation of production and the making of items of much greater
size and importance. Joseph Bottom, who was in charge of the Petersburg Lapidary Factory for thirty years, dealt particularly well with this
new demand. Because of a series of innovations, it became more advan-
tageous over time to work with raw materials on site, rather than transport them in blocks to distant places. Thus in 1765, the Ekaterinburg
Lapidary Factory began its work in the Urals, while in 1786, in far-
away Altai, a factory was founded attached to the Loktevsky
Bronze Foundry. (This factory was moved to Kolyvan in 1802
and is known today as the Kolyvan Factory.)

Among the work of the 1770s and 1780s, clear forms of
Classical proportions dominate; these look as beautiful in
large-scale works as in small table decorations.

The creation of the Agate Rooms in Tsarskoye Selo pro-
vides a wonderful example of the use of Russian and other
precious stones. The concept behind this architectural complex belonged to the Scot, Charles Cameron, who came to St
Petersburg in 1780 on the invitation of the Empress herself.
Not satisfied with the work of the architects who had been
trained in Paris – and who, even when they had turned to
Classical Doric, continued to use 'grace' and 'elegance' as their

main criteria – Catherine had been searching for more profound interpreters of Antiquity.

Cameron and the Italian architect, Giacomo Quarenghi, fulfilled Catherine's needs, demonstrating an exquisite knowledge of the buildings of Ancient Greece and Rome; their architectural philosophy was similar to that which was already being built in St Petersburg. Both architects were distinguished by their new understanding of the organization of space, the role of coverings, walls and Classical order. Instead of the Baroque-style illusion of endlessness, expressed in a single line of corridored rooms, a rationally thought-out closed composition of a single space was created. This use of space changed a person's feeling about themselves; they became not merely a small part of the world order, but more a thinking personality, an individual.

Quarenghi, Cameron, and the Russian architect Ivan Starov who created a similar type of architecture alongside them, were able to reach the very roots of Ancient art. According to a number of researchers, 'Cameron was the first person in Russia who showed the Classical world not as an abstraction, as a luxurious scheme, but as an immortal ideal able to exist with feeling in an artistic work'.[2]

A remarkable example of ancient harmony, of that 'Greco-Roman rhapsody' about which the Empress was dreaming, was one of Charles Cameron's most ambitious projects – the Thermal Baths in Tsarskoye Selo. This outstanding architectural ensemble, which still stands today, consists of the Cold Baths, Agate Rooms, Hanging Garden, Gallery, and the stairs. The arrangement of the 'Agate' and 'Jasper' areas is especially unusual. Here the walls, columns, pilasters, niches and doors are decorated with natural jasper (one of the types of jasper used is referred to as 'meat agate' to this day). All shades of green, red and brown, enriched with multi-coloured veins and stripes, come together here in a single and unique natural decoration.

The ornamentation has been carefully thought out by its creator. Closer inspection reveals that not only the walls, but the columns, have been covered with small pieces of stone, delicately running into each other. This kind of mosaic, assembled from stone of a single colour, was later named 'Russian Mosaic', in honour of its most talented masters.

Elegant doors in true Classical style, vases, table-altars,

105

table-consoles, lamps – all of these added to the adornment of interiors. A wide use of stones for interior decoration, with their inimitable natural beauty, became not only the creative signature of Charles Cameron, but of other architects of this period of 'strict Classicism'.

On more than one occasion, Cameron made use of the skills of Russian stone-cutters, and he did so when planning the rooms of the Great Palace at Tsarskoye Selo. Each room here was unique. And unlike the other architects of the capital, Cameron's talent was especially evident in the country parks of residences and in the surrounding landscape. Thus, in the decor for the Green Dining Room, Cameron created a poetic image, reminiscent of the beauty of the park, with its transparent ponds and marble sculpture set against a background of leaves. The white moulded decor of the walls, created by the sculptor Ivan Petrovich Martos, with its pistachio tones in the background, was without doubt inspired by the well-known relief panels of Josiah Wedgwood, which were made at his Etruria factory in Staffordshire, England.

For the Lyons Guest Room, however, Cameron created a completely different decor, where the main element was patterned French silk. The upper frieze of the walls, the window surrounds and the doors were a sky-blue colour, while the doors themselves, and the floor, were created out of panels of wood encrusted with mother-of-pearl. The large stoves in the Lyons Guest Room were constructed in the shape of a rotunda and made from earthenware, while the lights were decorated with garlands of glass amethysts, garnets, topazes and rubies.

In the Light-Blue Guest Room, the arrangement of console-tables is of particular interest. The supporting sections of the tables were made in the form of glazed painted vases and cups, interwoven with a golden design and with elegant engraved vases which, with their crossed legs, are a vivid reminder of the creative inheritance of the Scottish designer Robert Adam and his many followers.

Important elements of another main room, the Arabesque Room, include decorative arabesques and twelve wall mirrors with rectangular and oval golden frames. Particular attention was paid to the doors,

which were painted in deep blue, yellow, light blue, light green and pink.

Cameron's imagination was boundless. Each room was unique in its conception and form. Even traditional structures for early Baroque and Rococo interiors with 'chinoiserie' style were created differently by Cameron. His Large Chinese Room is striking, with its refined and varied decor. Authentic lacquered panels and ceramic dishes made in China are intertwined with the engraved and painted decor of the walls in a stylized Eastern fashion. Serpents and lizards meander over not only the wall, but also the furniture, which is decorated additionally with metal insets with picturesque scenes of Chinese life.

Two rooms, however, deserve special mention among all these magnificent interiors – the Bed-chamber of the Empress and her elegant Deep-Blue 'Snuff-Box' Study.

Cameron covered the walls of the Bedchamber with fine layers of milky-white polished glass, mirrors, double columns of amethyst glass and gilded bronze. Twenty-nine plaques from Wedgwood's factory completed the decor of the room. The Bed-chamber was divided into two parts: two small arches led into the rear recess, where the bed and the alcove were located, and in the front area, in the space between the arches, the sofa was situated. Such use of space was highly innovative.

Catherine had a similar arrangement installed in her bedchamber in the Winter Palace. As she wrote to Baron Friederich Melchior Grimm in 1782:

ABOVE

Design for the Lyons Drawing Room in the Great Palace at Tsarskoye Selo, *c.*1780.

Charles Cameron
(1743/5–1812)

CATALOGUE NO. 97

I have found the way to set out my bedroom such as you cannot imagine. I had great depth but now no longer. My bed is next to the windows; but so that the light does not aggravate my eyes a mirror has been placed next to the bed and the mirror is turned towards the windows and under them is the sofa. … And this invention your Humble Servant will now spread to all Petersburg homes. In addition, my bed does not have a baldaquin around it – it only has curtains.[3]

In the Deep-Blue 'Snuff-Box' Study, the ceiling, walls, card table and two stools were made from milky-white and deep blue glass with silver foil underneath. Later, a similarly unusual but effective decor would appear in the rooms of the Winter Palace, from the plans of Ivan Starov for the wedding of the Tsarevich Alexander Pavlovich.

This impressive variety of materials, styles and shapes, which enabled the architects to carry out even the most refined creative fantasies, bears witness to the high level of development of many industries. The processes which began back in the reign of the Empress Elizabeth reached a climax during the reign of Catherine II. The experiments of Mikhail Lomonosov, for example, who had been working on making coloured glass in the 1750s and '60s, took fully ten years to yield their outstanding results.

Some of the craftsmen from the glassworks in Ust-Ruditse, which was closed in 1768, came to work in the state factory originally founded in Petersburg in 1735. The factory was eventually presented by Catherine in 1774 to her secret husband, Prince Grigory Potemkin. Educated, talented and blessed with an incredible energy, Potemkin took over the running of this enterprise entrusted to him. At his command, two glass factories were immediately built close to Ozerki, on the River Neva: one for the making of pharmaceutical glass items, and the other for crystal. Later, the production of mirrors would be added to the output. From the 1780s, mirrors, various glass items and chandeliers with coloured parts were frequently used as diplomatic gifts.

The standard of the St Petersburg glass production, its variety and the extent of its use in interior design, may be judged, for example, from the description of the festive reception given by Potemkin in 1791 in the Tauride Palace on the occasion of the arrival of the Empress. A 'Hill with a Waterfall', based on designs of I. Kulibin, a self-taught craftsman, was made at the glass factory for Potemkin's winter garden. This was an installation with a winding mechanism, which gave the effect of flowing glass streams of water. There was also a grotto-summer house made out of mirrors. Around the marble statue of Catherine, columns were built and floral garlands wound around them. Among these garlands, according to an eye-witness account, 'small, low, crystal lamps made from coloured glass had been attached'. From this improvised altar, there were small paths leading outwards and Pomeranian trees had been planted which, instead of real fruit, had 'plums, cherries and various kinds of grapes which had somehow been made out of glass'. Inside, there were lit candles, and 'cedars' which had … 'pineapples, melons and watermelons … all of which looked completely natural in colour, size and in appearance. The leaves and stalks were made of light material, but the fruit itself was made of glass. All these fruits were lit from within.'[4]

These fantastical creations – which excite the imagination in description alone – demonstrate the high level of mastery of those who produced them. Foreign visitors were simply astounded by the luxury of those in the Russian court circles.

The ceremonial table service alone at the Tauride Palace was intended for five hundred people; the gentlemen would attend at the tables to serve the ladies. In order to illuminate the table, in addition to the chandeliers and candelabra hanging within the room itself, huge uplighters in the form of cups were used. These were in the shape of a Russian 'cup for toasting fraternal ties' and tinted with a reddish hue.

As well as traditional glass, silver and gold dishes, it became more usual, from the 1770s, to use porcelain ware at the dinner table.

Apart from dinner and dessert services, enough for hundreds of guests at court gatherings, various sculptural compositions were introduced to honour the rule of the 'Semiramis of the North', the decoration of which had their own special symbolism. On the plates of the Cabinet Service, for example, which were decorated around the edges with garlands of wild flowers on a gold background, there were central medallions with views of Rome and its outlying districts.

From 1779 until 1804, the head of the sculpture workshop at the Imperial Porcelain Factory was the talented sculptor Jean-Dominique Rachette, a former pupil of the Academy of Arts of Copenhagen. He was the maker of the great allegorical 'surtout de table' for the large Arabesque service, the first of the series of ceremonial palace services which matched the famous services of Vienna, Meissen or Sèvres in size, composition and beauty.

The Empress Catherine inspected this huge dinner and dessert service in the Winter Palace in September 1784. It consisted of sixty

BELOW

Pieces from the service of
the Order of St George,
made by the Gardner
Factory in Moscow
Province, 1777–78.

CATALOGUE NO. 171

settings and a total of 973 pieces, made up of fifty different types of items. Most of the main pieces were decorated with medallions in the form of cameos with heads in profile and vases, details of decorative murals discovered in Herculaneum and Pompeii, and cartouches containing allegorical representations of Justice, Industry, Art and other such subjects. These evenly and finely distributed compositions looked wonderful against the snowy-white porcelain.

Virtually the entire production of the Imperial Porcelain Factory during Catherine's reign was distinguished by such high-quality workmanship and high artistic ideals.

The notion of the 'ideal' is especially obvious in the ensembles created for special ceremonies. To these belonged, for example, the 'Order' services which were used only during receptions for gentlemen of the four highest Orders in Russia. The four services were made in the factory close to Moscow founded in 1766 by the English merchant and forestry dealer, Francis Gardner. Each service, with settings for the maximum number of gentlemen in the Order, had in its decoration the corresponding ribbon and an image of the Order – 'Andrew', 'Alexander Nevsky', 'George' and 'Vladimir'. This decoration was tastefully painted onto the dishes themselves, which had been influenced by the famous service of Berlin manufacture given to Catherine II in 1772 by Frederick the Great of Prussia. The English traveller William Coxe, who observed the ceremonial reception in the Winter Palace of the Order of St Andrew, described it thus:

The Empress was wearing a green velvet dress which was trimmed with ermine and she wore a diamond brooch depicting the Order; the attire of the gentlemen stood out because of its great luxury, but at the same time this was too shiny and lacked taste: the top part was trimmed with silver material and the tunic was trimmed with this same silver material; the waistcoat and the pantaloons were of golden shiny material and their stockings were of red silk; their hats were a la Henri IV studded with diamonds and decorated with feather plumes …[5]

This pomposity of court receptions inspired Coxe to admit that

… the luxury and splendour of court attire, and the vast amounts of precious stone, leave the grandeur of other European courts far behind. On the costumes of Frenchmen and on the dresses of the ladies there is not as much ornamentation – there are long hanging sleeves with some adornment. … Nobody made such an impression on us, the foreigners, as the Russian nobility did with their luxury, the abundance of precious stones which shone forth from various parts of their attire …[6]

At this time in St Petersburg, a '*pléiade*' of famous jewellers was at work, including Jean-Pierre Ador, Johann Gottlieb Sharff, Jean-François-Xavier Bouddé, Louise David Duval and Georg Heinrich Køonig. Their creations were remarkable for the elegance of their forms, the delicately thought-out decoration, the high quality of the materials used, and the exquisite quality of the workmanship.

Catherine's burgeoning collection of rare works of art awoke in her the idea of creating in the premises of the Small Hermitage a special 'Gallery of Precious Stones', to be sited close to the Hanging Garden. As well as the items brought here specially, the gallery would exhibit the best work of skilled Russian craftsmen. Masters such as Osip Dudin and Ivan Vereshchagin, for example, had no equal in Europe. Their work in ivory is incredible in its delicacy and detail, with surfaces which have an appearance of carved azure lace, with elegant silhouettes.

From the first years of Catherine's 'Hermitage', then a private museum, she filled it with objects made by the masters in Tula, famed for the exquisite beauty of the decorative items they made from steel. By order of the Empress in 1785, two experienced Tula masters, who had worked in the weapon factory there, were sent to England.

Aleksei Surnin and Andrei Leontiev did not go to study the processes for working with metal – they had already mastered the finer details – but to look at the production and widen their range of creative skills. Surnin, being especially talented, was offered a good position to stay in England, but he turned the offer down and returned to Tula.

Tula, with its 'Kremlin' fortress, had long been the defence border of the southern part of the Moscow State. The majority of the town's inhabitants were blacksmiths and, since the 16th century, many weapons for the Russian army had been made there. Professional weapon-making skills and a sense of patriotic duty were handed down from generation to generation, and from 1712, with the founding of the Tula Weapon Factory by a decree of Peter the Great, the Tula masters were favoured by the court, undertaking large orders for special items for diplomatic gifts.

In 1785, on the invitation of Prince Potemkin, an Englishman Ferdinand Davie came to Tula to build a workshop for mathematical and scientific equipment. Three of Davie's pupils later opened their own factories and thus widened the variety of goods traditionally made in Tula. Catherine visited the weapon factory in person, in 1775 and 1787. On both occasions, according to the *Manuscript of Court Life*, the craftsmen greeted her with a ceremonial welcome and brought her 'bread and salt [traditionally used as a welcome in Russia] and samples of their workmanship'.

It is well known that on 21 May, at the annual Sophiisky Fair, held not far from Tsarskoye Selo, the Empress and members of her family acquired various items brought for them from Tula, such as steel tables, umbrellas and 'all kinds of bits and pieces'. Ordinary citizens who could afford it would eagerly buy up what was left over by the court.

Catherine knew true craftsmanship when she saw it and this also applied to the making of furniture, which was only developed in Russia from the 1700s. To promote this domestic production, the Empress would set out the best items of furniture in the rooms of the Hermitage where they would stand alongside priceless art, bronze, porcelain, glass and jewellery brought in from various countries throughout the world. Johann Georgi, a St Petersburg physician and natural scientist who wrote the first travel guide for the Russian capital, noted:

> ... here there stood a large wooden bureau on which various events and journeys of Her Highness were depicted in the Tavricheskii area and this was the work of a serf of [A. V.] Soltykov ...[7]

This bureau is now in the collection of the Palace-Museum in Tsarskoye Selo, although in later publications it is ascribed to famous German or French craftsmen. However, within the collection of the State Historical Museum, there are two card tables bearing a signature that confirms without doubt that the bureau was indeed the work of one Matvey Yakovlevich Veretennikov, a serf of A. V. Soltykov. Having a great aptitude for furniture-making, it is likely that Veretennikov was sent to St Petersburg to carry out the making of ceremonial items of furniture for the wealthy nobility.

There exist in a number of museum collections a range of objects that may have been made in the workshop of Veretennikov. All are tastefully decorated using the technique of marquetry. In the 1790s, however, during the period of strict Classicism, extravagant ornamentation was no longer popular; indeed it had already gone out of fashion in Europe. As Russia had come later than other countries to the production of fashionable furniture, local craftsmen were still attempting to make maximum use of the techniques already learned.

Veretennikov began to fashion his pieces in a new way, bringing in complex multi-figured scenes and giving them three-dimensional qualities. In so doing, the viewer experiences something like an act in an 18th-century theatre. In this 'scenic space', typically Classical motifs are used and 'heroes' are dressed in a style close to Ancient times.

Veretennikov's workshop existed in St Petersburg for more than ten years. The proximity of his creative style to that of the court masters

BELOW

The lid and sides of this box show the new factory at Tula which was designed by Kozma Sokolnikov, the Tula factory's principal architect. Although the project was approved in 1782, the complex was never built. The box itself was made by Andrian Sukhanov. There were originally 80 chess pieces, but only 44 have survived.

Tula Factory, Tula
(late 18th century)

CATALOGUE NO. 130

is confirmed not only by the subjects and themes of his work, but also by the drawing of decorative elements.

Other outstanding examples of Russian work using marquetry, include a chest of drawers with the monogram 'EII' and emblems of Siberia, and a toilette table dated to the 1770s, the work of the Naskovy carpenters from Okhta. Both pieces are highly significant items within Russian furniture-making as a whole. The decoration of the chest of drawers, created in lozenge-shaped patterns like a trellis fence, with ivory inlay, is frequently used. Catherine's monogram 'EII' is also used, with the two-headed eagle and emblem of Siberia.

The Naskovys' toilette table, made in the form of a trefoil on three elegant folding legs, has rich chequered ornamentation. In the background, the monogram of the Grand Duchess Maria Fedorovna is visible. The simple geometric design of the background, together with the addition of ivory details, became a characteristic feature used by Russian furniture-makers of the 1760s–80s.

In addition to the 'Naskovy carpenters', there were also masters based in St Petersburg who used the technique of marquetry. Nikifor Vasiliev is particularly well known. In 1770, Vasiliev decorated wood for two pieces which had been commissioned by the Tver nobility for presentation to the Empress – a desk and a small toilette table (now in the Russian Museum and the Museum of the City of Tver respectively). It is worth noting that the construction of these pieces, decorated with engraved views of Tver, is carried out in a different style. The small table has undulating contours, while the desk has strict, Classical straight-line details.

Nikifor Vasiliev's professional style is very well known, with its characteristically complex architectural views. He used virtually a filigree technique in his production of the smallest details, and was able to compose subjects of choice in any size and form on the surface of his work. It is thought that Vasiliev was a qualified craftsman from Okhta, one of the outlying districts of St Petersburg, as in the 1770s his name was mentioned among the Okhta masters who had laid floors in the Great Palace at Tsarskoye Selo.

Another master noted for his wood-working skills, Gerasim Kozlov, was also involved in the decoration of the Great Palace. A table, signed 'G. Kozlov', has been decorated with filigree ornamentation including elements of 'chinoiserie' with ivory details. Koslov considered himself to be an apprentice in 'amber work', that is to say he took part in the decoration of the famous Amber Room at Tsarskoye Selo.

Apart from the Russian masters, there were many other craftsmen at the time of Catherine II who came to St Petersburg from other European countries. From 1770–80, 'Master of Carpentry' Johann Schmidt carried out a variety of work for the Marble Palace designed by Antonio Rinaldi. As documents show, Schmidt was persuaded to make 'from pinewood foundations' parquet floors, card tables of 'overseas wood', fitted with 'velvet and bronze items', corner cupboards, chest-of-drawers, and many other items.

Masters such as Leopold Heim, Johann Kimel, and Christian and Andrei Meyer, are also frequently mentioned as makers of parquet floors and furniture. The two Meyers made floors from 'overseas' wood and ivory.

Christian Meyer deserves special mention as, from the beginning of the 1780s, he was practically in charge of the furniture workshop which worked exclusively on court commissions. The tasteful use of marquetry in his early work, covering almost the entire surface of the piece, is strongly reminiscent not only of French decorative graphics, but also the artistic achievements of English architects working in the elegantly restrained style of Robert Adam.

It is thought that Meyer likely met the Empress in person. From 1782–84 he taught carpentry to the Grand Dukes Alexander and Constantine. Catherine, who carefully supervised the education of her oldest grandsons, wrote more than once to Baron Grimm about their successes in various crafts.

From the end of the 1780s, architectural elements increasingly began to be brought into furniture and these were highlighted in even the smallest detail. This is evident in the work of Christian Meyer. The merit of this new style, which was eventually introduced into Russian art, was that while there was external simplicity, special attention was paid to the natural beauty of the materials, the quality of the work and the perfection of the construction.

From 1784, David Roentgen, owner of a large business in Neuwied on the River Rhine, supplied Catherine with many outstanding examples of such 'simple' restrained furniture:

Having been assured of the support and the recommendation of his acquaintance Baron F.-M. Grimm, the former Parisian correspondent of Catherine II, and having received a gracious answer from the Empress – 'We with great pleasure will meet this Herr Furniture Maker and Mechanic since we are building more than ever before' – Roentgen

*started working in a most meticulous manner to prepare an enterprise
which would win him great success in the Russian capital.*[8]

And he was not mistaken – the Russian nobility very willingly gave him
commissions to supply expensive but highly presentable items made
with mahogany veneers, other woods, and metal mounts of the most
perfect quality.

Apart from original and 'exclusive' items, which were made mech-
anically, Roentgen also brought to Russia a greater quantity of veneered
furniture which was simple, yet practical. These found suitable homes
in the studies, libraries and rooms of learning used by the nobility of
the Enlightenment.

Some of the distinctive features of Roentgen's work in the 1780s
included 'square furniture legs … which ended in a characteristic way
in cubic form, or like acorns, and which had corrugated bronze attach-
ments on them; … there were handles made in the shape of entwined
scarves, frames made of ornamental strips, grooves into which brass
was inserted and bronze rose windows'.[9]

Many of these details began to find their way into the creative styles
of court master, Christian Meyer. It is worth noting that he frequently
had to furnish the same ceremonial interiors already fitted out with
items manufactured by the Neuwied factory. The eminent expert on
Russian furniture, P. Veiner, noted at the turn of the 20th century that

> … [Meyer] *was precisely one of those Masters who in Petersburg made
> large quantities of furniture based on French models or close to the
> sketches of these items; Catherine herself turned to him with commissions
> for the furnishing of many of her Palaces and the researcher on French
> furniture in Russia, Denis Roche, correctly suggests that we owe to these
> Masters the majority of items made from red wood, almost without
> decoration – perhaps just with a few beads or bronze strips inserted –
> and this was called the 'Jacob Style' which began to be popular in
> Russia at the end of the c.18th century.*[10]

The immediate visual impact of these plain but dramatic pieces, together with the relatively cheap cost of the materials used, helped the
'Jacob Style' of furniture to spread rapidly throughout Russia.

Christian Meyer's workshop continued in production for more
than twenty years in St Petersburg, making parquet floors, doors and
items of furniture, based on the drawings of leading architects, for the

Winter Palace and Marble Palace, the Hermitage, the Imperial residences at Tsarskoye Selo, the Tauride Palace and many more.

Having become a supplier to the court, and with so much work to be done, Meyer acted not only as a master but also as a contractor, bringing craftsmen with many specialities into his service, such as joiners, engravers, gilders and bronze-workers. With masters of many different nationalities working alongside him, items appeared which combined traits of French, German and English furniture schools. Under the 'watchful gaze' of Meyer, a whole new artistic style in furniture-making emerged, aimed at aristocratic taste and with the possibility of significant sales. Fashionable styles of furniture, at the specific demand of those who commissioned it, were frequently repeated, and such items began to acquire their own special appearance, although the elements of decoration were subject to variation.

Another master who quickly became a leading furniture-maker in St Petersburg was the German Heinrich Gambs, a pupil of Roentgen. Gambs appeared in St Petersburg around 1790, initially working principally for the Small Palace where he made furniture for Grand Duke Paul and his wife, Maria Fedorovna. Five years later, however, having acquired financial support from an Austrian merchant, Jonathan Otto, Gambs was in a position to receive the permission of the Empress to set up a furniture factory and to open a shop at the Kalinkin Bridge.

Thus began the brilliant career of Heinrich Gambs, who was to gain Russian citizenship in 1807 and the title of 'Court Mechanic' by 1810. Gambs created furniture of exceptional quality, not only from his own designs, but from those of the leading architects of the capital, collaborating during the 1790s with the architect Vincenzio Brenna in particular.

Gambs remained faithful to the Classical style of Roentgen – the impeccable quality of the veneer and metalic details – but he also added his own touches. In the decoration of furniture and other items destined for the Small Palace, Gambs was the first to use details of ivory and *verre églomisé* (glass with the reverse side covered with gold or other metalic leaf). Gambs' shop proved popular with the wealthy courtiers, satisfying the market with items of the highest taste and quality.

Johann Georgi's travel guide observed that in the 1790s, even citizens of modest wealth 'had in their houses a hall, dining-room, guest room, and in all of these there could be found tables, chairs, sofas, large mirrors, with card and mirror tables, wall and table clocks, pianos, several cupboards and desks'.[11]

ABOVE

The doors from this cabinet for carved gems came from the workshop of David Roentgen, 1786–87, while Christian Meyer made the cabinet. Later, Heinrich Gambs created the lower portion of the piece (early 19th century).

CATALOGUE NO. 235

Georgi recalled that in the Guild of Russian Carpenters in the capital, there were 124 masters, 285 apprentices and 175 pupils. Out of these, 90 were German. Georgi wrote separately about the craftsmen in Okhta, who came under the jurisdiction of the Admiralty Colleges:

In holiday times they worked for themselves in the town or in their own homes with carpenters, joiners and others, and they worked even with black wood and various other things, just like the city Masters but much less expensive.[12]

It is also worth noting that many craftsmen came to St Petersburg by special invitation of one or other of the architects who worked in the capital. Charles Cameron arranged for around a hundred craftsmen to come from Scotland to settle in Sophia, the nearest suburb to St Petersburg. Quarenghi, for example, had Italians in the 'team' of master decorators that he always worked with – including the famous engraver and gilder Telesforo Bonaveri.

Charles Cameron and the French sculptor and decorator Jean-Baptiste Charlemagne, who came to St Petersburg in 1770, formed a close working relationship. Charlemagne became a member of the Academy of Arts, and later an academician, and had an excellent knowledge of the decorating and craft market in the capital. This enabled him to take upon himself the role of contractor and to distribute the many commissions Cameron received to make furniture, lights or bronze-ware, all of which were necessary for the Imperial homes in Tsarskoye Selo.

Throughout the 18th century, admiration for French art at the Russian court remained as strong as the constant attraction to English culture. However, if the French dictated fashion in the decoration of palace interiors, satisfying the ambitions of their owners, the more rational comfort of the English was perhaps more practical for everyday life.

During the years of Catherine's reign, the most varied forms of production and purchase of items of decorative and applied art took place in the Imperial capital. By the end of the century, there were many shops in existence, the most well-known being that of M. Nechaev which housed an impressive range of goods. Judging from announcements in the newspapers, one could buy 'different kinds of lights, lamps, girandoli, card tables and ladies' tables tastefully decorated with red wood and bronze, bureaux, desks, cupboards, large and small toilette sets, sets of mirrors in frames, sofas, canopies, armchairs and goatskin leather chairs, fireplaces with and without bronze'.[13] Inhabitants from other Russian cities, especially Moscow, eagerly bought up these goods from the shops in the capital.

As a result of her reign, Catherine II, in the words of one of her contemporaries, left behind many 'flourishing crafts' and 'industries'. The very fruits of her 'European education' began to find their way 'into the very heart of Russia', and even there they gave birth to 'taste', to 'general opinion' and to 'the adherence to the dignity of the Russian name'.[14] One can state, with all certainty, that the foundations of the later bright dawning of Imperial culture in Russia, at the beginning of the 19th century, were all laid during the years of the wise rule of the Great Empress.

NOTES

1. N. A. Evsina, *Architectural Theory in Russia* (Moscow, 1975), p. 109.
2. D. Shvidkovskii, *Charles Cameron at the Court of Catherine II* (Moscow, 2001), p. 93.
3. This quotation is taken from G. N. Komelova, 'Catherine's Apartments in the Winter Palace', in the Winter Palace, Special Collection, 2000, p. 93.
4. Quotation from *300 Years of Applied Decorative Arts in St Petersburg: An Illustrated Encyclopaedia*, Special Collection, vol. 1, 2004, pp. 134–35.
5. 'Russia a Hundred Years ago, 1778. William Coxe's journey', *Russian Antiquity 1877*, pt 2, vol. 19, p. 31.
6. Ibid.
7. J. Georgi: I – *A Description of the Imperial Russian capital and Sights in its Locality 1794–1796*, Special Collection, 1996, p. 342.
8. *The Furniture of David Roentgen in the Hermitage*, exhibition catalogue, compiled by B. Geres (Leningrad, 1980), p. 5.
9. Ibid., p. 6.
10. P. Veiner: 'Gatchina', Special Collection, 1995 (reprint), p. 84.
11. J. Georgi, op. cit., pp. 602–603.
12. Ibid., p. 249, pp. 602–603.
13. St Petersburg Departments, 1793, no. 99, p. 301.
14. F. F. Vigel: *Notes, Russian Archive*, 1892, p. 73.

CHAPTER VII

Catherine the Great and European Decorative Art

TAMARA RAPPE

Catherine the Great commissioned and purchased porcelain, furniture, tapestries, silver and jewellery from abroad so that she could live in luxury and wealth and not fall behind any of the other European courts. The most famous European craftsmen were called upon to decorate her homes with fashionable and expensive items. Large quantities of Western products were imported into the Russian capital. They blended with the furnishings in the Imperial palaces and mansions of the nobility, and introduced the Neo-Classical style which was then the height of fashion in Europe. In their memoirs, foreign travellers noted that the 'richness and splendour of the Russian court exceeds even the most extravagant descriptions: traces of ancient Asian magnificence are mixed with European refinement'.[1] Many orders were placed in the West, foreign craftsmen arrived in St Petersburg, and the capital of Russia became a centre of attraction for Europeans. The Empress's own taste, along with her wisely-chosen advisers, enabled her to acquire some of the most important and interesting items made during the second half of the 18th century.

FURNITURE

It may have been her German background, or some intuition about which craftsmen to patronize, that encouraged Catherine to involve the German furniture maker David Roentgen in the furnishing of her apartments. Having learned from her correspondent in Paris, Baron Friedrich Melchoir Grimm, of the reputation of the renowned, German craftsman, her decision led to many spectacular acquisitions, with Roentgen shipping a great deal of furniture to the Russian court.

Indeed, almost all the European monarchs made use of Roentgen's services, with his furniture long occupying important spaces in the royal palaces of Paris, Berlin and Stockholm. In the mid-1700s, Roentgen's workshop in the town of Neuwied on the River Rhine produced amazing sets of furniture with mechanical curiosities in the spirit of the Rococo style which prevailed in Europe at the time. In the second half of the century, with changes in taste and the rising interest in Antiquity, Roentgen began to create furniture in the Classical style. This meant that his pieces became rectilinear and austere, with a contrast between the veneers – which were usually mahogany, with a very fine texture – and splendid gilt bronze mounts or decoration. It is thought that Roentgen developed a special, so-called 'architectural style' just for Russia. It is certainly true that the best and most significant of his works were created according to architectural principles, with a balance of supporting and load-bearing parts, and that they incorporated columns, pilasters and pediments.

While not going beyond the limits of the Neo-Classical style, Roentgen's furniture is distinguished by its surprising monumentality, precision, and the severity of its proportions. Indeed, it has no exact parallel among the simpler works of this style created in Europe. The style created for Roentgen's Russian furniture has a number of salient features and can immediately be recognized by his use of large quantities of bronze sculpture and such decorative components as hanging drapery, small chains of pearls, and rosettes.

The consignments of furniture for the Empress Catherine began in 1784 and over a period of several years resulted in a steady stream of items for the decoration of the palaces and homes in St Petersburg. These included various types of tables, desks and clocks. In order that Catherine should be aware that she was dealing with 'the best furniture maker and mechanic of the century', as Baron Grimm described him, Roentgen sent a large bureau surmounted by a statue of Apollo, on which he had concentrated all his skill and craftsmanship. Along with the mechanic Peter Kinzing, who worked in his Neuwied workshop, Roentgen equipped this astonishing bureau with multiple mechanisms that made it possible to open the desks, doors and drawers by means of hidden levers and knobs. These explosive operations were carried out to the accompaniment of music recorded on special cylinders.

Such a wonder was bound to attract the attention of the Empress. To judge from her correspondence, Catherine, who had initially been somewhat cool towards the Neuwied master, very quickly valued his virtuoso skills and ordered furniture for the Winter Palace and her summer residences.

Roentgen was also commissioned to furnish Catherine's palace in Pelle, which was designed by Ivan Starov but never completed. It was assumed that Roentgen would not only supply furniture, but also rich interior decorations, including doors. At any rate, the actual doors

The Apollo Bureau, with
its mahogany and gilded
bronze decoration and
elaborate opening
mechanisms, was well-
received by the Empress.

David Roentgen
(1743–1807)

that he created have survived. These doors, as well as other furniture destined for the palace at Pelle, arrived in Russia in 1787 in Roentgen's third consignment. They were intended for a small cabinet for storing engraved gemstones, and led Catherine to order another five cabinets for her beloved collection of cameos and intaglios. These large double-door cabinets still exist in the Hermitage collection. They have bronze numbers and are decorated with medallions representing Cicero and Plato. A similar medallion with a portrait of Plato adorned a bureau which was in Roentgen's second consignment of furniture for Russia.

Today, all that remains of Roentgen's many deliveries are approximately two dozen items. However, these pieces provide us with a great deal of information about this outstanding German cabinet-maker of the late 18th century.

Although Catherine brought in furniture, porcelain and silver, such items did not form 'special collections'. There can be no doubt, however, that the Empress's collection of engraved gemstones occupied a very special place in her collecting and patronage, and also her appreciation of history and art. They were systematically and passionately amassed, and were more highly prized than her collection of paintings which was intended to strengthen her political position. Catherine absolutely loved engraved gemstones, and it was not by chance that her passion was variously referred to as 'cameo disease', 'cameo sickness' or 'cameo fever'.

Not only did Catherine personally collect cameos and intaglios, but she also infected her family, friends and favourites with this 'sickness'. Her lover, Count Alexander Lanskoy, was the first to fall victim to this 'fever', and it was he who helped the Empress to develop the lapidary factories at Ekaterinburg and Kolyvan. After Lanskoy's sudden death in 1784, his personal collection went to the Empress.

Catherine was also given a collection acquired abroad by her friend, Princess Ekaterina Dashkova, President of the Academy of Sciences. Another favourite, Count Alexander Dmitriev-Mamonov, made a cameo with a portrait of the Empress, while Catherine's daughter-in-law, Maria Fedorovna, also carved and engraved cameos.

Catherine's collection included engraved examples from Antiquity to the 1790s. By the end of her reign it contained 10,000 original engraved gemstones and 34,000 copies.

The history of the creation of the Catherine II's cameo collection has been studied extensively.[2] Art agents, diplomats serving in foreign countries, travelling aristocrats, antiquarians and artists were all engaged in the acquiring of engraved gemstones for the Empress. Her correspondence with Baron Grimm and Etienne-Maurice Falconet is full of information about purchases. In 1787, the collection of the Duc d'Orléans arrived at court and was placed in the cabinets made by Roentgen. The French Revolution (1789) provided more opportunities to purchase French aristocratic collections. No less significant was the arrival of the collection of Jean-Baptist Casanova, Director of the

BELOW

Princess Ekaterina Romanovna Dashkova and Maria Fedorovna in later life.

By Gavriil Ivanovich Skorodumov (1754–92)

CATALOGUE NO. 47

By Jean-Henri Benner (1776–1836)

CATALOGUE NO. 197

Dresden Academy of Arts. Catherine encouraged the development of her collection in every way possible. 'Only God knows what a joy it is to touch them every day,' she wrote, '… they contain an inexhaustible source of knowledge'.[3]

Contemporary pieces were also purchased, including a unique collection by the English engravers William and Charles Brown. The work of these masters is well represented in the Hermitage and reveals that a love of Classical models profoundly influenced their work. However, the Browns always interpreted Classical originals in their own particular way. Their works are distinguished by such originality and a 'painterly way' of creating images.

Catherine also collected copies of engraved gemstones by the Scot James Tassie. These were supplied in specially commissioned cabinets designed by the architect James Wyatt, who worked in the style of the Scottish architect and designer Robert Adam (whom Catherine had tried to bring to her court). Thirteen of these cabinets survive in the Hermitage. They were described by Rudolf Erich Raspe, who catalogued Tassie's work for Catherine, as 'beautifully built' and among the 'best of the magnificent décor of her Majesty the Empress'.[4] A plaque attached to one of the cabinets bears the name of the little-

---

This 13th-century Italian cameo of an *Eagle holding a Hare in its Talons* was acquired from the collection of Jean-Baptist Casanova, Dresden, 1792.

CATALOGUE NO. 258

This cameo, dated *c.*1575–90, bears the profile of *Queen Elizabeth I of England*. It was acquired with the Duc d'Orléans' collection of gemstones in 1787.

CATALOGUE NO. 265

James Tassie's London workshop produced portrait medallions from potassium silicate or lead glass. This is *Alexander putting Homer's* Iliad *in a casket*.

CATALOGUE NO. 292

known London furniture-maker 'F. Roach', and suggests that he was responsible for these satinwood-veneered pieces. Indeed, Catherine loved these cabinets so much that she commissioned a similar one for Lanskoy, for his gems.

PORCELAIN

Catherine's exquisite taste and her love of Antiquity is evident in the strikingly beautiful Cameo Service, commissioned for her lover, Grigory Potemkin. Catherine ordered it from the French royal porcelain factory at Sèvres, Paris, in 1777 and it was completed and sent to the Russian capital two years later. Intended for sixty people, it consisted of 744 pieces. As the service was being made for the Empress of All the Russias, it was produced at the very highest quality and in the latest style, involving dozens of craftsmen and painters.

The order specified that the service should be based on Classical models ('*sur les modèles antiques*') and that it should reflect Catherine's passion for Classical cameos. Consequently, cameos were specially made and inserted into the decoration. As customary at this time, the centre of the table was decorated with pieces of biscuit or unglazed porcelain, of which there were an exceptional number of pieces: over forty sculptural groups and vases surrounded a sculpture of the Empress herself, who was represented as Minerva. Not surprisingly, this extremely refined, beautifully painted and gilded service cost far more than Catherine expected, and she was highly annoyed at the final bill of 331,362 *livres*. A long correspondence ensued and the payments were eventually spread out over twenty-four years.

ABOVE

Allegory of Victory over the Turkish Fleet by Charles Brown, London, 1789–90, and *Catherine II instructing her Grandsons* by William and Charles Brown, London, 1789–91

CATALOGUE NOS. 275 AND 276

The Empress herself was frequently portrayed in porcelain. Her image was represented in biscuit porcelain, sitting on a throne, under a large *baldacchino* or canopy, surrounded by figures wearing costumes of the different nationalities of Russia, in the great service produced by the Berlin Porcelain Factory given to her by Frederick the Great of Prussia. The Meissen Factory at Dresden also produced small sculptures of the Empress, most notably on a rearing horse, modelled by Johann Joachim Kändler.

TEXTILES

Catherine was also portrayed in textiles. The painter Fedor Stepanovich Rokotov's state portrait of the Empress was turned into a tapestry by the Gobelins Factory in Paris, while the Lyons weaver Philippe de La Salle produced a profile of the Empress in silk, as seen by Princess Dashkova in Voltaire's house at Ferney, Switzerland. However, the most interesting European textiles associated with the Empress are the hundreds of metres of silk fabric which were sent by the Pernon Manufactory at Lyons to decorate the walls of the Imperial palaces. These included scenes relating to the military victories over the Turks and the famous 'peacocks and pheasants' design by de La

RIGHT

This stunning centrepiece from the exquisite Cameo Service represents *Odysseus recognizing Achillles among the Daughters of Lycomedes*, a scene from the beginning of the Trojan Wars.

Sèvres Porcelain Factory, Paris (1776–79)

CATALOGUE NO. 96

Salle, used on the walls of the Lyons Drawing Room at Tsarskoye Selo. The latter evidently made a considerable impact, as it was copied by the Lazarev Factory, near Moscow.

INTRODUCING EUROPEAN TASTES INTO THE CAPITAL

As mentioned above, Catherine obtained many items from France. Most of her principal silver services were made by leading Parisian goldsmiths. The remarkable roll-call of eminent makers includes François-Thomas Germain, Jacques-Nicolas Roettiers and Robert-Joseph Auguste. Auguste, who undertook numerous commissions for the French court, including the crown worn by Louis XVI at his coronation, supplied no fewer than four of the services issued to Catherine's governor-generals. The Empress also commissioned one of the most important French Neo-Classical gilded bronze and enamel pieces – the huge 'inkstand' or desk decoration commemorating the great Russian naval victory over the Turks at the battle of Chesme in 1770, produced by the enameller and jeweller Barnabé Augustin de Mailly between 1775 and 1777.

Catherine also brought or attracted French craftsmen to work in St Petersburg. Among the Parisian masters were the bronze makers Antoine Simond, who made the ballot box designed by Gavriil Kozlov between 1767 and 1770, and Pierre-Marie-Louis Agi (1752-1828), who was responsible for the even more refined bust of Catherine as Minerva (1781) and the 'Crimean Inkwell' (1794).

BELOW

'Catherine II's Crimean inkwell' was made for the 'Judge's Table' in the Military College in St Petersburg.

Pierre-Marie-Louis Agi (1752–1828)

CATALOGUE NO. 147

Large quantities of British goods were also imported into Russia during the reign of Catherine II. English mahogany furniture could be purchased in the English shops, which were abundant in St Petersburg in the late 18th century, and it was popular in the palaces and homes of the élite. *The Saint Petersburg Gazette* often included advertisements for English goods.

In 1773 Catherine commissioned an extensive creamware service of 944 pieces

from Josiah Wedgwood's Etruria Factory in Staffordshire, England, for the Kekerekeksinen or Chesme Palace. This palace served as a rest-stop between St Petersburg and her main country estate of Tsarskoye Selo, about fifteen miles south of the capital. Intended for sixty people, the service consisted of 680 items for dinner and 264 pieces for dessert. It was decorated with 1222 numbered views of British landmarks, and Wedgwood's partner, Thomas Bentley, provided Catherine with a catalogue in French which identified all the scenes. As the Kekerekeksinen Palace was named after the Finnish for 'frog marsh', the service was also decorated with a green frog. Not surprisingly, it is known as the 'Green Frog Service'. The Scottish views that feature on the pieces include Ailsa Craig, Bridge of Don, Duntulm Castle on the Isle of Skye, Edinburgh Castle, Elgin Cathedral, the Falls of Foyers near Loch Ness, Inverness, Melrose, Abbey and Stirling Castle.

Wedgwood undertook many other Russian commissions, including blue and white medallions of Catherine (one as Minerva), and his factory probably supplied large jasper plaques that were used to decorate some of architect Charles Cameron's new rooms at Tsarskoye Selo.

During the 1770s, Catherine also acquired stone vases with gilt bronze mounts from Matthew Boulton, observing they were 'superior to those of France in all respects'. This was high praise indeed from the owner of the Imperial Lapidary Factories and someone who knew a great deal about contemporary French decorative art. The Empress would subsequently add the large stone desk set that had been commissioned in Rome by Baron de Breteuil in 1777, as well as Roman mosaics and micromosaics, to her large collection of cut stone and related items.

As one would expect, Catherine commissioned jewellery and accessories such as snuff-boxes and watches, both for her own use and to give away as gifts and rewards. She set up a special 'diamond room' with cabinets containing 'a lot of jewellery and other precious stones … from which the Sovereign chose whatever she wished to present as gifts'.[5] A number of highly talented snuff-box makers and jewellers were drawn to St Petersburg to work for the Empress and her court. They included Johann Gottlieb Scharff, who was born into a German family of immigrants in Moscow and moved to St Petersburg in 1767. Scharff made the famous 'Useful' snuff-box, which belonged to the Empress. It was decorated with Catherine's emblems of a beehive, bees and rose bush and the word '*polenoye*', meaning useful.

Other prominent makers include Swiss enameller and goldsmith Jean-Pierre Ador, who arrived in St Petersburg in the early 1760s, the Frenchman Jean-François-Xavier Bouddé, who moved from Hamburg to St Petersburg in 1765, and David Rudolph, born in Copenhagen, who became a master craftsman in St Petersburg in 1779.

Contemporary interest in stone, in Russia and in Dresden where Johann Christian Neuber was making large numbers of small boxes decorated with dozens of different stones, led to some St Petersburg boxes being decorated with specimens of Russian stones. A good example is the snuff-box by Rudolph, set with amethysts, topazes and other semi-precious stones from Siberia and a cameo portrait of Catherine. It also has the arms of Siberia on the base and appears to have been owned by the Empress.

This chapter barely scratches the surface of the 'great splendour and pomp' of Catherine's court. As the French ambassador Count L. P. Ségur noted, some aspects were 'similar to what was enjoyed by the élite of Paris and London'.[6] A later commentator also noted that 'the ability of Russians, including artists, to adopt an "outside" art form and make it their own and to take it further along its path, is a typical feature of the swift artistic development of Russia'.[7]

BELOW

This snuff-box by David Rudolph is decorated with Siberian stones and is dated to the 1780s. It belonged to Catherine II.

David Rudolph
(active 1779–93)

CATALOGUE NO. 67

NOTES

1   M. I. Pilyaev, *Old Petersburg* (St Petersburg, 1889), 1990 edition, pp. 193–94.

2. J. O. Kagan, 'Catherine II – A Collector and Commissioner of the Modern Glyprics', Papers of the State Hermitage, vol. 29, *Western European Art*, issue 8 (St Petersburg, 2000), pp. 174–94.

3. SIRIO, *Collection of the Russian Historical Society*, vol. 23, 1878, p. 329.

4. J. Holloway, *James Tassie* (Edinburgh, 1992), p. 14.

5. J. Georgi, *Description of Imperial St. Petersburg –* the Capital of the Russian Empire (St Petersburg, 1794), vol. 1, p. 77.

6. L. P. Ségur, 'Memoirs and Recollections', quoted in the anthology *Eighteenth-century Russia through the Eyes of Foreigners* (Leningrad, 1989), p. 327.

7. N. N. Kalitina, 'Russian and French Artistic Relations in the First Half of the Nineteenth Century', in *The Art of France and Russian-French Artistic Links*, Abstracts of Conference Papers (St Petersburg, 1996), p. 48.

CHAPTER VIII

Scots in the Service of the Great Catherine

———

ANTHONY CROSS

BELOW

Snuff-box presented to
Dr Robert Erskine by
Peter the Great, *c.*1716[?].

CATALOGUE NO. 3

'We, English of the Scottish nation' ['*my, aglichane skotskoi natsii*'] – so began a petition to the Empress Catherine II from the group of workmen recruited by her architect Charles Cameron. It acknowledged the Russian use of the word '*aglichane*' to designate all coming from the British Isles, but it stressed equally a distinct sense of Scottish nationality.

It was, however, the fate of many Scots to be designated English in 18th-century Russia (and before and after), when to scratch an Englishman was more often than not to find a Scot. Scots were to be found in Russia from the days it was called Muscovy, principally if not exclusively as mercenaries, but it is in the 18th century that their presence might be said to be all-pervasive and detected in so many areas of activity and expertise that were vital to the smooth running of the Russian Empire.

Within the limited space available, it is obviously impossible to do full justice to the Scottish input, or to even include a roll-call of all those who deserve mention; what follows highlights a number of outstanding personalities within the context of particular areas – medical, naval, technical and artistic – in which Scots made a significant and lasting contribution.

* * *

Before the Acts of Union of 1707 and the merging of English and Scottish into British – nicely reflected in Daniel Defoe changing the title of his journal *Review of the State of the English Nation* (1705) to *Review of the British Nation* two years later – it was English doctors who found positions as body-physicians to the tsars from Ivan IV ('The Terrible') to Aleksey Mikhailovich, the father of Peter the Great.

Under Peter a fundamental reorganization of the Russian medical services led to the creation of the post of *archiater* or chief physician that was almost invariably combined with that of body-physician. The first appointee was a Scot, the celebrated and erudite Dr Robert Erskine FRS (1677–1718), who served Peter from 1706 until his death; the last was also a Scot, Dr James Mounsey FRS (1700–73), who had been in Russia since 1736 but served only a few months as *archiater* in 1762 before his patron, Peter III, was assassinated and he was 'retired' by his widow, Catherine II, who soon abolished the post. Back in Scotland, the learned doctor, who earned the sobriquet 'Rhubarb Mounsey' for his role in introducing the medicinal rhubarb, *rheum palmatum*, into Britain, did not hesitate, however, to recommend for service in Catherine's Russia two young doctors who were to achieve particular eminence during her reign.

John Rogerson (1741–1823), the son of Mounsey's half sister, went to Russia in 1766 and within three years became a court physician, when it was said that the Empress

BELOW

Dr John Rogerson, painted *c.*1792–96, and a cabinet of Russian medals reputed to have been presented to him by Catherine II (CAT. 175).

Painting by Johann Baptist Lampi the Elder (1751–1830)

SCOTTISH NATIONAL PORTRAIT GALLERY

> ... *consults him occasionally about her health and follows his advice and takes what he prescribes, but she much oftner, most graciously entertains him with other discourse, and all about her pay him the respect of a body physician, and tho' he wisely courts none of them, the courtiers do the same and his practise increases.*

This captures the relaxed relationship that Rogerson was to enjoy with the Empress to the end of her days, when he wrote of *'les grandes, rares et admirables qualités de Catherine'* ['the great, rare and admirable qualities of Catherine'], describing his service as *'la liberté la plus parfaite'* ['the most perfect freedom'].

Rogerson became the Empress's personal physician in 1776 and thereafter enjoyed a reputation not only as a good doctor – though his prescriptions seem invariably to have been laxatives, James's Powders and bloodletting – but also as a man of wide learning, elected to the Russian Academy of Sciences, the Royal Society and other scientific societies (without publishing any scientific or medical papers). He was well rewarded by Catherine with rank, gifts and land for his devoted service and he enjoyed the friendship of many of the eminent people of the time, including Princess Ekaterina Dashkova and her brother Semyon

135

Vorontsov, the long-serving Russian ambassador in London, with whom he shared a commitment to the cause of friendship between Britain and Russia. Rogerson was also known for his love of gambling and was denounced by his enemies for his political intriguing and dabbling in court affairs, to the extent that it was said that he *'connait mieux que personne tout ce qui se fait à notre cour, dans notre capitale, dans nos provinces, dans nos maisons, dans nos familles'* ['knows better than anyone everything that takes place at our court, in our capital, in our provinces, in our homes, in our families'].

The career of Matthew Guthrie (1743–1807), who arrived from Edinburgh three years after Rogerson with letters of recommendation from Mounsey, was to follow a different curve. He was assigned to the Russian army of the south in 1771 under Field Marshal Pyotr Rumyantsev, where his involvement with questions of quarantine and plague prevention was to be the subject of a later scholarly paper. Writing incessantly on a wide range of subjects was his passion, and his appointment as chief physician to the Noble Land Cadet Corps back in St Petersburg in 1778 allowed ample time to devote to his scholarly pursuits during the last thirty years of his life in Russia.

Described by a British visitor to the Russian capital in 1804 as a 'gentleman of the most aimable manners, a philosopher, and well known to the world for his various scientific and literary productions', and earlier, less flatteringly by another as 'the most pompous man I have met with [...] a perfect Quixote in physick and mineralogy', Guthrie was a member of an incredible number of learned societies including the Royal Society, the Society of Antiquaries of Scotland, the Royal Society of Arts and the Imperial Free Economic Society. He was also an indefatigable scientific popularizer and 'communicator' to British journals.

An indication of his range and versatility were the regular contributions he made under the pseudonym 'Arcticus' to James Anderson's Edinburgh journal *The Bee* in 1792–94, covering subjects from gemmology and ornithology to folklore and literary translations. The latter included 'Ivan Czarowitz, or the Rose without Prickles that Stings not', a version of an allegorical tale by the Empress herself that he later published as a separate booklet. His research into all aspects of Russian folk culture led to his important *Dissertations sur les antiquités de Russie* (St Petersburg, 1795), part of his vast '*Noctes Rossicae*, or Russian Evening Recreations' that remained in manuscript and is now held in the British Library. His last publishing venture, the considerable 'editing' of his wife Maria's *Tour Performed in the Years 1795–96 through the Taurida, or Crimea* (1802), provided the British public with detailed information about the history and geography of an area that was increasingly attracting the interest of travellers.

Within the confines of the 18th century, Guthrie's work represents the culmination of the transference of scientific, geological, geographical, botanical and zoological knowledge from Russia to Great Britain, initiated by Dr Erskine and continued by a whole line of Scottish doctors.

* * *

The creation of a navy was of the utmost importance for Peter the Great. To learn how ships were built and sailed, he spent much time in Holland and England during the Great Embassy of 1697–98 and took the opportunity to recruit the shipwrights and naval officers Russia obviously lacked. These men were predominantly English, but there was one exceptional Scot – Henry Farquharson, Liddell mathematical tutor at Marischal College, Aberdeen – whom Peter appointed to head his proposed Moscow school of navigation and mathematics. For more than forty years, Farquharson trained young Russian navigators and was arguably the most able and influential person the Tsar brought into his service. It was only following the uprising of 1715, and the dismissal or resignation from the British navy of officers with Jacobite sympathies, that Scots were recruited in numbers for Peter's navy. These included Thomas Gordon and Thomas Saunders, both of whom were to become admirals.

Soon after Catherine came to the throne, she reviewed her fleet off Cronstadt, comparing their manoeuvres to those of herring boats, and set about reorganizing her navy. She sent young Russians for training on British ships and recruited waves of British half-pay officers, first during the years following the Seven Years War and later, after the war against the American colonies and France and Spain, and the end of the Armed Neutrality of 1780.

Between 1764 and 1772, fifty British officers joined the Russian navy; in 1783 no fewer than thirty-eight officers arrived in a body and many more followed in subsequent years. One of the earliest groups, arriving in the summer of 1764, consisted of five experienced Scottish officers, headed by Charles Douglas. Douglas was given the rank of rear-admiral by Catherine, but he and one of the other officers returned to England, leaving Samuel Greig (1735/6–88), a captain of the first rank, William Roxborough, a captain of the second rank and Greig's kinsman, and a lieutenant, William Gordon, who died in 1768. Catherine sought a replacement for Douglas in another Scot, Captain John Elphinstone (1722–85), who was promoted to rear-admiral soon after his arrival in June 1769.

Elphinstone, a courageous and enterprising officer, but also impetuous, obstinate and vainglorious, was to command one of the squadrons of the Russian fleet under the overall command of Count Aleksey Orlov in the great Russian victory over the Turks at the bay of Chesme the following year. His role in the victory, extolled for a British public in the anonymous *Authentic Account of the Russian Expedition against the Turks by Land and Sea* (London, 1772), was considerable, but in Russian eyes the national hero was naturally Orlov, who was allowed to add as the second barrel to his name 'Chesmensky'. Nonetheless, Orlov and the Empress were generous in their praise of Greig, who commanded the *Trekh Ierarkhov* (*The Three Bishops*), Orlov's flagship, but transferred to the *Rostislav* to direct the crucial action with fire-ships against the Turkish line. Elphinstone was soon to be re-called to St Petersburg to face charges for the loss of his own flagship, the *Sviatoslav*, on a sandbank during a later engagement in the Russian-Turkish war; never the model of tact, he sealed his fate by appearing before the Empress in his Royal Navy uniform, the *Scots Magazine*

noting that she had apparently commented that 'it was high time that a man should quit her service, who had thrown off her livery'. In late 1771 an aggrieved Elphinstone returned to England and service in the Royal Navy.

Meanwhile, the careers of Greig and several other British officers from the Mediterranean campaign were set to flourish, particularly that of Lieutenant Thomas Mackenzie (d.1786), who commanded one of the four fire-ships and who eventually became a rear-admiral, responsible for the construction of the harbour at Sebastopol, where a monument to his memory was built on an overlooking hillside.

It was, however, Greig, the master's mate from Inverkeithing, who was the undoubted success story among the many British naval officers serving Russia's cause and earning, according to the compiler of the *Dictionary of Notable People of the Russian Land* (1836), 'the indubitable right to stand alongside the most distinguished Russians of the age of Catherine II'. Immediately promoted to rear-admiral after Chesme, Greig flew his flag in a number of further engagements during the Mediterranean campaign before returning briefly to Russia. He then sailed back to Leghorn (Livorno) with his wife Sarah, daughter of the Scottish owner of a rope-walk at Cronstadt. In February 1775, however, Greig was involved in the abduction of the alleged daughter of the Empress Elizabeth by Count Aleksey Razumovsky and pretender to the Russian throne, the so-called Princess Tarakanova, who was to die in a St Petersburg prison. It was an unhappy event, undoubtedly undertaken on the instructions of Catherine, writing to Greig that, 'I shall always remember your services and shall not fail to give marks of my benevolence towards you' – and she was true to her word.

A knight of the Order of St George and St Anna for his prowess during the Mediterranean campaign, Greig was promoted to vice-admiral and appointed commandant of Cronstadt in July 1775. A year later, he received the Order of St Alexander Nevsky. The following year he returned in triumph to Britain and was presented to King George III in London and received the freedom of the city of Edinburgh on 3 October 1777. Further British recognition came in March 1782 when he was elected a fellow of the Royal Society 'for many eminent services in his Profession as well as for a very extensive knowledge in the various branches of Physics'. It was a year that, in many ways, signalled the high point of Greig's career, for he became also an honorary member of the Russian Academy of Sciences and was promoted to the rank of full admiral.

Greig's appointment as commandant of Cronstadt was of major significance not only for himself personally, but also for the improvements and reforms that were to be introduced into the Russian Baltic fleet. The Russian ambassador in London believed that it was through the efforts of the elderly Admiral Sir Charles Knowles, the highest ranking British officer recruited by Catherine and serving for three and a half years until July 1774, and in particular of Greig, that the Russian navy was placed on what he termed *'le pied anglais'*, or what the *Scots Magazine* called 'the English exercise'. Greig was able to build on the planning initiatives of Knowles, and in the thirteen years to his death he did much to modernize the naval dockyards and installations at Cronstadt. This included the supervision of the installation of the steam engine, designed to empty the dry docks, that had been ordered by Knowles from the Carron Iron Works at Falkirk in Scotland. This

OPPOSITE

Admiral Samuel Greig (1735/6–88) was born at Inverkeithing in Fife, Scotland. As a member of Catherine II's navy, he distinguished himself at the battle of Chesme in 1770. At the start of the war with Sweden, in 1788, he commanded the Baltic fleet and successfully defended the maritime approaches to St Petersburg.

Unknown artist (19th century)

CATALOGUE NO. 138

same steam engine was visited by Catherine in 1782, when she also noted the progress made on replacing the rotting wooden linings of the docks with granite. Then, following the great fire that led to the transfer of the Admiralty from St Petersburg in 1783, Greig produced his masterplan for the development of Cronstadt that included not only the new buildings for the Admiralty, but also the construction of barracks, a prison, cadet college and hospitals, and the dredging and reconstruction of the naval and commercial harbours. Cronstadt under Greig began to take on the appearance of the granite impregnability that faced the British fleet in the Crimean War.

It was as supreme naval commander of the Russian navy that Greig entered the war against Sweden that began in 1788, but his war was short. He died on 26 October, not in battle but from a fever from which the administrations of Dr Rogerson could not save him. His death occasioned national mourning on an unprecedented scale, including the holding of memorial lodges in the capital, for Greig had been a committed Freemason and master of the 'Neptune' Lodge at Cronstadt since 1781. Catherine was genuinely moved. She not only had a gold medal struck in his memory, but also ordered the Italian architect Giacomo Quarenghi to design the marble mausoleum for the Lutheran cathedral of Revel (now Tallin) where his state funeral took place.

* * *

Both Knowles and Greig recognized the need to turn to Britain, and specifically Scotland, for the technical expertise and quality products to equip and modernize the Russian fleet (and army). Knowles's secretary, John Robison (1739–1805), later professor of natural philosophy at the University of Edinburgh, attempted in 1771 to attract James Watt into Russian service as 'Master Founder of Iron Ordnance'. It was, however, the Carron Iron Works at Falkirk, founded in 1759, and its employees, that were to play a major role in hastening Russia's 'industrial revolution' during Catherine's reign, despite the existing British laws that forbade the foreign recruitment of skilled workmen and the export of sensitive machinery and instruments.

Carron had delivered its first consignment of cannon as early as 1772, but many failed their proofing, and two of its cannon founders, Adam Ramage and Joseph Powell, had entered Russian service the previous year, achieving little success. It was only with the arrival of a group of Carron workmen, under the engineer Adam Smith, in early 1775 to install the Smeaton-designed fire engine ordered by Admiral Knowles two years earlier, that a productive connection was made. Smith stayed on in Russia to maintain the engine in working order, and his son Alexander, who had joined him in 1783, was given the task in 1791 of assembling a further engine ordered by Admiral Greig

BELOW

Carron Iron Works was located on the banks of the River Carron near Falkirk in Scotland.

*Unknown artist,
c.1790*

NATIONAL MUSEUMS
SCOTLAND

shortly before his death. This, however, was thwarted by the lack of several vital parts.

In the interim, Greig had succeeded in persuading the director of Carron, Charles Gascoigne (1738–1806), to come to Russia with a group of some dozen skilled workmen and specialist machinery to establish an iron foundry and produce the reliable cannon that the Russians needed. Gascoigne arrived in June 1786 with the permission of a badly-informed British government, but his actions were widely seen as treachery both in Britain and among the British community in St Petersburg. Within months, Gascoigne was writing to Greig to persuade the Empress to order cannon and carronades directly from Carron for 'the Country in Scotland are outrageous gainst the Company & me, under the notion that we are doing a national prejudice to Scotland'. The orders were placed and more workmen came to join Gascoigne at Petrozavodsk, where he was made director of both the Alexandrovsky cannon works and the nearby Konchezersky iron foundry, which he fundamentally reorganized 'according to the Carron system; and began to produce the cannon so necessary in the imminent conflicts with Turks and Swedes'.

In 1789 Gascoigne established a small foundry at Cronstadt, and a few years later another state foundry on the Peterhof Road that much later became the famous Putilov works, re-named after the October Revolution, the Kirov. Towards the end of Catherine's reign, he was sent to prospect for coal and to survey suitable sites for a foundry that could serve the Black Sea fleet: this led to the establishment of the Ekaterinoslavsky (later Lugansky) foundry on the River Lugan. Construction was completed in 1799, already well into the reign of Paul I, when Gascoigne was involved in designing a new mint on Sadovaya Street. Meanwhile, the famous mint in the Peter and Paul fortress was reconstructed by English engineer, Matthew Boulton.

Early in Alexander I's reign, Gascoigne reorganized the Admiralty's old Izhora works at Kolpino, and in 1805 he became director of the great Aleksandrovskaya manufaktura or textile mill in St Petersburg. His input and influence over the twenty years he spent in Russian service up to his death were immense and rivalled those of his friend and fellow-countryman, Samuel Greig.

Charles Gascoigne amassed a considerable fortune by fair means and foul, living in style in mansions at

Petrozavodsk and, later, at Lugansk in New Russia. There he married off his daughters, and, at age sixty, was married himself to the beautiful teenage daughter of Dr Matthew Guthrie, Anastasia-Jessy, who was soon allowed a discreet divorce on the grounds of 'Disparity of Age and Disposition'. Enjoying the modest rank of collegiate councillor and the Order of St Vladimir (third class) under Catherine, Gascoigne received 2000 serfs from the Emperor Paul, the rank of actual state councillor, and the Order of St Anna (second, then first class).

Among the workmen Gascoigne brought with him in 1786 was the young cannon-turner master Charles Baird (1766–1843) who, six years later, went into partnership with the long-established English instrument-maker Francis Morgan, marrying Morgan's daughter Sophia two years later. It was the beginning of an impressive industrial empire that reached its height in the reigns of both Alexander I and Nicholas I, when the phrase *'kak u Berda'*, 'like clockwork' – just as in Baird's factories – became proverbial.

Baird is perhaps most famous for instituting the first steamship service with the *Elizaveta* between the capital and Cronstadt in 1815, and for the ironwork on Auguste de Montferrand's St Isaac Cathedral, as well as for many of the St Petersburg bridges, including Hastie's Police Bridge. His ever-growing industrial complex, which included his iron foundry, sawmill and machine shops, occupied a virtual island site on the left bank of the River Neva, to the west of the Admiralty, where today his name is still celebrated in Baird's Bridge (*Berdov most*). A fellow Scot wrote of him in 1805:

> [Baird] *is about 40 Years of age – certainly very active & intelligent, – knows the Russian language well, which, rest assured is a very essential point & work of time: – is pretty intimately acquainted with the Mechanical Professors in general, both Russian & Foreigners – also with many of the principal Nobility; & with the proper mode of applying the Key to the private Doors of the Chief-Officers in most of the Govt Departments.*

It is the same writer who coined the phrase 'the Caledonian Phalanx', of which Baird was an undisputed leader.

* * *

Characterized by Catherine shortly after his arrival in Russia in 1779, as '*écossais de nation, jacobite de profession, grand dessinateur nourri d'antiquités, connu par un livre sur les bains romains*' – 'Scottish by nationality, Jacobite by allegiance, great designer nourished on antiques, known for a book on the Roman baths' – Charles Cameron (1743/5–1812) has of more recent times been dubbed 'Russia's most famous Scot'. This accolade is largely explained, one suspects, by his creation of the Cameron Gallery at Tsarskoye Selo, a virtually unique example of a building known by its architect's name, if not during his lifetime then within years of his demise.

Well versed in the appeal – and measurements made *in situ* – of Roman *thermae*, the London Scot was tailor-made for the Empress's aesthetic tastes and sympathies in the first decades of her reign. This pre-eminence in her affections and commissions Cameron shared with the Italian architect Giacomo Quarenghi, who arrived in the same year. Unlike Quarenghi, whose buildings were to adorn St Petersburg, Cameron is known for what he designed, built and decorated outside the capital at two of the Imperial residences, Tsarskoye Selo and Pavlovsk, venues *de rigueur* for the multitudes of present-day visitors.

Cameron began work on the redesign of internal apartments for the Empress within the sprawling palace known as the Catherinian (after Catherine I) and brought the delicacy of classical interiors in the spirit of Robert Adam to replace the heavy baroque of the Empress Elizabeth's architect Francesco Bartolomeo Rastrelli. His versatility in styles other than the Graeco-Roman was evident in the Arabesque Room, Lyons Drawing Room and Chinese Hall in the reception rooms of the Fourth Apartment, and in the six private rooms of the Fifth Apartment, including a bedroom with twenty-two Wedgwood plaques.

Cameron, the author of *The Baths of the Romans* (1772), was soon preparing for his Imperial mistress her own sumptuous bath complex beneath the Agate Pavilion, where the natural stone in which Russia abounds was used to stunning effect. The pavilion opened onto the Hanging Garden and led to the gallery or colonnade that contained a central glazed area, where the Empress could sit or entertain in inclement weather, and ended with a portico, from which descended the two graceful staircases, merging into one. When the portly empress was unable to negotiate the stairs, Cameron added, in 1792, a *pente douce* (in Russian, *pandus*) at right angles to the gallery, allowing a more gentle access to the park.

A year or so after his arrival in Russia, Cameron was given a

further commission at nearby Pavlovsk, designing a palace for the future Paul I and his consort, set within an English landscape park that rivals his gallery as his most famous creation. In the park itself, the Temple to Friendship was in fact the first building he designed after his arrival in Russia. For the palace, Cameron chose the beloved model of the Palladian villa, creating a central three-storeyed building surmounted by a shallow dome on a column-encircled drum, which was flanked by two curving single-storeyed colonnaded galleries.

Cameron was replaced in 1787 by the Italian architect Vincenzo Brenna before his work at Pavlovsk was finished, but he saw to completion the third of the great projects on which he was involved in the 1780s; his modest Palladian Cathedral of St Sophia, begun in 1782, was consecrated in 1788. It stood in a wide square surrounded by other Cameron-designed buildings as the central part of a model town that was to be viewed from the Cameron Gallery. Directly recalling the renowned Hagia Sophia in Constantinople, it played a key role in the symbolism of Catherine's 'Greek Project' embodied in the layout of the park of Tsarskoye Selo.

Cameron was also much involved in the planning of Pavlovsk's

BELOW

The Cameron Gallery
c.1780.

ANY Parent or Guardian, defirous of fixing a well-educated Youth, expert in accounts, to a Genteel Profeffion (a married family) in an extenfive trade, either for four or feven years; in cafe the latter fhould be preferred, that term will make him jointly, with his freedom of London, a member of one of their richeft companies. Any know-ledge of the trial of metals, fmelting, refining, &c. would have a prefe-rence.

Pleafe to mention name and addrefs to Mr Slomon, at the Chapter Coffeehoufe, London.

For her Majefty the Emprefs of all the Ruffias.

WANTED,

TWO CLERKS, who have been employed by an Architect or very confiderable Builder, who can draw well, fuch as figures and or-naments for rooms, &c. &c.

Two Mafter Mafons,

Two Mafter Bricklayers,

A Mafter Smith, who can make locks, hinges, &c.

Several Journeymen Plafterers,

Several Journeymen Bricklayers

It is expected that none will apply who are not fully mafters of the above work, and who cannot bring with them proper certificates of their abilities and good behaviour.

The mafter mafons, bricklayers, and fmith, muft have been employ-ed as foremen in their different lines. The mafter bricklayers and men will have a pice of ground given them. As the encouragement to each will be confiderable, the beft of tradefmen will be expected.

For further particulars apply to Meffrs Peter and Francis Forrefter and Company, Leith, who will have a good veffel ready to carry them out by the 1ft of April next, provided the Baltic is by that time open.

W R E C K.

THE SOPHIA of Leith, Captain James Chriftie, from Bourdeaux and Guernfey for Leith, was wrecked near Alemouth, in North-umberland, on Friday night laft, the 16th inftant.—Several veffels were next day feen from the fhore, picking up part of the cargo of wine, &c. which had floated from the fhip.

It is intreated that the mafters of thefe veffels will, upon their arrival at their deftined ports, land the goods they may have picked up in the Cuftom-houfe, and advife Meffrs Bell and Rannie, merchants in Leith

renowned landscape garden, and to a lesser extent at Tsarskoye Selo, where the chief gardener was John Bush, formerly of Hackney in London, whose daughter Cameron married in 1784. Inevitably, British gardeners were much in demand in Catherine's Russia, employed both by the Empress and grandees such as Orlov and Potemkin. Scots were much in evidence, beginning with the brothers Charles and John Sparrow, recruited in 1769 to work for Orlov at Gatchina, and including James Meader, an experienced practitioner who is far less known than his skill warrants. His major creation, the great English Park at Peterhof, along with its Quarenghi-designed English Palace, was sadly obliterated during the Second World War.

Meader, formerly gardener to the Duke of Northumberland at Syon House and author of *The Planter's Guide: or Pleasure Gardener's Companion* (1779), was dispatched soon after his arrival in 1779 to Peterhof, where he remained until his return to Britain in 1792. Of his activities in Russia during the first eight years of his stay, we have the invaluable record of his extant letter-book. Of what he achieved, we have the evidence of four watercolours that he painted in 1782.

Fellow-countrymen Andrew Swinton wrote in 1790 that he found the park 'a very beautiful spot; and when the natural flatness of the ground is considered, it is amazing what art and taste have been exerted in finishing it. – Here are winding rivulets, cascades dashing over moss-clad rocks, antique bridges, temples, ruins, and cottages amazing.'

Embarking on his work at Tsarskoye Selo, Cameron soon realized that the Russian workmen did not possess the skills as stonemasons, bricklayers, plasterers and smiths vital to the success of his projects. An advertisement in the *Edinburgh Evening Courant* in January 1784 led to the recruitment of seventy-three tradesmen who, with their families, were soon on their way to St Petersburg. They would be accommodated in a row of small wooden houses in Sophia known as the English Line. Relations between workmen and the architect were often fraught and not all the workmen enjoyed the Russian experience, many leaving after the expiry of their initial three-year contracts, while others stayed until 1790. Yet others remained for the rest of their lives, creating notable careers of their own. None was more successful than Adam Menelaws (1749–1831) and William Hastie (1755–1832), whose independent careers spanned four reigns.

Adam Menelaws, whose portrait was painted in the 1790s by the renowned Russian artist Vladimir Lukich Borovikovsky, was an experienced master stonemason who was almost immediately seconded from Tsarskoye Selo to work under the Russian architect Nikolai L'vov on the St Joseph Cathedral at Mogilev, and also on the Cathedral of Boris and Gleb at Torzhok. Early in the 19th century, he worked for Count Razumovsky on estates near Moscow and was responsible for rebuilding in a strictly Classical idiom the Moscow mansion, damaged in the great fire of 1812, that was to become the Museum of the Revolution in Soviet times.

It was, however, precisely at Tsarskoye Selo that he was to spend the last fifteen years of his life, producing a number of garden pavilions and buildings in the fashionable neo-Gothic style in the park of the Alexander Palace, including the Llama House, the Arsenal and White Tower. He left as his ultimate monument the great forty-foot Egyptian Gate with its cast-iron bas-reliefs copied from Egyptian originals.

Hastie, who died the year after Menelaws, achieved even more contemporary fame in two completely unpredictable areas. The young stonemason revealed a talent for architectural drawing that brought him to the attention of Catherine and, without a building to his credit, he was appointed chief architect to the Empress's favourite, Count Platon Zubov, in the southern territories recently acquired by Russia. It was, however, as the foremost designer and builder of cast-iron arched bridges – including the Politseisky Bridge on Nevsky Prospekt crossing the Moika – that he established a reputation in Alexander's reign. Concurrently he was appointed chief architect at Tsarskoye Selo in 1808, producing a new town plan that ironically involved the obliteration of Cameron's Sophia (apart from its cathedral, now happily restored to its former glory), and was the first in an astonishing spate of often controversial plans for over a score of towns throughout the length and breadth of Russia.

* * *

The Scottish contribution to Catherine's Russia in the informed application of medical and surgical expertise, the efficient manning and

ABOVE

The Politseisky Bridge in
St Petersburg, *c.*1830.
Named Green Bridge after
being painted in 1730, the
bridge was renamed
Politseisky (Police) Bridge
in 1768 due its close
proximity to the home
of St Petersburg's Police
General. It became Green
Bridge again in 1998.

Vasily Sadovnikov
(1800–79)

running of the Russian navy, the introduction of new industrial and scientific technology, and the beautifying of the capital and its environs with buildings and gardens, and indeed in much else, was immense; but it was a contribution that went far beyond the end of her reign, extending virtually to the Crimean War, over half a century later.

Menelaws, Hastie and Baird are examples of men, the major accomplishments of whose careers fall outside the confines of Catherine's reign, and they were in no way exceptions.

Among doctors, mention has not been made of Sir James Wylie (1768–1854), the longest serving and most celebrated of British doctors in Russia, who arrived in 1790 but whose glory days were as head of all Russian medical services under Alexander I.

Scottish naval officers served with distinction and high rank in Alexander's navy and it was not so much legacy as progeny, for the sons of Elphinstone and Greig were prominent, none more so than Alexis Greig (1775–1845), who emulated his father by becoming an admiral and honorary member of the Academy of Sciences.

From the ranks of Cameron's workmen came not only Menelaws and Hastie, but also the daughter of the plasterer William Lyon, the formidable Jane or Jenny (b. 1771), the 'nanny-lioness' (*niania-l'vitsa*), who cared for the infant Grand Duke Nikolay Pavlovich from 1796 and stayed with the Imperial family for more than forty years; and the son of the master smith James Wilson, Alexander (1774–1866), who followed Gascoigne as director of the Kolpino works and the Aleksandrovskaya manufaktura and rose to the rank of major-general of engineers. The list goes on ….

(A) GENERAL

The Caledonian Phalanx: Scots in Russia (Edinburgh: National Library of Scotland, 1987) (series of essays).

Anthony Cross, *By the Banks of the Neva: Chapters from the Lives and Careers of the British in Eighteenth-Century Russia* (Cambridge University Press, 1997).

(B) INDIVIDUAL CASE STUDIES

Anthony Cross, 'John Rogerson: Physician to Catherine the Great', *Canadian Slavic Studies*, IV (1970), pp. 594–601.

Jesse M. Sweet, 'Matthew Guthrie (1743–1807): An Eighteenth-Century Gemmologist', *Annals of Science*, XX (1964), pp. 245–302.

Anthony Cross, 'Arcticus and The Bee (1790–1794): An Episode in Anglo-Russian Cultural Relations', *Oxford Slavonic Papers*, NS II (1969), pp. 62–76.

K. A. Papmehl, 'Matthew Guthrie – the Forgotten Student of Eighteenth-Century Russia', *Canadian Slavonic Papers*, XL (1969), pp. 167–82.

John H. Appleby, 'St Petersburgh to Edinburgh – Matthew Guthrie's Introduction of Medicinal Plants in the Context of Scottish-Russian Natural History Exchange', *Archives of Natural History*, XIII (1987), pp. 28–40.

Anthony Cross, 'The Elphinstones in Catherine the Great's Navy', *Mariner's Mirror*, LXXXIV (1998), pp. 268–77.

Anthony Cross, 'Samuel Greig, Catherine the Great's Scottish Admiral', *Mariner's Mirror*, LX (1972), pp. 173–97.

Margaret M. Page, 'Admiral Samuil Karlovich Greig: A Scot in the Service of Catherine the Great', *Scottish Slavonic Papers*, no. 15 (1990), pp. 7–18.

Anthony Cross, '"A Sort of Connexion with that Country": John Robison's Contribution to Scoto-Russian Cultural Relations', *Filosofskii vek*, XV (St Petersburg, 2001), pp. 47–63.

R. P. Bartlett, 'Scottish Cannon founders and the Russian Navy, 1768–1785', *Oxford Slavonic Papers*, NS X (1977), pp. 51–72.

R. P. Bartlett, 'Charles Gascoigne in Russia: A Case Study in the Diffusion of British Technology, 1786–1806', in A. G. Cross (ed.), *Russia and the West in the Eighteenth Century* (Newtonville, Mass.: Oriental Research Partners, 1983), pp. 354–63.

Anthony Cross, 'Cameron's Scottish Workmen in Russia', *Scottish Slavonic Review*, no. 10 (1988), pp. 51–74.

Anthony Cutler, 'Recovering St Sophia: Cameron, Catherine II, and the Idea of Constantinople in Late Eighteenth-Century Russia', in Henry A. Millon and Susan Scott Munshower (eds), *An Architectural Progress in the Renaissance and Baroque Sojourns in and out of Italy*. Papers in Art History from the Pennsylvania State University, VII (Philadelphia, 1992), pp. 888–910.

Dmitry Shvidkovsky, *The Empress & the Architect: British Architecture and Gardens at the Court of Catherine the Great* (New Haven: Yale University Press, 1996).

Anthony Cross, 'In Cameron's Shadow: Adam Menelaws, Stonemason Turned Architect', *Scottish Slavonic Review*, no. 17 (1991), pp. 7–19.

Dmitrij Shvidkovsky, 'Architect to Three Emperors: Adam Menelas in Russia', *Apollo* (January 1992), pp. 36–41.

A. J. Schmidt, 'William Hastie, Scottish Planner of Russian Cities', *Proceedings of the American Philosophical Society*, CXIV (1970), pp. 226–43.

Tamara Korshunova, 'William Hastie in Russia', *Architectural History*, XVII (1974), pp. 14–21.

D. Shvidkovskii, 'Classical Edinburgh and Russian Town-Planning of the Late 18th and early 19th Centuries: The Role of William Hastie (1755–1832)', in *Scottish Architects Abroad: Architectural Heritage*, II (1991), pp. 69–78.

EXHIBTION CATALOGUE

6.

7. SNUFF-BOX DECORATED WITH PUG DOGS

Nevskaia Porcelain Factory (later the Imperial Porcelain Factory), St Petersburg, dated 1752
Porcelain, decorated with overglaze enamels, and with a gold mount, 4.7 x 7.8 x 6.1 cm
State Hermitage Museum, inv. no. ЭРФ–150

The inventor of Russian porcelain, Dmitry Ivanovich Vinogradov (1720–58), made this porcelain snuff-box, decorated by the enamel painter Ivan Chorny. Pug dogs were fashionable in the 18th century. They could symbolize fidelity and also indicate that the owner of the box was a Freemason.

8. SNUFF-BOX DECORATED WITH PASTORAL SCENES AND 'THE PILGRIMS ON THE ISLAND OF CYTHERA'

Nevskaia Porcelain Factory (later the Imperial Porcelain Factory), St Petersburg, c.1750–60
Porcelain, decorated with overglaze enamels, and with a gold mount, 4.1 x 8.4 x 6.3 cm
State Hermitage Museum, inv. no. ЭРФ–151

The Greek island of Cythera was said to be the birthplace of Venus, goddess of love. The scene is copied from an engraving by Bernard Picart of 1708.

7.

8.

9. PARCEL-SHAPED SNUFF-BOX ADDRESSED 'TO HER IMPERIAL MAJESTY ELIZABETH PETROVNA, THE AUTOCRAT OF ALL RUSSIA, THE MOST GRACIOUS SOVEREIGN'

Nevskaia Porcelain Factory (later the Imperial Porcelain Factory), St Petersburg, dated 1753
Porcelain, decorated with overglaze enamels and gilding, and with a gold mount, 3.8 x 9.6 x 7.6 cm
State Hermitage Museum, inv. no. ЭРФ–159

These so-called parcel- or packet-shaped boxes were intended to look like postal envelopes and had the owner's name and address inscribed on the lid. The calligraphy is by Lev Tersky and the gilding and decoration by Andrei Chorny (son of Ivan Chorny).

10. SNUFF-BOX WITH RELIEF DECORATION IN THE FORM OF SHELLS, CORAL AND SEAWEED

Nevskaia Porcelain Factory (later the Imperial Porcelain Factory), St Petersburg, 1750–60
Porcelain, decorated with overglaze enamels, and with a gold mount, 6.3 x 9.1 x 7.6 cm
State Hermitage Museum, inv. no. ЭРФ–154

The inside is painted with a depiction of one of the Five Senses after the 17th-century Flemish-Dutch artist Adriaen Brouwer.

10.

11. SNUFF-BOX WITH 'CHINOISERIE' DECORATION

Nevskaia Porcelain Factory (later the Imperial Porcelain Factory), St Petersburg, c.1760
Porcelain, decorated with overglaze enamels and gilding, and with a gold mount, 4.9 x 8.2 x 6.0 cm
State Hermitage Museum, inv. no. ЭРФ–152

12. CHESS PIECES

Nevskaia Porcelain Factory (later the Imperial Porcelain Factory), St Petersburg, mid-18th century
Porcelain, decorated with overglaze enamels and gilding
State Hermitage Museum, inv. nos.
ЭРФ–166, pawn (black), 6.5 x 2.9 x 2.6 cm
ЭРФ–169, pawn (white), 7.1 x 2.5 x 2.5 cm
ЭРФ–170, knight (horse) (white), 8.4 x 5.5 x 3.2 cm
ЭРФ–171, bishop (elephant) (white), 9.5 x 5.8 x 3.3 cm
ЭРФ–172, castle (white), 6.6 x 5.6 x 3.2 cm
ЭРФ–173, queen (white), 11.2 x 4.2 x 4.0 cm

13. PIECES FROM THE PRIVATE DINNER AND DESSERT SERVICE OF EMPRESS ELIZABETH

Nevskaia Porcelain Factory, St Petersburg, 1756–62
Porcelain, decorated with overglaze enamels and gilding
State Hermitage Museum, inv. nos.
ЭРФ–4494, basket, 9.8 x 28.5 x 21.2 cm
ЭРФ–8788, salt, 3.0 x 11.0 x 9.8 cm
ЭРФ–135, plate, 3.5 x 24.2 cm
ЭРФ–137, salt cellar, 2.9 x 11.0 x 9.5 cm
ЭРФ–139, spoon, 18.6 x 4.0 x 2.3 cm
ЭРФ–6701, 19th-century small plate, 3.0 x 25.0 cm
ЭРФ–6961, small basket for biscuits, 9.8 x 29.5 x 21.0 cm

These items come from Elizabeth's 'Own Special Service'. This was the first dinner service made for the Empress's private use and consisted of several hundred pieces. In 1838 the Imperial Porcelain Factory was commissioned to replace items that had been broken and to enlarge the service for Emperor Nicholas I. One of the plates here is an example of these additions.

14. ICON OF *THE VIRGIN OF KAZAN*

Icon painted second half of 18th century; setting by
Yakov Frolov, Moscow, 1775
Tempera on panel; silver-gilt setting, on wood,
decorated with pearls, amethysts, almandines and
glass, 33.1 x 28.5 cm
State Hermitage Museum, inv. no. ЭРО–8912

This icon represents the Heavenly Protectress of St
Petersburg. It is one of the most venerated in Russia.

15. RELIQUARY IN THE SHAPE OF GOLGOTHA

Justus Nicolaus Lundt, St Petersburg, 1787
Partly gilt silver, 40.5 x 39.5 x 27.5 cm
State Hermitage Museum, inv. no. ЭРО–5714

Golgotha or Calvary was the hill on which Christ
was crucified.

16. ALTAR CROSS

Unidentified master, Moscow, 1763
Silver-gilt and wood, 45.6 x 27.5 x 2.5 cm
State Hermitage Museum, inv. no. ЭРО–8391

17. MYRRH BEARER, WITH TWO SMALL BOTTLES

Unidentified master, St Petersburg, 1779
Partly gilt silver, wood and glass
State Hermitage Museum, inv. nos.
ЭРО–8785, myrrh bearer, 6.6 x 18.2 x 11.6 cm
ЭРО–8786/1.2, bottle, 3.9 x 4.7 x 4.2 cm
ЭРО–8787/1.2, bottle, 3.9 x 5.5 x 5 cm

This myrrh bearer was made for the baptism of the
Grand Prince Constantine, the second grandson of
Catherine II. It is decorated with the Imperial eagle
and Catherine II's monogram.

14.

18.

Russian, 1772
Brocade, silk and canvas, 136.0 cm (back length)
State Hermitage Museum, inv. no. ЭРТ–19004

These vestments were presented by Catherine II to the Cathedral of Holy Prince Vladimir, in St Petersburg. The lining is inscribed: 'These robes were bestowed by her most pious Highness the Empress Catherine II on the 9th of September on the day after the consecration of the new side-chapel of the Assumption of Our Lady.'

SONS AND LOVERS

19. PIECES FROM THE ST ANDREW SERVICE

Meissen Porcelain Factory, Dresden, Germany, 1744–45
Porcelain, decorated with overglaze enamels and gilding
State Hermitage Museum, inv. nos.
ГЧ– 1779, plate, 3.1 x 24.5 cm
ГЧ–1426 a, б, oval bowl, 27.5 cm (height with lid), 14.3 cm (height of lid), 24.5 cm (length of bowl), 18.0 cm (width of bowl)
ГЧ–1439, candlestick, 28.5 x 16.5 cm
ГЧ–1466, double salt-cellar, 6.5 x 14.5 x 7.5 cm
ГЧ–1498 a, б, chocolate cup with saucer, 7.8 cm (height of cup), 7.7 cm (cup diameter), 9.8 cm (length of cup with handle), 15.0 cm (diameter of saucer)
ГЧ–1538, teaspoon, 12.0 x 2.8 x 1.3 cm
ГЧ–1779, plate, 3.1 x 24.5 cm
ГЧ–1731, plate, 3.1 x 24.5 cm

This service was created as a gift from Augustus III, King of Poland and Elector of Saxony, to Empress Elizabeth on the occasion of the marriage of Catherine and Peter. Made up of over 400 dinner and tea/coffee items, it was the largest collection of Meissen porcelain sent to a foreign court. The service is decorated with the Russian coat-of-arms, the two-headed eagle, and the crucified Apostle St Andrew – hence its name, 'The St Andrew Service'.

20. MINIATURE OF THE GRAND DUKE PETER

Jean-François Samsois, French, 1752–62
Watercolours and gouache on parchment, in bronze frame, 6.9 x 9.0 cm (framed)
State Hermitage Museum, inv. no. OPM–84

Peter is depicted wearing the Order of St Andrew.

21. PIECES FROM THE ORLOV TOILET SERVICE

Imperial Porcelain Factory, St Petersburg, 1765–70
Porcelain, decorated with underglaze blue, overglaze enamels, gilding and silvering
State Hermitage Museum, inv. nos.
ЭРФ–160, plate, 23.5 x 3.7 cm
ЭРФ–8280 a, б, teapot and lid, (a) 19.7 x 22.5 x 13.5 cm, (б) 6.0 x 11.1 cm
ЭРФ–8282 a, б, ice cream bowl and cover, (a) 6.0 x 8.6 x 5.5 cm, (б) 2.5 x 5.1 cm
ЭРФ–8284 a, б, toilette box and cover, (a) 5.6 x 5.5 x 4.4 cm, (б) 3.2 x 5.7 x 4.3 cm
ЭРФ–8285 a, б, toilette box and cover, (a) 5.6 x 5.5 x 4.4 cm, (б) 3.2 x 5.7 x 4.3 cm
ЭРФ–8286 a, б, snuff-bottle and stopper, (a) 7.5 x 5.0 x 4.2 cm, (б) 2.5 x 1.4 cm
ЭРФ–8289, tray, 2.0 x 12.8 x 15.4 cm
ЭРФ–8290, tray, 2.0 x 12.8 x 15.4 cm
ЭРФ–8291, tray, 1.0 x 17.0 x 11.2 cm
ЭРФ–8294, spoon, 9.9 x 2.2 x 1.0 cm

The service was commissioned by Catherine as a gift to Count Grigory Orlov, who was her lover from 1760 until 1773. Orlov played a crucial role in bringing her to power in 1762. Decorated with his monogram 'GGO', the 300-piece service was one of the most important works produced by the Imperial Porcelain Factory during the early years of Catherine's reign. The gift is associated with Orlov's promotion to chief of the artillery in 1765.

21.

19.

23.

22. PETER III'S OFFICER'S CAPE OF THE IMPERIAL DRAGOON REGIMENT OF HOLSTEIN-GOTTORP

Russian, 1750s
Cloth, silk and metallic thread, 135.0 cm (back length)
State Hermitage Museum, inv. no. ЭРТ–12700

23. PETER III'S OFFICER'S CAFTAN OF THE IMPERIAL DRAGOON REGIMENT OF HOLSTEIN-GOTTORP

Russian, 1750s
Cloth, silk, metal thread, 100.0 cm (back length)
State Hermitage Museum, inv. no. ЭРТ–12701

24. COUNT ALEKSEY BOBRINSKY AS A CHILD

Carl-Ludvig Christinek (1732/3–1792/4), Swedish, signed and dated 1769
Oil on canvas, 90.0 x 73.5 cm (framed)
State Hermitage Museum, inv. no. ЭРЖ–1407

Aleksey Bobrinsky (1762–1813) was the illegitimate son of Catherine and Grigory Orlov. In 1782 he completed training in the Territorial Cadet Corps and entered the army as a lieutenant. After a stay in Paris (1785–87), Bobrinsky returned to Russia in 1788. His final years were spent in Bogorodintsk, in the Tula Province, where he engaged in agricultural pursuits, mineralogy and astronomy.

THE CORONATION

25. PETER III'S OFFICER'S CAFTAN OF THE ESSEN GRENADIER BATTALION OF HOLSTEIN-GOTTORP

Russian, 1762
Cloth, silver stripes and gold thread, 101.0 cm (back length)
State Hermitage Museum, inv. no. ЭРТ–11041

26. COCONUT CUP, DECORATED WITH THE INITIALS OF PETER III AND CATHERINE

Unidentified master, Moscow, mid-18th century
Coconut and silver-gilt
State Hermitage Museum, inv. no. ЭРО–4739 а, б,
(а) 22.5 x 7.8 cm, (б) 6.2 x 7.5 cm

27. EMPEROR PETER III

Unknown artist, 1762
Oil on canvas, 132.5 x 99.0 cm; 153.7 x 119.5 x 9.0 cm (framed)
State Hermitage Museum, inv. no. ЭРЖ–562

This is a copy of a portrait by Aleksey Petrovich Antropov, of 1762.

COUP D'ÉTAT, 28 JUNE 1762

The four scenes which record the events that took place on 28 June 1762 are early 19th-century copies of watercolours by German artist Joachim Konrad Keestner, commissioned by Catherine. The originals were completed in the 1760s.

28. CATHERINE II DEPARTING FROM PETERHOF ON THE DAY OF THE COUP D'ÉTAT ON 28 JUNE 1762

Watercolours on cardboard, 25.9 x 35.0 cm
State Hermitage Museum, inv. no. ЭРР–8032

29. THE SWEARING OF ALLEGIANCE TO CATHERINE II BY THE IMPERIAL GUARD OF THE IZMAILOVSKY REGIMENT ON THE MORNING OF 28 JUNE 1762

Watercolours on cardboard, 25.5 x 34.7 cm
State Hermitage Museum, inv. no. ЭРР–8034

30. CATHERINE II ON THE STEPS OF THE CATHEDRAL OF OUR LADY OF KAZAN BEING GREETED BY THE CLERGY ON 28 JUNE 1762

Watercolours on cardboard, 25.7 x 35.0 cm
State Hermitage Museum, inv. no. ЭРР–8035

31. CATHERINE II ON THE BALCONY OF
THE WINTER PALACE BEING ACCLAIMED BY
TROOPS AND THE PEOPLE ON 28 JUNE 1762

Watercolours on cardboard, 25.6 x 34.5 cm
State Hermitage Museum, inv. no. ЭРР–8036

32. EQUESTRIAN PORTRAIT OF CATHERINE II

Vigilius Eriksen (1722–82), Danish, signed, after 1762
Oil on canvas, 196 x 178 cm
State Hermitage Museum, inv. no. ГЭ–1312

CATHERINE'S CORONATION IN 1762

33. DISH WITH CATHERINE II'S MONOGRAM
'EII' UNDER A CROWN

Andrei Gerasimov and Alexei Vasilevich Polozov,
Moscow, 1762
Silver-gilt, 58.0 x 46.0 cm
State Hermitage Museum, inv. no. ЭРО–5058

34. GOBLET WITH A CORONATION
PORTRAIT OF CATHERINE II, COATS OF
ARMS, A LION WITH A GLOBE, A DOG WITH
A PALM BRANCH, AND MILITARY TROPHIES

St Petersburg Glass Factory, St Petersburg, 1762
Colourless glass with wheel-cut and wheel-engraved
decoration, 24.2 cm (height)
State Hermitage Museum, inv. no. ЭРС–2416

During Catherine's reign, the laying out of the table
was carefully planned. Glass goblets were often
decorated with an engraved portrait of the Empress.

35. GOBLET WITH A CORONATION PORTRAIT
OF CATHERINE II, THE ALL-SEEING EYE OF
GOD AND CATHERINE'S MONOGRAM 'EA'

St Petersburg Glass Factory, second half of 18th century
Colourless glass with wheel-cut and wheel-engraved
decoration, 24.5 x 12.5 cm
State Hermitage Museum, inv. no. ЭРС–130

The air bubbles in this and other glasses helped
create sparkling effects in candlelight.

33.

36. GOBLET DECORATED WITH A CORONATION PORTRAIT OF CATHERINE II, THE ALL-SEEING EYE OF GOD AND CATHERINE'S MONOGRAM

St Petersburg Glass Factory, St Petersburg, second half of 18th century
Colourless glass with wheel-cut and wheel-engraved decoration, 21.0 cm (height)
State Hermitage Museum, inv. no. ЭРС–3220

37. COVERED GOBLET DECORATED WITH A PORTRAIT OF CATHERINE II AND MARS

St Petersburg Glass Factory, St Petersburg, 1762–65
Colourless glass with wheel-cut and wheel-engraved decoration, (a) 22.2 x 10.2 cm, (б) 7.0 x 9.5 cm
State Hermitage Museum, inv. no. ЭРС–2951 a, б

The portrait of the Empress on this goblet was based on one on a silver rouble.

38. CATHERINE II IN HER CORONATION ROBES

Attributed to Vigilius Eriksen (1722–82), Danish, after 1762
Oil on canvas, 216.0 x 147.0 cm
State Hermitage Museum, inv. no. ГЭ–9499

This impressive portrait depicts Catherine in magnificent state robes, with all the symbols of Russian Imperial power. The painter has made the Empress appear even more powerful and dominant by representing her very close to the viewer. He has further emphasized her Imperial power by showing her standing on porphyry, a red-purple stone that is associated with great rulers of the past.

ENLIGHTENED EMPRESS

39. BUST OF CATHERINE II

Marie-Anne Collot (1748–1821), French, signed and dated St Petersburg 1769
Marble, 61.0 cm
State Hermitage Museum, inv. no. Н.ск.–1391

40. BUST OF VOLTAIRE

Workshop of Jean-Antoine Houdon (1741–1828), Paris, 1778–79
Marble, 48.0 x 25.0 x 24.0 cm
State Hermitage Museum, inv. no. ЭРСк–71

François-Marie Arouet de Voltaire (1694–1778) was a philosopher, writer, journalist, historian and orator. He criticized all aspects of feudal relationships, despotic forms of government and clerical views. This bust was made after his return to Paris after a twenty-year exile at Ferney, in Switzerland.

41. BUST OF DENIS DIDEROT

Marie-Anne Collot (1748–1821), French, signed and dated 1772
Marble, 57.0 cm
State Hermitage Museum, inv. no. Н.ск.–2

Denis Diderot (1713–84), the famous philosopher and man of the Enlightenment, was also an art critic and the friend and supporter of the French sculptors Falconet and Collot. A model for this bust was in Collot's luggage when she set out with Falconet for Russia. Catherine commissioned this marble bust from her.

42. MODEL OF VOLTAIRE'S HOUSE AT FERNEY

Pierre Morand, 1777
Wood, paper, glass, metal and plaster, 48.0 x 100.0 x 65.0 cm
State Hermitage Museum, inv. no. ЭРТх–1785

This model of Voltaire's house in Switzerland was created under Voltaire's personal supervision by his niece's valet. It was made and sent to Catherine, along with drawings, plans and measurements of the château, so that the Empress could build a small but exact copy of Voltaire's house at Tsarskoye Selo. Catherine subsequently decided not to proceed with the project.

43 · BUST OF ETIENNE-MAURICE FALCONET

Marie-Anne Collot (1748–1821), French, signed and
dated St Petersburg 1773
Marble, 56.0 cm
State Hermitage Museum, inv. no. Н.ск.–6

The French sculptor Falconet (1716–91) was a
friend of Diderot and came to St Petersburg with
his assistant Collot in 1766. He had many conver-
sations with Catherine and produced a great bronze
equestrian statue of Peter the Great for her. This is
one of Collot's finest works and was purchased by
the Empress.

44 · BUST OF GEORGE-LOUIS LECLERC, COUNT OF BUFFON

Jean-Antoine Houdon (1741–1828), French, signed
and dated 1782
Marble, 61.0 cm
State Hermitage Museum, inv. no. Н.ск.–225

Catherine was impressed with the work of the
French naturalist and scientist Buffon (1707–88)
and commissioned this bust from Houdon in 1781.
It arrived in St Petersburg in June 1782 and was
placed on display in the Hermitage.

45 · BUST OF ROUSSEAU

Workshop of Jean-Antoine Houdon (1741–1828),
Paris, 1778–79
Marble, 50.0 x 26.0 x 25.0 cm
State Hermitage Museum, inv. no. ЭРСк–72

Jean-Jacques Rousseau (1712–78) was a philosopher,
writer and composer. He was close to Diderot and
other men of the Enlightenment and collaborated
on the *Encyclopédie*. Diderot criticized contemporary
civilization which was based on inequality and the
ruthless exploitation of people.

46 · MODEL OF THE MONUMENT TO THE EMPRESS CATHERINE II IN THE SQUARE IN FRONT OF THE ALEXANDRINSKY THEATRE IN ST PETERSBURG

Designed by Mikhail Osipovich Mikeshin; made by
Matvei Afanasevich Chizhov; cast by A. N. Sokolov,
Russian, 1862
Bronze, marble and granite, 90.0 x 88.0 x 88.0 cm
State Hermitage Museum, inv. no. ЭРСк–275

This one-sixteenth scale model was shown to St
Petersburg City Council in 1862 and approved by
them and by the Emperor Alexander II. The 4.4
metre-high statue was started in the same year and
finally unveiled on 24 November 1873.

THE THISTLE AND THE EAGLE

47 · PRINCESS EKATERINA ROMANOVNA DASHKOVA

Gavriil Ivanovich Skorodumov (1754–92), London, 1777
Engraving, 26.8 x 21.9 cm
State Hermitage Museum, inv. no. ЭРГ–13114

48 · NOTEBOOK, WITH PENCIL, DECORATED WITH A PORTRAIT OF PRINCESS DASHKOVA AND HER MONOGRAM

Notebook, goldsmith Jean-Jacques Prevost, Paris, *c.*1765
Miniature, painted by miniaturist Ozias Humphry
(1742–1810), 1770
Gold, and watercolours and gouache on ivory,
9.4 x 5.8 x 1.2 cm
State Hermitage Museum, inv. no. ОРм–3087/1–5

In November 1770, Ozias Humphry recorded in his
account book that the miniature cost twelve guineas
(£12.60 equivalent).

49. BUST OF CATHERINE II

Imperial Porcelain Factory, St Petersburg, after 1793
Biscuit (unglazed) porcelain, 28.0 x 19.3 x 14.0 cm
State Hermitage Museum, inv. no. ЭРФ–453

Jean-Dominique Rachette, the head of the sculpture workshop of the Imperial Porcelain Factory, made the model for this piece after a marble bust of Catherine by Fedot Schubin, of 1783. The porcelain bust was reproduced many times in the 18th and 19th centuries so that it could be given to esteemed visitors and guests.

50. FIGURES FROM THE *PEOPLES OF RUSSIA* SERIES

Imperial Porcelain Factory, St Petersburg,
late 18th century
Porcelain, decorated with overglaze enamels and gilding
State Hermitage Museum, inv. nos.
ЭРФ–176, woman from Kamchatka, 20.5 x 9.4 x 7.9 cm
ЭРФ–177, Tartar woman from Kazan, 22.3 x 9.7 x 8.2 cm
ЭРФ–788, Tartar man from Kazan, 22.0 x 9.5 x 8.3 cm
ЭРФ–790, Mamista or Chukhonets woman (Protestant Finn living in St Petersburg region), 20.8 x 10.1 x 7.7 cm

ЭРФ–791, man from Kamchatka, 20 x 8.8 x 6.9 cm
ЭРФ–3357, Estland or Estonian Woman, 22.3 x 9.7 x 7.7 cm

Jean-Dominique Rachette modelled these and other related figures on engravings in the famous traveller and explorer Johann Gottlieb Georgi's *Description of All the Peoples inhabiting the Russian Empire*, published in 1776–77.

51. CATHERINE II'S IMPERIAL GUARD CAVALRY REGIMENT UNIFORM

Russian, outer dress 1786; under dress 1779
Silk, metallic thread, bronze and gilding, (1) 201.0 cm (back length), 600.0 cm (circum. of skirt), (2) 144.0 cm (back length), 96.0 (circum. of waist)
State Hermitage Museum, inv. nos. (1) ЭРТ–15587, (2) ЭРТ–15589

On special military occasions the Empress would wear so-called 'Officers' Dresses', which were fashioned according to the uniform of a particular regiment. The style of these costumes combined in a unique way features of French fashion (the open dress with special decorations) and the old Russian dress style (a free form dress with long folded sleeves).

52. *DISSERTATIONS SUR LES ANTIQUITÉS DE RUSSIE*

Matthew Guthrie, published in St Petersburg, 1795
National Museums Scotland, inv. no. DK GUT (Library)

An added note records that this copy was presented 'For the library of the Society of Antiquarians of Scotland with the respectfull Compliments of the Author'.

53. CATHERINE II HOLDING THE MANUSCRIPT OF HER 'NAKAZ'

Unknown miniaturist, c.1770
Enamels on copper and gilt bronze, 8.0 x 10.7 cm;
15.3 x 13.8 x 1.4 cm (framed)
State Hermitage Museum, inv. no. ЭРР–8014

The 'Nakaz', or Instruction, was a philosophical-legal treatise which Catherine wrote and published in 1767. Inspired by Enlightenment ideas, it was intended to guide the deputies of the Legislative Commission for Drafting a New Code of Laws.

54. TABLE WRITING SET GIVEN TO THE EMPRESS CATHERINE

Factory of Alexei Tyrchaninov, Urals, 1760s
Bronze, 47.0 x 48.0 x 38.0 cm
State Hermitage Museum, inv. no. ЭРМ–5246

In 1771 Alexei Tyrchaninov (1704–87), owner of the Sistertsky Bronze Foundry Factories, gave Catherine this writing set for making him a member of the Free Economic Society. It was 'made from the finest red bronze' and Catherine presented it to the Society, which she had established in 1765 to encourage the modernization of industry and agriculture.

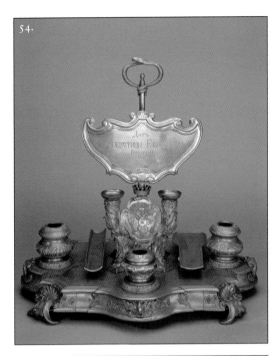

54.

55.

55. 'TANKARD' OF THE FREE ECONOMIC SOCIETY

Unidentified goldsmith 'G.B.', St Petersburg, 1789
Silver-gilt, 42.0 x 40.0 x 25.4 cm
State Hermitage Museum, inv. no. ЭРО–4759

This tankard or jug is richly decorated with references to abundant crops of cereals, two Russian roubles of Peter the Great and the Empress Elizabeth, and sixty-seven 17th and 18th-century coins minted in Denmark, Sweden, Switzerland, Germany, France, Italy, Mexico and elsewhere. The handle was made in Vienna during the first quarter of the 19th century.

56. BALLOT BOX BEARING CATHERINE II'S MONOGRAM

Antoine Simond, St Petersburg, 1767–70
Gilt bronze, silk and velvet, 39.7 x 21.6 x 20.6 cm
State Hermitage Museum, inv. no. ЭРМ–5218

This ballot or voting box was made by a Parisian master craftsman who worked in St Petersburg for the Russian court between 1767 and 1770. It seems to have been commissioned by the Nobility Cadet Corps (the first Russian cadet corps) in 1767. The design of the box is attributed to the artist Gavriil Kozlov, who produced drawings for decorative art items for the Imperial court and Prince Potemkin.

57. TAPESTRY OF VLADIMIR AND ROGNEDA

Imperial Tapestry Factory, St Petersburg, 1823–24
Wool and silk, 103.0 x 143.0 cm
State Hermitage Museum, inv. no. ЭРТ–16277

This tapestry is based on a painting by Anton Pavlovich Losenko, of 1770, depicting an episode in Russian history around 980. It represents the pagan Prince Vladimir of Kiev and Princess Rogneda of Polotsk. Rogneda was betrothed to Vladimir's half-brother, but Vladimir captured Polotsk and forced Rogneda to marry him. The tapestry is a smaller version of a work completed in 1799.

58. *VIEW OF THE PALACE EMBANKMENT, ST PETERSBURG, FROM VASILYEVSKY ISLAND*

Johann Georg De Meyr (1760–1816), German, signed and dated 1796
Oil on canvas, 76.5 x 116.5 cm; 89.5 x 129.8 x 6.0 cm (framed)
State Hermitage Museum, inv. no. ЭРЖ–2219

WINTER PALACE

59. EWER AND BASIN

François-Thomas Germain (1726–91), Paris, 1765
Silver-gilt, (1) 26.0 cm (height of ewer) x 15.0 cm (width), (2) 12.0 x 37.5 x 21.5 cm (basin)
State Hermitage Museum, inv. nos. (1) Э–512 (ewer), (2) Э–513 (basin)

These two superb rococo-style items are part of a toilet set made up of 20 pieces. The maker, François-Thomas Germain, was one of the outstanding gold-smiths of the 18th century. Sadly, he was forced into bankruptcy around this time and these are two of his last major works.

60. PIECES FROM THE ARABESQUE DINNER AND DESSERT SERVICE

Imperial Porcelain Factory, St Petersburg, 1784
Porcelain, decorated with overglaze enamels and gilding
State Hermitage Museum, inv. nos.
ЭРФ–348 a, б, ice cream bowl and lid, (a) 6.0 x 7.5 x 5.8 cm, (б) 3.5 x 4.6 cm
ЭРФ–350, wine bottle cooler, 12.8 x 16.2 x 13.3 cm
ЭРФ–351 a, б, в, sauce tureen with lid and stand, (a) 6.6 x 20.5 x 12.3 cm, (б) 7.3 x 16.2 x 12.0 cm, (в) 3.0 x 22.8 x 16.5 cm
ЭРФ–353, egg cup, 4.0 x 4.5 cm
ЭРФ–355, dinner plate, 4.0 x 24.3 cm

The Arabesque Service was the first great ceremonial service produced by the Imperial Porcelain Factory for Catherine's court and was used for the most important dinners and receptions. It consisted of 60 settings and a total of 973 items, made up of more than 50 different shapes. The pieces were decorated with allegorical female figures and cameos, which reflected Catherine's taste for the Neo-Classical style and her passion for collecting Classical cameos.

61. WINE COOLER

Robert-Joseph Auguste (1723–1805), Paris, 1778
Silver, 22.3 x 19 cm (height)
State Hermitage Museum, inv. no. Э–8623

This cooler for wine was part of the Kazan Service. Catherine II decreed that governors or governor-generals of the provinces should be supplied with silver services so that they could entertain in the style and dignity befitting their rank. This also meant that Catherine did not have to take so much with her when she travelled around the country.

Auguste was one of the leading French gold-smiths working in the Neo-Classical style, undertaking many commissions for the French court, including the crown worn by Louis XVI at his coronation. Auguste made four of Catherine's governor-general services.

After Catherine's death, Emperor Paul I recalled the governor-general services to St Petersburg.

62. TUREEN AND STAND FROM THE SALTYKOVSKY-CHERNYSHEVY SERVICE

Robert-Joseph Auguste (1723–1805), Paris, 1786–87
Silver, 36.0 x 50.0 cm
State Hermitage Museum, inv. no. Э–7171 a, б, в

This is part of the service commissioned to mark the 15th wedding anniversary of Countess Darya Petrovna Chernishevaya (1739–1802) and Count Ivan Petrovich Saltykov (1730–1805), a field marshal and holder of many Russian Orders and awards. In 1883 the great-grandson of the Countess sold the service to the Winter Palace.

63. PIECES FROM THE CABINET SERVICE

Imperial Porcelain Factory, St Petersburg, 1793–1801
Porcelain, decorated with overglaze enamels and gilding
State Hermitage Museum, inv. nos.
ЭРФ–343, monteith or cooler for wine glasses, painted
    with views of the Palazzo Solviati and the Hospice of
    St Michael, 12.5 x 28.5 x 17.0 cm
ЭРФ–344, liqueur-bottle cooler with moveable partition
    painted with views of Tivoli and the Egeria Spring,
    near Rome, (a) tureen, 13.7 x 31.8 x 22.4 cm, and
    (б) cover, 17.3 x 19.9 cm
ЭРФ–6810, a, б, в, tureen with cover on stand, painted
    with views of the Pont Molle and the Temple of Janus
    in Rome, (a) 15.3 x 34.5 x 20.5 cm, (б) 11.2 x 29.0 x
    21.8 cm, (в) 10.0 x 37.5 x 30.0 cm
ЭРФ–6811 a, б, covered circular dish painted with a
    view of the Capitoline Hill, (a) 5.4 x 28.2 cm, (б) 12.7
    x 33.3 cm
ЭРФ–6818 a, б, covered square dish painted with a
    view of the ruined Temple of Juno Lucina, (a) 4.2 x
    30.8 cm, (б) 14.5 x 20.4 cm
ЭРФ–6844, plate painted with a view of St Paul's Gate
    in Rome, 3.5 x 24.5 cm

The so-called Cabinet Service was commissioned
by Catherine in 1793 for presentation to Count
Alexander Bezborodko, one of the most influential
and wise statesmen of her reign. It was a development of the Arabesque Service and was decorated
with views of Rome based on engravings published
in books.

Part of the service was given to the Emperor
Paul I in 1796, who ordered additional pieces.
Alexander I decided not to use his murdered father's
service and the 'Cabinet of His Imperial Majesty'
(the body that looked after the personal belongings
of the Emperor) ordered that it should be kept in
the Service Store of the Winter Palace. As a result,
it became known as the Cabinet Service.

64. BUST OF CHARLES JAMES FOX

Joseph Nollekens (1737–1823), English, signed and
dated London, 1791
Marble, 66.0 x 51.0 cm
State Hermitage Museum, inv. no. Н.ск.–13

Catherine wanted a bust of Fox, the leader of the
Whig party in the House of Commons, because he
had convinced the British government not to take
military action against Russia to force her to return
lands seized during the Second Turkish War. Learning of the Empress's request, Earl Fitzwilliam let
Catherine have his own recently completed bust of
Fox. Catherine ordered that it should be displayed
in the Hermitage and a bronze copy made for
Tsarskoye Selo.

SMALL HERMITAGE: *OBJETS D'ART*

FAMILY CONNECTIONS

65. *NÉCESSAIRE* PRESENTED TO CATHERINE II

Unknown master, London, *c.*1760
Gold, heliotrope, silver, mother-of-pearl, glass, steel and
leather, 12.4 x 6.8 x 4.9 cm
State Hermitage Museum, inv no. Э–1811/1–13

This *nécessaire*, containing 12 items, was given to
Catherine on the occasion of her Name Day on 24
November. Inside is the inscription: 'I congratulate
our Gracious Beloved Lady Sovereign on the
occasion of her Highness's Name Day. May God
bestow His blessings on Your Highness for many
years and may you have mercy on your servants.
God's mercies are great as are Your Majesty's.'

66. THE 'USEFUL' SNUFF-BOX

Johann Gottlieb Scharff, St Petersburg, 1780
Gold, silver, diamonds, rock crystal and enamel,
6.9 x 4.9 x 2.2 cm
State Hermitage Museum, inv. no. Э–4692

67. SNUFF-BOX WITH A CAMEO PORTRAIT OF CATHERINE II

David Rudolph, St Petersburg, 1780s
Gold, agate, quartz-citrine, acquamarines, topazes,
amethysts, semi-precious stones and enamels,
8.3 x 2.8 cm
State Hermitage Museum, inv. no. Э–4204 а, б

This box is decorated with Siberian stones and there
is a medallion with the arms of Siberia on the base.
Rudolph was born in Copenhagen and became a
goldsmith in St Petersburg in 1779.

68. SNUFF-BOX DECORATED WITH A MINIATURE

Jean-François-Xavier Bouddé, St Petersburg, 1789
Gold, enamels, watercolours on paper and glass,
6.1 x 1.7 cm
State Hermitage Museum, inv. no. Э–4104 а, б

69. SIX MEMORIAL LOCKETS

Unknown master, St Petersburg, early 19th century
Gold, glass and hair, 4.7 x 4.2 cm
State Hermitage Museum, inv. no. Э–2867 а–е

Engraved inscriptions identify the hair as coming
from Emperor Peter the Great, Emperor Peter II,
Anna, Duchess of Holstein, Empress Elizabeth, Tsar
Michail Theodorovich and Tsar Aleksey Michailovich.

PERFECT PRESENTS

70. SNUFF-BOX DECORATED WITH FALCONET'S MONUMENT TO PETER THE GREAT

Unknown master, Swiss, after 1782
Gold, enamel, miniature, glass and hair, 7.5 x 2.3 cm
State Hermitage Museum, inv. no. Э–4025 а, б

The image is based on a medal by Johann Balthasar
Gass and Johann Georg Waechter made for the
unveiling of Falconet's monument in 1782.

71. SNUFF-BOX DECORATED WITH A MAP OF THE CRIMEA

Box, Claude-Pierre Pottier, Paris, 1784–85; miniature, map probably added in St Petersburg
Gold, pearls, avanturine glass, glass and paper, 6.4 x 2.2 cm
State Hermitage Museum, inv. no. Э–4107 а, б

72. PIN WITH MINIATURE OF CATHERINE II

Unknown master, St Petersburg, late 18th century
Gold, silver, diamonds, miniature painted on bone, and rock crystal, 7.9 x 1.7 cm
State Hermitage Museum, inv. no. Э–299

Catherine II is depicted wearing a small crown, a laurel wreath made of diamonds and the chain of the Order of St Andrew the First-Called.

73. SNUFF-BOX DECORATED WITH A PORTRAIT OF A MAN

Johann Gottlieb Scharff, St Petersburg, 1786
Gold, pearls and enamel, 8.3 x 2.0 cm
State Hermitage Museum, inv. no. Э–11550/1.2

The portrait may depict Peter Ivanovich Panin (1721–89), an outstanding military figure of Catherine's reign.

74. SNUFF-BOX WITH A REPRESENTATION OF CATHERINE II

Unknown master, St Petersburg, late 18th century
Sandstone and gold, 7.6 cm x 3.3 cm
State Hermitage Museum, inv. no. Э–10754/1–2

Many snuff-boxes decorated with medals of the Empress or important events were produced during Catherine's reign. These snuff-boxes were often made especially as gifts and would have been owned by the St Petersburg nobility.

75. FINGER RING DECORATED WITH A PORTRAIT OF CATHERINE II

Unknown master, St Petersburg, second half of 18th century
Gold and lazurite, 2.1 cm (diameter)
State Hermitage Museum, inv. no. Э–6655

TIME FLIES

76. WALL CLOCK

Johann Salomon Mayer, Zerbst, Germany, mid-18th century; clock mechanism by London clockmaker Charles Cabrier
Gold, silver, mother-of-pearl, carnelian, glass, diamonds, emeralds, garnets, topazes, turquoises, metal alloys and enamel, 14.2 cm (diameter)
State Hermitage Museum, inv. no. Э–2038

The clock is decorated with two cameos representing Roman emperors. An almost identical example, dated 1738, is in the Victoria and Albert Museum, London.

77. WATCH AND CHATELAINE

Watch, Joseph Dudds, London, mid-18th century
Gold, silver, rock crystal on metal leaf, glass, metal alloys and enamel, 4.7 cm (diameter), 16.1 cm (height)
State Hermitage Museum, inv. no. Э–1998/1–4

78. SNUFF-BOX

Unidentified master, St Petersburg (?), mid-18th century
Gold, rock crystal and coloured foil, 8.0 x 4.3 x 6.1 cm
State Hermitage Museum, inv. no. Э–4205

79. POCKET WATCH WITH KEY

Léonard Bardier, Paris, late 18th century
Gold, silver, enamel, pearls, glass and metal alloys, 5.4 cm (diameter)
State Hermitage Museum, inv. no. Э–10566/1.2

80. WATCH AND CHATELAINE

Watch, John Ellicott II; embossed decoration by Henry Manly, London, 1760–61
5.1 cm (diameter); 14.5 cm (height)
State Hermitage Museum, inv. no. Э–2056/1–4

The Empress Elizabeth acquired a huge collection of English watches and clocks, which is still the pride of the Hermitage collection of precious stones. This example is decorated with 'Hannibal at Nine Years of Age, Swearing Enmity to the Romans', after Gravelot, while the links of the chatelaine have embossed allegorical figures of Justice, Wisdom, Meekness and Strength. Manly was the son of an Augsburg silversmith and changed his name from Heinrich Mannlich when he settled in London.

ARISTOCRATIC AMUSEMENTS

81. FINGER RING DECORATED WITH A PUG DOG

Unknown master, St Petersburg, late 18th century
Gold and enamel, 1.7 cm (diameter)
State Hermitage Museum, inv. no. Э–4407

The ring is inscribed with the word 'FIDELITE'.

82. CHARM (FOR BRACELET)

Unknown master, Russian, late 18th century
Gold, metal alloys and enamel, 2.8 x 3.6 cm
State Hermitage Museum, inv. no. Э–4886

Inside the charm is a musical mechanism, which can be wound up by turning the ring. On the lower surface is the monogram of Catherine the Great with the date 1793.

83. NOTEBOOK WITH A PENCIL AND A CALENDAR FOR 1766

Goldsmith 'DFP', Paris, mid-1760s
Gold, enamel, fabric and printed paper, 8.8 x 5.6 x 0.9 cm
State Hermitage Museum, inv. no. Э–11149/1.2

84. MAGNET

Urals, Russia, mid-18th century
Magnet, gilt bronze and mica, 26.0 x 20.0 x 8.0 cm
State Hermitage Museum, inv. no. ЭРМ–8021

Although magnets could be used for scientific experiments, expensive and decorated magnets such as this were probably intended for amusement.

85. SCENT BOTTLE

Unknown goldsmith, French, mid-18th century
Jasper, gold, silver, diamonds and paste, 6.0 x 3.3 cm
State Hermitage Museum, inv. no. Э–1926/1.2

86. TWO THREE-BRANCH CANDELABRA

Potemkin Glass Factory, St Petersburg, second half of 18th century
Colourless and green glass, gilt bronze and marble
State Hermitage Museum, inv. nos. ЭРС–2174, 69.0 x 50.0 cm; ЭРС–2188, 54.0 x 41.0 cm

87. CARD TABLE

Russian, late 18th century
Rosewood and other woods, cloth and metal, 74.0 x 97.0 x 48.0 cm
State Hermitage Museum, inv. no. ЭРМ6–573

88. DISH AND COUNTERS FOR CARD GAMES

Johann Meisner, St Petersburg, late 18th century
Silver-gilt and silver, 3.8 x 19.3 cm (dish),
5.6 cm (maximum length of counters)
State Hermitage Museum, inv. nos. Э–5162 (dish), Э–8687 to 89, 8693 to 95, 8700. 8702, 8704 (counters)

The side of the dish is decorated with Catherine's emblem of a beehive, bees and a rose bush.

77.

80.

The Empress Catherine wrote these rules for her guests, laying down an 'etiquette without etiquette'.

IMPERIAL TAPESTRY FACTORY

During Catherine's reign, the Imperial Tapestry Factory, founded by Peter the Great in 1717, had about 150 Russian staff and occupied many buildings along the River Neva and elsewhere. It produced a wide variety of work, including portraits of Catherine and other prominent individuals, scenes from Classical and Russian history, and copies of Old Master paintings acquired by the Empress.

91. TAPESTRY PORTRAIT OF CATHERINE II

Imperial Tapestry Factory, St Petersburg, 1782–83
Wool, silk and metal threads, 82.0 x 65.0 cm;
111.0 x 94.0 cm (framed)
State Hermitage Museum, inv. no. ЭРТ–16192 а, б

This portrait is based on the artist Fedor Stepanovich Rokotov's painted portrait of Catherine. Such tapestries were displayed in palace halls, but were also given as diplomatic gifts.

89. ALEXANDER LANSKOY

Unknown artist, Russian, late 18th century
Oil on canvas, 97.0 x 79.3 x 6.0 cm (framed)
State Hermitage Museum, inv. no. ЭРЖ–92

The handsome young guard's officer Alexander Lanskoy (1758–84) became Catherine's new lover in 1780. Lanskoy had great influence upon the Empress; however, he tried not to involve himself in state matters and never voiced his own views openly. Unfortunately, his health was very poor and he died suddenly at the age of only 26.

92. TAPESTRY PORTRAIT OF COUNT NIKITA IVANOVICH PANIN

Imperial Tapestry Factory, St Petersburg, second half of 18th century
Wool and silk, 68.0 x 57.0 cm
State Hermitage Museum, inv. no. ЭРТ–16194

93. CATHERINE II

Fedor Stepanovich Rokotov (1732/35–1808),
Russian, 1780s
Oil on canvas, 263.0 x 188.0 cm; 294.5 x 219.0 x 9.5 cm (framed)
State Hermitage Museum, inv. no. ЭРЖ–II–678

90. CATHERINE II'S RULES OF BEHAVIOUR FOR VISITORS TO THE HERMITAGE

Unknown craftsmen, St Petersburg, late 1760s
Lacquered wood and gilding, 78.0 x 60.0 x 3.0 cm
State Hermitage Museum, inv. no. ЭРД–3300

94. PIECES FROM THE 'GREEN FROG SERVICE'

Josiah Wedgwood, Etruria Factory, Staffordshire,
decorated in Wedgwood's painting workshop, London,
1773–74
Queen's ware, decorated with overglaze enamels
State Hermitage Museum, inv. nos. and measurements:
ГЧ–8467, cover with view of Melrose, Scotland,
　13.0 x 26.0 cm
ГЧ–8545, dish with view of Falls of Foyers, Scotland,
　3.6 x 21.5 cm
ГЧ–8552, dish with view of Bridge of Don, Scotland,
　3.6 x 21.5 cm
ГЧ–8568 a, б, rectangular dish with cover, with views of
　Inverness and Stirling Castle, Scotland, 25.0 x 21.0 x
　8.5 cm
ГЧ–8717, dish with view of River Thames, from
　Chiswick, England, 1.7 x 30.0 cm
ГЧ–8940, plate with view of Duntulm Castle, Scotland,
　ГЧ–8941, plate with view of Elgin Cathedral,
　Scotland, ГЧ–9005, plate with view of Ailsa Craig,
　Scotland, 2.5 x 24.3 cm (all)
3Ф–20836, wine cooler with view of Edinburgh Castle,
　16.5 x 16.5 cm

The famous 'Green Frog Service' was designed for
50 people and consisted of 680 items for dinner and
264 pieces for dessert. It was decorated with 1222
numbered views of Britain. Wedgwood's partner,
Thomas Bentley, gave Catherine a catalogue in
French, with a full record of all the scenes.

The selection of pieces on display show views of
the following Scottish scenes: Ailsa Craig, Bridge of
Don, Duntulm Castle on the Isle of Skye, Edinburgh
Castle, Elgin Cathedral, the Falls of Foyer by Loch
Ness, Inverness, Melrose Abbey and Stirling Castle.

The 'Green Frog' service was made for
Kekerekeksinen Palace, which took its name from
the surrounding boggy area. This was called 'frog
marsh' in Finnish – hence the green frog on the
majority of the pieces in the service. Built between
1774 and 1777, Kekerekeksinen Palace served as a
rest stop on the way to the main Imperial country
estate of Tsarskoye Selo. In 1780 it was renamed
Chesme Palace in honour of Russia's great naval
victory over the Turks at the battle of Chesme in
1770.

94.

95. PIECES FROM THE CAMEO SERVICE

Sèvres Porcelain Factory, Paris, 1776–79
Soft-paste porcelain, decorated with overglaze enamels
and gilding
State Hermitage Museum, inv. nos. and measurements:
ГЧ–51, small plate, 26.0 x 2.7 cm
ГЧ–382, stand for sugar bowl, 27.7 x 17.0 x 2.3 cm
ГЧ–432, saucer for coffee cup, 12.0 x 3.2 cm
ГЧ–489, coffee cup, 5.5 x 5.6 cm
ГЧ–501, 502, 542, 544, ice-cream cups, 8.5 x 6.3 cm
ГЧ–609, cooler for wine glasses, 12.5 x 26.0 x 15.0 cm
ГЧ–624 а, б, в, ice-cream bowl with insert and lid,
    24.0 x 19.0 cm
ГЧ–641, bottle cooler with handle, 12.0 x 26.0 x 12.0 cm
ГЧ–660, stand for four ice-cream cups, 5.3 x 22.0 x
    15.8 cm
ГЧ–672, cream jug, 16.0 x 15.2 cm
ГЧ–682 а, б, coffee pot with lid, 17.2 x 18.9 cm
ГЧ–684 а, б, sugar bowl with cover, 14.0 x 17.0 x
    10.4 cm

In 1776 Catherine placed an order with the famous
French factory of Sèvres for a service for 60 people,
which would be a gift to Prince Potemkin. The
decoration reflected Catherine's interest in Classical
history and mythology and in cameos. Louis XVI of
France let his collection of cameos be used as models,
and tiny versions were made in biscuit porcelain
and then inserted into the pieces in the service.

The grateful Potemkin gave Catherine an angora
cat and the Empress was simply delighted with this
'cat of all cats'. Unfortunately, the outstanding 744-
piece Cameo Service cost the vast sum of 328,188
livres, which annoyed the Empress, and the payments
were spread out over 24 years.

96. ODYSSEUS RECOGNIZES ACHILLES AMONG THE DAUGHTERS OF LYCOMEDES: CENTREPIECE FROM THE TABLE DECORATION OF THE CAMEO SERVICE

Sèvres Porcelain Factory, Paris, 1776–79
Hard-paste biscuit (unglazed) porcelain, 28.5 x 34.6 x 24.5 cm
State Hermitage Museum, inv. no. ГЧ–7197

The table decoration of the Cameo Service consisted of a central bust of the Empress Catherine as the goddess Minerva and more than 30 biscuit groups, vases and other ornaments of various types after models by the sculptor Louis-Simon Boizot.

This group shows a scene from the beginning of the Trojan Wars. Achilles' mother sent her young son to hide as a girl at the court of King Lycomedes of Scyros, to avoid him being killed in the conflict. Odysseus was dispatched to recruit Achilles and tricked him by placing jewellery and other fine items before the women. Achilles revealed his true identity when he picked up a helmet, sword and shield.

TSARSKOYE SELO

97. DESIGN FOR THE LYONS DRAWING ROOM IN THE GREAT PALACE AT TSARSKOYE SELO

Charles Cameron (1743/5–1812), British, c.1780
Pen and ink with wash and watercolour on paper, 40.8 x 60.3 cm
State Hermitage Museum, inv. no. OP–10975

The Lyons Drawing Room was one of the state rooms of the Great Palace and was directly attached to Catherine's private rooms, which were also designed by Cameron. On the walls, Cameron intended to use Lyons silk, woven to his own design. However, due to the haste with which the work was carried out, French 'Peacock and Pheasants' pattern silk, designed by Philippe de La Salle and manufactured by Camille de Pernaune, was used.

98. 'PEACOCKS AND PHEASANTS' FABRIC

Lazarev Factory, Frianovo, near Moscow, late 18th century
Silk and satin, stamped 'F:S:S:I:L:L:V:S:F' (Factory of the State Counsellor Ivan Lazarevich Lazarev in the Village of Frianovo), 331.0 x 80.0 cm
State Hermitage Museum, inv. no. ЭРТ–15995

The factory of the Lazarev merchants was one of the oldest silk-making enterprises in Russia and produced excellent work.

99. DESIGN FOR THE WINDOW WALL OF THE CHINESE HALL IN THE GREAT PALACE AT TSARSKOYE SELO

Charles Cameron (1743/5–1812), British, c.1780
Pen and ink with wash and watercolour on paper, 44.0 x 71.0 cm
State Hermitage Museum, inv. no. OP–11029

Cameron created the Chinese Hall on the second floor of the Great Palace at Tsarskoye Selo. Onto the clear-cut, Neo-Classical layout of the wall, he placed Chinese-style ornamentation. This design shows that Cameron originally intended to use Chinese landscapes; however, he ended up using Chinese black lacquer panels.

100. TWO ARMCHAIRS

Designed by Charles Cameron; made in workshop of Jean-Baptiste Charlemagne, St Petersburg, 1784
Gilt wood, metal, paint and silk, (1) 119.0 x 72.0 x 61.0 cm, (2) 119.0 x 72.0 x 61.0 cm
State Hermitage Museum, inv. no. (1) ЭРМб–817, (2) ЭРМб–1193

These armchairs come from the suite prepared for the Large Chinese Room of the Great Palace at Tsarskoye Selo. Cameron also represented the dragons and crawling lizards on the walls of the Chinese Room.

101. CROSS-SECTION OF THE STAIRCASE IN THE AGATE PAVILION AT TSARSKOYE SELO

Charles Cameron (1743/5–1812), British, c.1780
Pen and ink with wash and watercolour on paper,
64.0 x 44.5 cm
State Hermitage Museum, inv. no. OP–10990

102. *CATHERINE II WALKING IN THE PARK AT TSARSKOYE SELO*

Unknown artist, late 18th or early 19th century
Oil on canvas, 103.5 x 73.7 x 5.5 cm (framed)
State Hermitage Museum, inv. no. ЭРЖ–568

This is a copy of a picture painted by Vladimir Borovikovsky of 1794, now in the State Tretyakov Gallery, Moscow. The original was commissioned by the court administration, but was not purchased by the Empress due to its very informal nature.

IMPERIAL PORCELAIN FACTORY

The Imperial Porcelain Factory was founded in St Petersburg by the Empress Elizabeth in 1744. It was soon making very fine table services, snuff-boxes and figures. During Catherine's reign, it produced Neo-Classical-style vases, biscuit (unglazed porcelain) figures similar to those made at the French royal porcelain factory of Sèvres, and even items imitating Josiah Wedgwood's jasper wares.

VASE MANIA

103. VASE WITH HANDLES, MASKS AND RELIEF GARLANDS

Imperial Porcelain Factory, St Petersburg, 1780–96
Porcelain, decorated with underglaze blue, overglaze enamels, lustre and gilding, 41.5 x 16.0 x 18.0 cm
State Hermitage Museum, inv. no. ЭРФ–482

104. VASE DECORATED WITH A PORTRAIT OF CATHERINE II, THE EMPRESS'S MONOGRAM AND A BOUQUET

Imperial Porcelain Factory, St Petersburg, 1780s
Porcelain and biscuit (unglazed) porcelain, decorated with overglaze enamels and gilding, 34.5 x 15.8 x 12.2 cm
State Hermitage Museum, inv. no. ЭРФ–486

The biscuit medallion of Catherine II as Minerva is a copy of Johann-Georg Vechter's medal of 1762, commemorating Catherine's accession to the throne. Vechter's representation was frequently reproduced during Catherine's reign. The vase originally had handles in the form of two cupids, but these have been lost.

105. COVERED VASE MADE FOR CATHERINE II'S NAME DAY

Imperial Porcelain Factory, St Petersburg, late 1780s–1796
Porcelain, decorated with underglaze blue, overglaze enamels and gilding, (a) 50.5 x 41.6 x 31.4 cm, (б) 27.0 x 21.0 cm
State Hermitage Museum, inv. no. ЭРФ–488 a, б

This vase was made especially for Catherine's Name Day on 24 November. On one side is the figure of Fame with a trumpet, holding a shield with the Empress's monogram under the Imperial crown. On the other side, Fame points to a shield bearing the number 24 and the Archer sign of the Zodiac for Sagittarius (22 November to 21 December), which signify 24 November.

106. COVERED VASE DECORATED WITH RELIEF GARLANDS, MEDALLIONS AND MASKS

Imperial Porcelain Factory, St Petersburg, 1785–95
Porcelain, decorated with underglaze blue, overglaze enamels and gilding, (a) 37.6 x 21.2 cm (vase), (б) 15.0 x 20.7 cm (cover)
State Hermitage Museum, inv. no. ЭРФ–9539 a, б

107. CANDELABRUM VASE FOR SIX CANDLES

Imperial Porcelain Factory, St Petersburg, 1780s
Porcelain, decorated with underglaze blue, gold powder
and gilding, with porcelain flowers and enamelled and
gilded metal, 70.0 x 25.5 x 26.5 cm
State Hermitage Museum, inv. no. ЭРФ–818 a, б

CLASSICAL CERAMICS

108. CHILDREN PLAYING WITH A GARLAND

Imperial Porcelain Factory, St Petersburg, signed
'J:H […]very' for J. H. Xavery and dated 177[?]
Biscuit (unglazed) porcelain, 47.5 x 26.0 x 20.0 cm
State Hermitage Museum, inv. no. ЭРФ–7218

The Flemish sculptor Johann Xavery worked in
St Petersburg from 1766 to 1777. He produced
sculpture for the Small Hermitage and also collaborated with the Imperial Porcelain Factory, which
made small copies of his marble works in biscuit
porcelain.

109. PAN OR SATYR

Imperial Porcelain Museum, St Petersburg, 1780–90
Biscuit (unglazed) porcelain, 28.5 x 16.0 cm
State Hermitage Museum, inv. no. ЭРФ–816

Modelled by Jean-Dominique Rachette after a work
by the French sculptor Clodion.

110. PAIR OF KRATER VASES DECORATED WITH CLASSICAL SCENES

Imperial Porcelain Factory, St Petersburg, late 18th or
early 19th century
Porcelain, decorated with overglaze enamels and
gilding, 35.0 x 24.5 cm (both vases)
State Hermitage Museum, inv. nos. ЭРФ–5221 and
ЭРФ–5222

111. CUP AND SAUCER DECORATED IN THE 'ETRUSCAN STYLE'

Imperial Porcelain Factory, St Petersburg, 1780s
Porcelain, decorated with overglaze enamels and
gilding, 12.2 x 10.2 x 7.7 cm (cup), 3.4 x 15.6 cm (saucer)
State Hermitage Museum, inv. no. ЭРФ–9682 a, б

The decoration on the saucer is based on a drawing
of 'The Punishment of Pan' by the St Petersburg
architect Thomas de Thomon. Around the side of
the cup is the inscription in French, 'Do not touch
this cup without thinking about me'. These two
pieces are said to have been a gift from the Empress
Catherine to Prince Potemkin.

112. COVERED VASE DECORATED WITH PORTRAITS OF ANTIGONUS AND CASSANDER AND LION MASKS

Imperial Porcelain Factory, St Petersburg, 1780
Porcelain, decorated with overglaze enamels, gold dust
and gilding; gilt bronze rings, (a) 42.5 x 30.5 x 23.0 cm,
(б) 12.5 x 19.5 cm
State Hermitage Museum, inv. no. ЭРФ–480 a, б

During the wars that followed the death of
Alexander the Great in 323 BC, Cassander became
King of Macedonia, while Antigonus took over
what would become Turkey and Syria. This vase was
designed by Rachette and was probably produced in
connection with the Emperor Joseph II's visit to
Russia in 1780. It seems likely that it would have
been displayed with another vase decorated with
portraits of Seleucus and Ptolemy, the rulers of
Babylon and Egypt. The pinkish-purple finish was
intended to be read as porphyry, a stone associated
with Ancient rulers.

113. ERATO

Imperial Porcelain Factory, St Petersburg, c.1798
Biscuit (unglazed) porcelain, 37.0 x 18.3 x 10.5 cm
State Hermitage Museum, inv. no. ЭРФ–457

103.

107.

108.

112.

175

Erato was the muse of lyrical and love poetry and one of the Nine Muses. Jean-Dominique Rachette modelled this figure after the marble statue of Erato by Johann-Heinrich Dannecker, of 1785–89, now at Pavlovsk Palace. A figure of Erato was included in the service given to Catherine's granddaughter, the Grand Duchess Elena, for her wedding in 1799.

114. WINTER

Imperial Porcelain Factory, St Petersburg, 1790s
Biscuit (unglazed) porcelain, 38.0 x 16.4 cm
State Hermitage Museum, inv. no. ЭРФ–449

The sculpture is signed 'AB' for sculptor Alexander Bert, who finished his training in the school attached to the Imperial Porcelain Factory in 1795 and then worked under the supervision of Rachette.

IMPERIAL GLASS FACTORY

115. LIDDED BEAKER DECORATED WITH METROPOLITAN PLATON AND MONOGRAM OF PRINCE POTEMKIN

Potemkin Glass Factory, St Petersburg, 1780–90
Clear glass decorated with gold and silver, and inscribed 'We beg absolution for our sins through God's mercy', 14.0 x 9.0 cm
State Hermitage Museum, inv. no. ЭРС–2545 а, б

In 1763 Metropolitan Platon (1737–1812) was appointed by Catherine II as the religious teacher of her son, Grand Duke Paul. He became the Superior of the Alexander Nevsky Monastery in St Petersburg in 1766, and in 1777 helped Potemkin to acquire monastery land for the construction of his glass factory. Platon was Bishop of Tver and Kashinsk in 1770, Archbishop of Moscow in 1775, and Metropolitan of Moscow and Kolomensk in 1787.

116. TABLE DECORATION

Potemkin Glass Factory, St Petersburg, 1790s
Mirror and bronze, 14.0 x 69.0 x 43.0 cm
State Hermitage Museum, inv. no. ЭРС–2157

117. WINE GLASS DECORATED WITH CATHERINE II'S MONOGRAM 'EA' AND A TWO-HEADED EAGLE

Potemkin Glass Factory, St Petersburg, 1780–96
Clear glass decorated with wheel-engraving and gilding, 15.0 x 6.0 cm
State Hermitage Museum, inv. no. ЭРС–68

118. JUG ON STAND

Potemkin Glass Factory, St Petersburg, 1790s
Clear glass decorated with gilding, 15.0 x 8.5 cm (jug), 3.5 x 21.5 x 16.5 cm (stand)
State Hermitage Museum, inv. no. ЭРС–2989 а, б

119. COVERED JAM OR COMPOTE DISH

Potemkin Glass Factory, St Petersburg, 1780–90
Golden ruby glass decorated with gilding, 9.3 x 17.7, 12.0 x 18.5 cm
State Hermitage Museum, inv. no. ЭРС–147 а, б

Golden ruby glass was coloured by adding gold particles to the molten glass.

120. TABLE LAMP

Potemkin Glass Factory, St Petersburg, 1780–90
Manganese glass, bronze and marble, 46.5 x 23.5 cm
State Hermitage Museum, inv. no. ЭРС–2585

121. SHTOF DECORATED WITH A CROWNED TWO-HEADED EAGLE AND CATHERINE II'S MONOGRAM 'EA'

Potemkin Glass Factory, St Petersburg, second half of 18th century
Clear glass with wheel-engraved decoration, 28.0 x 12.0 x 7.3 cm
State Hermitage Museum, inv. no. ЭРС–90

A *shtof* was a unit of measurement and also the name of a special large, thick bottle with sloping shoulders for alcohol. During Catherine's reign, a *shtof* was 1/10th of a bucket or 1.23 litres.

116.

120.

125.

177

122. PERFUME BOTTLE DECORATED WITH
THE STAFF OF HERMES OR MERCURY AND
THE INSCRIPTION 'PEACE WITH THE TURKS
JULY 1774'

Petersburg Glass Factory, St Petersburg, after 1774
Clear glass decorated with gilding, 11.5 x 2.6 x 1.6 cm,
3.0 x 1.4 cm (stopper)
State Hermitage Museum, inv. no. ЭРС–230 а, б

The staff of Hermes or Mercury was believed to
bring peace between and amongst enemies.

IMPERIAL LAPIDARY FACTORIES

Peter the Great established the stone-cutting and
polishing mill at Peterhof in the early 1720s. Between
1748 and 1778, it was run by Englishman Joseph
Bottom. Many beautiful minerals were found in the
Urals and Siberia during Catherine's reign; these
discoveries led to the development of important
stone-cutting factories at Ekaterinburg and Kolyvan.

123. OBELISKS DECORATED WITH THE
ARMS OF THE RUSSIAN PROVINCES

Imperial Lapidary Factory, Peterhof, 1780s
Jaspers, quartzes, lazurite, topaz marble, gilded bronze
State Hermitage Museum, inv. nos. and measurements:
ЭРКm–502, 506 to 509, 513, 515, 517, 525, 528 to
529, 531 to 535 (all approximately 12.0 x 4.3 x 4.3 cm),
536 to 537 (both 18.8 x 4.3 x 4.3 cm)

These obelisks are associated with a decree establishing the Provinces of Russia in 1775 and with
two more decrees assigning uniform colours, coats
of arms and three colours for the Provinces in April
1782 and April 1784.

124. PAIR OF COVERED VASES

Made under the supervision of Joseph Bottom,
Imperial Lapidary Factory, Peterhof, signed/dated 1777
Yamsk jasper, 35.6 x 18.4 cm (both vases, inc. covers)
State Hermitage Museum, inv. nos. ЭРКm–935 а, б,
ЭРКm–936 а, б

Jasper was found at Yamsk in 1765, in the north-
west slope of the Irendyk mountain in the Southern
Urals.

125. PAIR OF COVERED VASES

Imperial Lapidary Factory, Peterhof, 1780s
Amazonite 25.5 x 13.8 x 13.8 cm (both vases)
State Hermitage Museum, inv. nos. ЭРКm–933, 934

Amazonite is a greenish-pale blue feldspar. New
deposits were discovered in the Southern Urals in
1784, in the Ilmensky mountains which have been
called the 'Mecca of Russian Minerals'. Catherine II
owned two pairs of Amazonite vase. She also gave
earrings 'from the Amazon stone' as gifts to her
ladies of the chamber, as it was believed to protect
from the 'evil eye'.

126. PAIR OF COVERED VASES

Imperial Lapidary Factory, Peterhof, c.1780
Urazovsky jasper, 19.8 x 15.6 x 15.6 cm
State Hermitage Museum, inv. nos. ЭРКm–944, 945

The deposit of Urazovsky jasper was found in 1752
on the southern slope of the Urals, close to the
village of Urazovo. Due to its unusual colouring, a
combination of warm dark red shades and cold ice-
white, reminiscent of quartz, it was known as 'meat
agate'. The stone was greatly loved by architects and
decorators and was used to decorate palace interiors
during the second half of the 18th century. One of
the outstanding examples was the Agate Rooms in
the Cameron Gallery at Tsarskoye Selo.

127. PAIR OF COVERED VASES

Imperial Lapidary Factory, Kolyvan, about 1793
'Tigiretsky' quartz, 28.3 x 13.5 x 6.5 cm
State Hermitage Museum, inv. nos. ЭРКm–952, 953

Pink transparent quartz was discovered in the Altai,
in the Tigiretsky mountain range, at the end of the
18th century.

128. STONE FOUNTAIN

'Pyramid' or Grotto-Fountain made of the 'Treasures of Nature'
Imperial Lapidary Factory, Ekaterinburg, 1785–86
Agates, jaspers, quartzes, serdolik, cornelian, aquamarine, copper and gold, 59.5 x 22.7 x 22.7 cm
State Hermitage Museum, inv. no. ЭРО–6502

This 'Pyramid' or grotto-fountain, which has lost many of its parts, was probably intended as a table decoration. It was presented to the Empress Catherine with a map and a list showing where the minerals had come from in the Urals and Siberia.

It has been claimed that Catherine displayed the 'Pyramid' in her dressing room or bedroom. During the 19th century, it was exhibited in the 'Cabinet of Mineral Objects' and in the Raphael Loggia.

TULA FACTORY

The ancient city of Tula, to the south of Moscow, was the centre of the metallurgical and arms industries in Russia. As the manufacture of some weapons declined, the Tula armourers used their skills to produce luxury steel items. They made exceptional pieces for Prince Potemkin, who was in overall control of the Imperial Armoury and the private factories, and for the Empress Catherine, who visited Tula in 1775 and 1787. However, they also sold their goods in St Petersburg and other major Russian cities.

129. PAIR OF FOUR-BRANCH CANDELABRA

Tula Factory, Tula, late 18th century
Steel, bronze, niello and gilding, 27.5 x 11.0 x 11.0 cm
State Hermitage Museum, inv. nos. ЭРМ–981, 982

130. CHESS BOX AND CHESS PIECES PRESENTED TO CATHERINE II BY THE TULA ARMOURERS

Tula Factory, Tula, 1780s
Steel, bronze, silver, copper, niello and gilding, 17.0 x 50.0 x 31.0 cm (box)

State Hermitage Museum, inv. no. ЭРМ–4578 (box), ЭРМ–4579 to 4581, 4586 to 4587, 4589 to 4595, 4607 to 4609 (pieces)

131. TABLE

Tula Factory, Tula, c.1801
Steel, bronze, silver, copper, niello and gilding, 76.5 x 55.5 x 38.0 cm
State Hermitage Museum, inv. no. ЭРМ–7497

132. SEWING BOX WITH CATHERINE II'S 'EA' MONOGRAM

Tula Factory, Tula, late 18th century
Steel, bronze, gilding and velvet, 17.0 x 26.0 x 17.5 cm
State Hermitage Museum, inv. no. ЭРМ–7503

133. FOOTSTOOL

Tula Factory, Tula, late 18th century
Steel, bronze, gilding and silk, 18.0 x 39.0 x 28.0 cm
State Hermitage Museum, inv. no. ЭРМ–7535

134. CUSHION

Tula Factory, Tula, late 18th century
Steel, glass beads and velvet, 41.5 x 23.0 cm
State Hermitage Museum, inv. no. ЭРМ–2336

135. ARMCHAIR

Tula Factory, Tula, 1790s
Steel, bronze, silver, copper, niello, gilding and silk, 97.5 x 58.5 x 48.0 cm
State Hermitage Museum, inv. no. ЭРМ–2185

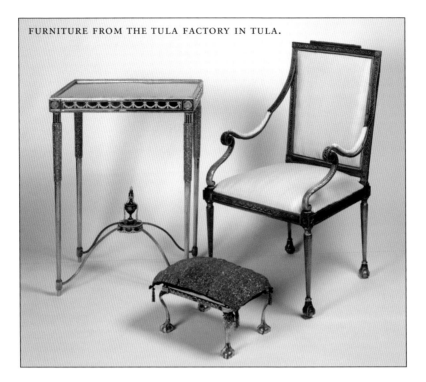

FURNITURE FROM THE TULA FACTORY IN TULA.

136. *THE DESTRUCTION OF THE TURKISH FLEET AT THE BATTLE OF CHESME*

Jacob Philipp Hackert (1737–1807), German, signed and dated Rome 1771
Oil on canvas, 162.5 x 220.0 cm; 166.0 x 224.0 x 5.0 cm (framed)
State Hermitage Museum, inv. no. ГЭ–2048

This painting was commissioned by Count Ivan Shuvalov, one of Catherine's art agents in Rome. It was presented to the Empress in 1772, along with Turkish trophies. Hackert went on to complete a series of twelve large paintings of the battle of Chesme and the First Turkish War for the Empress.

137. *COUNT ALEKSEY ORLOV AT THE BATTLE OF CHESME*

Unknown artist, 19th century
Oil on canvas, 120.0 x 95.5 cm; 137.5 x 112.5 x 6.0 cm (framed)
State Hermitage Museum, inv. no. ЭРЖ–4

140.

Count Aleksey Orlov (1735–1807) was the brother of Catherine's favourite, Prince Grigory Orlov, and also took part in the *coup* of 1762. During the First Turkish War he commanded the Russian fleet and won the victory at Chesme in 1770. He was awarded the Order of St George (First Class), a sword studded with diamonds, and the title 'Chesmensky'.

138. ADMIRAL SAMUEL GREIG

Unknown artist, 19th century
Oil on canvas, 71.5 x 56.7 cm (framed)
State Hermitage Museum, inv. no. ЭРЖ–5

139. PRINCE GRIGORY POTEMKIN

Johann Baptist Lampi the Elder (1751–1830), Austrian, *c.*1790
Oil on canvas, 73.5 x 60.5 cm
State Hermitage Museum, inv. no. ЭРЖ–1879

140. ARMCHAIR OF THE PRESIDENT OF THE MILITARY COLLEGE

Unknown master, St Petersburg, *c.*1784
Gilt wood, velvet and metal thread embroidery, 153.0 x 75.0 x 68.0 cm
State Hermitage Museum, inv. no. ЭРМб–109

This ceremonial armchair was apparently made for Potemkin, who was appointed President of the Military College in 1784. The symbolical-allegorical decoration alludes to the occupant's great services to the Fatherland.

141. PRINCE GRIGORY POTEMKIN

Ivan Petrovich Martos (1754–1835), St Petersburg, *c.*1794–95
Marble, 100.0 x 62.0 x 42.0 cm
State Hermitage Museum, inv. no. ЭРСк–270

142. CATHERINE II AS MINERVA

Pierre-Marie-Louis Agi (1752–1828), St Petersburg, signed and dated 1781
Gilt bronze and marble, 50.0 x 20.0 x 23.0 cm
State Hermitage Museum, inv. no. Энр–5609

Agi was the finest bronzesmith working in St Petersburg during Catherine's reign.

143. MODEL OF THE STATUE OF FIELD MARSHAL ALEXANDER SUVOROV

Mikhail Ivanovich Kozlovsky (1753–1802), St Petersburg, 1801
Bronze and granite, 69.0 x 22.0 x 22.0 cm
State Hermitage Museum, inv. no. ЭРСк–163

144. TANKARD PRESENTED TO FIELD MARSHAL SUVOROV

Unidentified goldsmith 'AZ', St Petersburg, 1796
Partly gilt silver, 27.4 x 19.2 x 26.0 cm
State Hermitage Museum, inv. no. ЭРО–7354

On the lid is a medal of the Empress Catherine. The eleven medals on the sides commemorate Suvorov's victories in 1787, 1789 and 1790.

145. TANKARD DECORATED WITH COMMEMORATIVE MEDALS OF THE RUSSIAN-TURKISH WARS

Carl Gustav Neumann, St Petersburg, 1793
Partly gilt silver, 28.8 x 21.0 x 26.0 cm
State Hermitage Museum, inv. no. ЭРО–5052

The tankard is decorated with medals honouring Counts Grigory Orlov, Aleksey Orlov and Pyotr Rumyantsev and others commemorating the peace with Turkey in 1774 and Catherine's visit to the Crimea in 1787.

146. TRAY ENGRAVED WITH MAP OF THE BLACK SEA

Unidentified goldsmith 'MN', Moscow, 1774
Partly gilt silver, 5.8 x 68.0 x 53.0 cm
State Hermitage Museum, inv. no. ЭРО–4819

This tray was presented by Moscow merchants to the Grand Duke Paul and his first wife, Natalia, in July 1775, during celebrations in Moscow to mark the end of the First Turkish War. The territory of Russia is represented in silver, while that of neighbouring states is gilt.

147. 'CATHERINE II'S CRIMEAN INKWELL'

Pierre-Marie-Louis Agi (1752–1828), St Petersburg, 1794
Gilt bronze, 40.0 x 30.0 x 40.0 cm
State Hermitage Museum, inv. no. Эпр–4974

This ink set was made for the 'Judge's Table' in the Military College, St Peterburg.

148. TROPHIES

Imperial Porcelain Factory, St Petersburg, 1783–91
Porcelain, decorated with overglaze enamels and gilding, 33.0 x 21.0 x 22.0 cm
State Hermitage Museum, inv. no. ЭРФ–6441

This piece would have formed part of the table decoration for a grand meal. It forcefully drew attention to the military successes of Catherine the Great and the Russian army.

149. THE PEACE OF JASSY (OR CONCLUSION OF TREATY OR THE APOTHEOSIS OF RUSSIA)

Imperial Porcelain Factory, St Petersburg, c.1791
Biscuit (unglazed) porcelain, 29.5 x 21.4 x 17.0 cm
State Hermitage Museum, inv. no. ЭРФ–445

This allegorical sculptural group by Rachette, representing Russia's victory over the Turks, shows the Classical goddess Cybele, patroness of cities and states, holding Hercules' club and a medallion of Catherine wearing a laurel wreath, seated in a boat on top of a pile of trophies taken from the Turks. Standing beside her is a woman holding a horn of plenty. On the other side lies the three-headed dog Cerberus, guarding Russia and the Empress.

150. ADMIRAL FEDOR FEDEROVICH USHAKOV

Unknown artist, 19th century
Oil on canvas, 120.0 x 98.0 cm (framed)
State Hermitage Museum, inv. no. ЭРЖ–9

In July 1788, Admiral Ushakov (1744–1817) led the advance Sebastopol squadrons and destroyed the Turkish navy at the battle of Fidonisi. In 1790 he was appointed to command the entire Black Sea fleet and twice defeated the Turks, blowing up their flagship.

151. COUNT ALEXANDER SUVOROV

Joseph Kreitzinger (1757–1829), Russian, 1799
Oil on canvas, 40.0 x 32.5 cm; 53.7 x 45.8 x 6.0 cm (framed)
State Hermitage Museum, inv. no. ЭРЖ–1916

152. ASSAULT ON THE OCHAZOV FORTRESS BY THE RUSSIAN ARMY IN DECEMBER 1788

Johann Adam Bernhard von Bartsch (1757–1821), Austrian, late 18th century
Engraving, 66.4 x 81.5 cm
State Hermitage Museum, inv. no. ЭРГ–16754

Prince Potemkin is the central figure in the composition. He is shown leading the army besieging the fortress. This engraving is based on a painting of 1792 by Francesco Giuseppe Casanova (1727–1802). Casanova produced a number of battle paintings focusing on Potemkin's feats for Catherine the Great.

153. *ASSAULT ON THE ISMAIL FORTRESS BY THE RUSSIAN ARMY IN DECEMBER 1790*

Russian, late 18th century
Engraving tinted with watercolours, 42.0 x 73.5 cm
State Hermitage Museum, inv. no. ЭРГ–21066

154. EMPEROR PETER I

Carlo Bartolomeo Rastrelli (1675–1744),
St Petersburg, signed and dated 1729
Bronze, 102.0 x 90.0 x 40.0 cm
State Hermitage Museum, inv. no. ЭРСк–162

The highly-talented Florentine sculptor Rastrelli began this bust in 1723 and many craftsmen were involved in its casting and completion. Rastrelli's son, the architect Francesco Bartolomeo Rastrelli, designed the Winter Palace in St Petersburg and the Great Palace at Tsarskoye Selo.

155. *ALLEGORY OF THE VICTORY OF THE RUSSIAN FLEET IN THE FIRST TURKISH WAR*

Heinrich Buchholtz (1735–80), Russian, signed and dated 1777
Oil on canvas, 75.0 x 127.2 cm; 88.8 x 141.5 x 5.0 cm (framed)
State Hermitage Museum, inv. no. ЭРЖ–1727

156. *THE TRIUMPH OF CATHERINE II: ALLEGORICAL REPRESENTATION OF CATHERINE'S VISIT TO THE CRIMEA IN 1787*

After Ferdinand de Mey's painting of 1787, 1790
Engraving, 60.3 x 79.3 cm
State Hermitage Museum, inv. no. ЭРГ–6798

157. *THE TRIUMPH OF CATHERINE II*

Unknown goldsmith, Russian, 1870s
Silver, 104.5 x 77.5 cm
State Hermitage Museum, inv. no. ЭРО–8203

This dish is inscribed 'Catherine II born 1729, crowned 1762, died 1796'. It was probably made in connection with the 150th anniversary of Catherine's birth in 1879. The composition is based on the engraving noted in the previous entry.

158. *CATHERINE II IN TRAVELLING COSTUME*

Unknown artist, after 1787
Oil on canvas, 52.2 x 65.8 cm; 75.0 x 61.7 x 4.5 cm (framed)
State Hermitage Museum, inv. no. ЭРЖ–2702

159. *THE DEATH OF PRINCE GRIGORY POTEMKIN ON THE BESSARABIAN STEPPES, 5 OCTOBER 1791*

Gavriil Ivanovich Skorodumov (1755–92),
St Petersburg, 1793
Engraving, 56.6 x 89.5 cm
State Hermitage Museum, inv. no. ЭРГ–6789

In the autumn of 1791, Potemkin was in Jassy, where he was carrying out peace negotiations with the Turks. Potemkin became seriously ill and left for Nikolaev, a town which he himself had founded. En route, he suffered agonizing convulsions and ordered that he be taken out of the carriage. He was put on the ground, murmured 'Forgive me, merciful Mother-Sovereign', and died aged only 51.

The text can be translated: '*Ovid weeps! Oh cruel death! / Who snatched you from us? / Like a spark in the flashing of an eye / Oh, Hero! Your famous times have been extinguished. / Our cities are covered in grief / You yourself ended your days on the plains / As you defended sweet peace / Nobody can touch your fame / How long will we be plunged into grief! / You will live in our hearts / Our eyes will never cease to pour forth bitter tears / And with them we will water your ashes.*'

This engraving was commissioned by Potemkin's niece, Countess Alexandra Branicka. It is based on a drawing by Mikhail Ivanov after a painting by Francesco Giuseppe Casanova.

160. *CATHERINE II LAYING THE TROPHIES OF THE BATTLE OF CHESME ON THE TOMB OF PETER THE GREAT*

Andreas Caspar Hühne (1749–1813), German, 1791
Oil on canvas, 74.5 x 91.0 cm; 94.5 x 110.0 x 6.0 cm (framed)
State Hermitage Museum, inv. no. ЭРЖ–1878

This is a sketch for one of three paintings commissioned by Catherine in 1791, at the end of the Turkish Wars. It shows Catherine pointing to the military trophies of the battle of Chesme that have been laid before the magnificent tomb of Peter the Great, which did not actually exist.

COURTLY PURSUITS

161. CARNIVAL SLEDGE, USED DURING WINTER CARNIVAL CELEBRATIONS

Unknown craftsmen, Russian, 1760–70
Carved and gilded wood, steel and leather, 174.0 x 350.0 x 116.0 cm
State Hermitage Museum, inv. no. ЭРРз–6450

COURT COSTUME

162. *CATHERINE II AMIDST MEMBERS OF HER FAMILY AND COURTIERS*

Ferdinand G. Sideau, St Petersburg, 1782
Engraving, 32.5 x 46.5 cm
State Hermitage Museum, inv. no. ЭРГ–13556

Catherine and her son's wife, Maria Fedorovna, are shown seated, with Catherine's grandson Alexander giving his grandmother a racquet for a game of shuttlecock, while his younger brother Constantine embraces his mother. Very appropriately, Catherine's son and heir Paul is represented standing directly behind her. On the left are Prince Potemkin and Falconet's equestrian statue of Peter the Great.

163. OPEN DRESS *ROBE À LA FRANÇAISE* OF TERRACOTTA-COLOURED SILK WITH A QUILTED UNDERSKIRT OF PINK SATIN

Western European or Russian, 1760s
Silk, satin and linen, (1) 140.0 cm (length), 78.0 cm (circum. of the waist), (2) 87.0 cm (length), 288.0 cm (circum. of the skirt)
State Hermitage Museum, inv. nos. (1) ЭРТ–16017, (2) ЭРТ–14964

The *robe à la française* was the basic type of women's dress in Europe right up to the French Revolution.

164. FOLDING FAN DECORATED WITH THE BATTLE OF CHESME, 1770

Russian, 1770s
Mother-of-pearl, silver plating, parchment, watercolours and glass, 25.5 cm (length)
State Hermitage Museum, inv. no. ЭРТ–12656

165. FOLDING FAN DECORATED WITH PASTORAL AND COURTLY LOVE SCENES

South German, 1770s
Ivory, paper, oil paint, varnish, watercolours and gilding, 27.3 cm (length)
State Hermitage Museum, inv. no. ЭРТ–6548

166. FOLDING FAN DECORATED WITH A COUPLE WALKING IN A LANDSCAPE

Dutch, 1770–80
Ivory, parchment, watercolours, gilding, 27.0 cm (length)
State Hermitage Museum, inv. no. ЭРТ–6518

163.

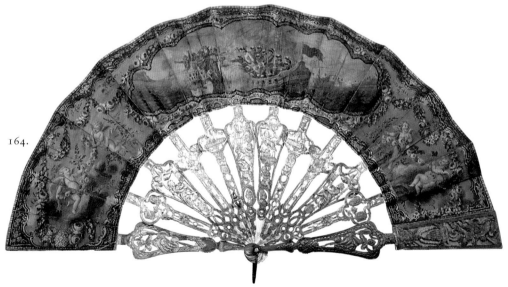

164.

167. FOLDING FAN DECORATED WITH THE LAUNCHING OF THE BALLOON OF JACQUES CHARLES AND NICOLAS-LOUIS ROBERT FROM THE GARDENS OF THE TUILERIES PALACE, PARIS, ON 1 DECEMBER 1783

French, c.1783–85
Ivory, paper, watercolours, gilding, glitter, 27.5 cm
State Hermitage Museum, inv. no. ЭРТ–6524

168. FOLDING FAN DECORATED WITH A SCENE FROM DRYDEN'S OPERA 'KING ARTHUR OR THE BRITISH WORTHY'

English, stamped with St Petersburg Customs mark and date '1789'
Ivory, paper, printed silk, watercolours and silver, 28.5 cm (length)
State Hermitage Museum, inv. no. ЭРТ–6520

The central medallion shows Emmeline, whose blindness has been cured, looking in a mirror and seeing a reflection of King Arthur standing beside her. Versions of Dryden's opera were performed in London in the 1770s and 1780s.

ORDER SERVICES

From 1777–83, Catherine II commissioned four services for the Knights of Russia's four highest Orders.

These services were used for the annual ceremonial receptions in the Winter Palace, which were held on the relevant Saint's Day or the date of the establishment of the Order. The members wore the correct attire of the Order, attended a religious ceremony in the large Church of the Winter Palace, and then enjoyed a banquet served on their particular porcelain service.

All four services were designed by the artist Gavriil Kozlov and were made in the factory founded by the English merchant Francis Gardner (1720–80) near Moscow in 1766.

167.

169. PIECES FROM THE SERVICE OF THE ORDER OF ST ANDREW

Gardner Factory, Moscow Province, 1777–80
Porcelain, decorated with overglaze enamels and gilding, and gilt silver
State Hermitage Museum, inv. nos.
ЭРФ–290, plate, 3.4 x 24.5 cm
ЭРФ–295, bowl, 4.3 x 19.3 x 11.5 cm
ЭРФ–297, cup, 7.0 x 8.6 x 6.2 cm
ЭРФ–9582, fork, 18.8 x 2.6 cm
ЭРФ–9591, knife, 22.2 x 2.9 cm

The Order of the Holy Saint and Apostle Andrew the First-Called was founded by Peter the Great around 1698. It was the first such Order in Russia and all male children of the House of Romanov became members. In 1777 Catherine commissioned a service with 30 settings for this exclusive Order. Decorated with the star and chain of the Order, the St Andrew service was supplied in 1780. It was used each year, on the anniversary of the Order, on 28 November.

170. PIECES FROM THE SERVICE OF THE ORDER OF ST ALEXANDER NEVSKY

Gardner Factory, Moscow Province, 1777–80
Porcelain, decorated with overglaze enamels and gilding, and gilt silver
State Hermitage Museum, inv. nos.
ЭРФ–278, openwork basket, 9.3 x 27.3 x 18.6 cm
ЭРФ–282, bowl in the form of a leaf,
    7.0 x 30.8 x 24.0 cm
ЭРФ–284, salt-dish, 3.8 x 9.6 x 8.2 cm
ЭРФ–7297 a, б, lidded ice cream bowl,
    (а) 8.0 x 9.0 x 6.3 cm, (б) 4.0 x 6.9 cm
ЭРФ–9600, fork, 18.7 x 2.5 cm
ЭРФ–9608, knife, 22.5 x 2.8 cm

The Order of St Alexander Nevsky was founded in 1725 by the Empress Catherine I. The service ordered by Catherine II consisted of 60 settings decorated with the star, cross and ribbon of the Order. The salt-dish was added during the reign of Alexander II (1855–81).

169.

171. PIECES FROM THE SERVICE OF THE ORDER OF ST GEORGE

Gardner Factory, Moscow Province, 1777–78
Porcelain, decorated with overglaze enamels and gilding, and gilt silver
State Hermitage Museum, inv. nos.
ЭРФ–310, openwork basket, 9.5 x 25.5 x 27.5 cm
ЭРФ–320 a, б, lidded ice-cream bowl (with squirrel on top), (a) 7.3 x 8.8 x 6.5 cm, (б) 4.7 x 7.1 cm
ЭРФ–321 a, б, lidded ice-cream bowl (with rose on top), (a) 7.6 x 8.8 x 6.2 cm, (б) 4.3 x 7.0 cm
ЭРФ–9572, knife, 22.3 x 2.9 cm
ЭРФ–9562, fork 18.5 x 2.6 cm
ЭРФ–314, salt-dish, 3.6 x 10.3 x 9.0 cm

The Order of the Great Martyr Saint and Glorious Victor, George, was established in 1769 to reward officers and generals for military successes. It had four classes, and only 25 people could hold the highest award.

The St George service consisted of 80 settings. It was decorated with the star, cross and ribbon of the Order and a squirrel, symbolizing constant and hard work. Ordered in 1777, the service was completed in 1778, at a cost of 6000 roubles. It was first used for a ceremonial dinner in the Winter Palace on 26 November 1778, on the ninth anniversary of the foundation of the Order. Extra pieces, like the salt dish, were added during the 19th century.

172. PIECES FROM THE SERVICE OF THE ORDER OF ST VLADIMIR

Gardner Factory, Moscow Province, 1783–85
Porcelain, decorated with overglaze enamels and gilding, and gilt silver
State Hermitage Museum, inv. nos.
ЭРФ–238 a, б, lidded ice cream bowl with handle, (a) 7.3 x 8.5 x 6.4 cm, (б) 4.0 x 7.0 cm
ЭРФ–247, small round bowl, 4.6 x 11.8 x 10.2 cm
ЭРФII–427 plate, 3.0 x 22.0 cm
ЭРФ–7060 a, б, lidded ice cream bowl with two handles, (a) 8.5 x 11.3 x 7.0 cm, (б) 3.5 x 7.0 cm
ЭРФ–9547, fork, 18.5 x 2.6 cm
ЭРФ–9553, knife, 22.6 x 2.8 cm

Catherine founded the Order of St Prince Vladimir, Equal to an Apostle, on 22 September 1782 to mark the 20th anniversary of her reign. The St Vladimir service was the largest of the Order services, with settings for 140 people. It cost 15,000 roubles – 1000 roubles more than the other services combined.

173. CUP DECORATED WITH A PORTRAIT OF COUNT ALEKSEY ORLOV

Meissen Porcelain Factory, Dresden, Germany, c.1770; decorated by unknown artist
Porcelain, decorated with overglaze enamels and gilding, 6.1 x 8.7 x 6.5 cm
State Hermitage Museum, inv. no. ЭРФ–9741

As the commander of the victorious Russian fleet at the battle of Chesme, Orlov was awarded the Order of St George, First Class, and the right to join the name 'Chesmensky' to his surname. The inscription on the cup reads: 'COUNT ALEKSEY GRIGOREVICH ORLOV: VICTOR OVER AND DESTROYER OF THE TURKISH FLEET'.

174. CHARTER OF CATHERINE II TO GENERAL-IN-CHIEF COUNT ALEKSEY ORLOV GRANTING HEREDITARY POSSESSION OF 4000 SERFS AS A REWARD FOR HIS VICTORY AT THE BATTLE OF CHESME IN 1770

A. N. Butovsky, Heraldry Workshop, St Petersburg, dated 11 December 1775
Parchment, ink, gold paint, watercolour and gouache; satin, silk, cord, tassels, gilt silver and sealing wax, 46.1 x 36.5 cm
State Hermitage Museum, inv. no. ЭРДр–2354 a, б

THE THISTLE AND THE EAGLE

175. CABINET OF RUSSIAN MEDALS PRESENTED TO DR JOHN ROGERSON BY THE EMPRESS CATHERINE II

White metal, mahogany, brass and other materials, 38.0 x 30.0 x 16.0 cm
National Museums Scotland, inv. no. A.1942.37

The 170 medals, on 13 trays, illustrate the rulers of Russia from Rurik in the 9th century to Catherine the Great. The cabinet is reputed to have been passed from Dr Rogerson's son to the lawyer James Walter Steuart (1802–86) and was given to National Museums Scotland by his granddaughter, Maria Steuart, in 1942.

176. *COUNTESS SHEREMETEVA AS BELLONA*

Unknown artist, not before 1769
Oil on canvas, 138.0 x 87.0 cm; 164.5 x 105.0 cm (framed)
State Hermitage Museum, inv. no. ЭРЖ–1872

Anna Petrovna Sheremeteva (1744–68), the elder daughter of the Chief-General Count Peter Borisovich Sheremetevo, wore this costume during the second carousel held in 1766, on 11 July, and won the third prize awarded to the ladies.

177. SET OF FLINTLOCK HUNTING WEAPONS WITH THE MONOGRAM OF CATHERINE II

Ivan Lyalin, Tula, *c.*1790
Steel, ivory, gold, silver and bronze, (1) 113 cm, (2) 119.5 cm, (3) 35.5 cm, (4) 35.5 cm
State Hermitage Museum, inv. nos.
(1) 3.0–6654/1–2, (2) 3.0–6655, (3) 3.0–6619/1–3, (4) 3.0–145,

This set belonged to Catherine the Great. The single-barrel gun has a sliding bayonet and is loaded with an insert cartridge at the breech end, a novel technological innovation at the time.

178. PAIR OF PISTOLS

Johann Adolf Grecke, St Petersburg, signed and dated 1780
Steel, wood, gold and silver, 36.1 cm (length of both)
State Hermitage Museum, inv. nos.
3.0–146/1–2, 3.0–818/1–2

These pistols were made for Catherine the Great.

179. WORKING MODEL OF FLINTLOCK REVOLVER GUN WITH SIX-SHOT CYLINDER AND FOLDING BAYONET

Made in Tula, *c.*1780
Steel, wood, gold and silver, 26.4 cm (length)
State Hermitage Museum, inv. no. 3.0–5436

A hunting revolver gun was considered a cutting-edge technological novelty around 1780. This working model was commissioned by Catherine II to enable her grandsons Alexander and Constantine to learn about military equipment and warfare.

180. SMALLSWORD

German (?), 1750–60
Steel, silver and gilding, 92.0 cm (length)
State Hermitage Museum, inv. no. 3.0–2642

181. COURT SMALLSWORD AND SCABBARD WITH THE MONOGRAM OF GRAND DUKE PAUL

Made in Tula, inscribed 'Tula, 1769'
Steel, wood, leather, snakeskin and gilding, 94.0 cm (length)
State Hermitage Museum, inv. no. 3.0–6801/1–2

This splendid example of Tula work was commissioned for the Grand Duke Paul.

177.

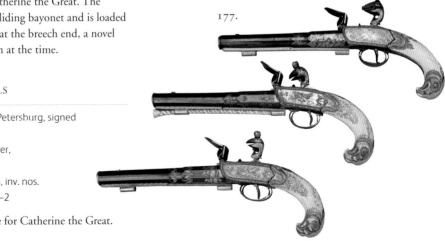

182. BOXED SET OF WORKING MODELS OF HUNTING FIREARMS WITH THE MONOGRAM OF GRAND DUKE CONSTANTINE

Made in Tula, *c*.1785
Steel, walnut and other woods, gold, silver and velvet
State Hermitage Museum, inv. nos.
3.0–5435/1–3, case, 32.0 x 16.7 x 4.5 cm
3.0–5435/1–3, 22.5 cm (length)
3.0–5437/1–2, 22.0 cm (length)
3.0–5438/1–2, 27.5 cm (length)
3.0–5443/1–2, 10.0 cm (length)
3.0–5444/1–2, 10.0 cm (length)

183. CHILD'S SABRE AND SCABBARD MADE FOR THE INFANT GRAND DUKE ALEXANDER

Made in Tula, *c*.1780
Steel, gold, silver, wood and velvet, 45 cm (length)
State Hermitage Museum, inv. no. 3.0–4661/1–2

These pieces are decorated with the monogram 'AP' under a crown, the arms of Tula, and St George killing the dragon.

184. COURT SMALLSWORD AND SCABBARD WITH THE MONOGRAM OF GRAND DUKE ALEXANDER

Made in Tula, *c*.1790
Steel, gold, silver, wood and leather, 87.5 cm (length)
State Hermitage Museum, inv. no. 3.0–6803

These items were designed to match the court dress of the Grand Duke Alexander.

185. HUNTING DIRK AND SCABBARD

Made in Tula, 1785–90
Steel, gold, wood and leather, 73.0 cm (length)
State Hermitage Museum, inv. no. 3.0–1364

This dirk is one of the greatest masterpieces of Tula armourers of this period. Weaponry of this quality was delivered to the court of Catherine the Great for royal hunting, and as gifts for members of the court and distinguished visitors from abroad.

186. CHILD'S HUNTING FLINTLOCK MUSKET WITH THE MONOGRAM OF GRAND DUKE ALEXANDER

Johann Adolf Grecke, St Petersburg, signed and dated 1779
Steel, brass, horn, wood and gilding, 46.5 cm (length)
State Hermitage Museum, inv. no. 3.0–5434/1–3

This musket was made by the court armourer Grecke for the Grand Duke Alexander when he was only three years old.

187. WORKING MODEL OF FLINTLOCK REVOLVER GUN

Made in Tula, *c*.1780
Steel, wood, gold and silver, 24.5 cm (length)
State Hermitage Museum, inv. no. 3.0–5439

188. CHILD'S FLINTLOCK GUN

Made in Tula, *c*.1780–85
Steel, wood, gold, silver and horn, 67.6 cm (length)
State Hermitage Museum, inv. no. 3.0–5431

To prevent accidents, the bayonet had a blunted tip.

189. CHILD'S FLINTLOCK GUN

I. Krapiventsov, Tula, 1780–85
Steel, wood, gold, silver and horn, 58.0 cm (length)
State Hermitage Museum, inv. no. 3.0–5430/1–2

190. CHILD'S FLINTLOCK GUN WITH THE MONOGRAM OF GRAND DUKE ALEXANDER

Made in Tula, 1780–85
Steel, wood, horn and silver, 65.0 cm (length)
State Hermitage Museum, inv. no. 3.0–5432/1–2

Catherine the Great presented this gun to the Grand Duke Alexander, along with other hunting weapons.

IMPERIAL CONNECTIONS

191. *THE GRAND DUKES ALEXANDER AND CONSTANTINE*

Johann Baptist Lampi the Elder (1751–1830),
Austrian, signed and dated 1795
Oil on canvas, 250.0 x 200.0 cm; 280.0 x 217.0 x 5.0 cm
(framed)
State Hermitage Museum, inv. no. ГЭ–4487

Catherine's two oldest grandsons are represented as close friends and their closeness is emphasized by the medallion representing the Classical heroes Castor and Pollux, who symbolize indestructable brotherly love and solidarity in battle. Alexander and Constantine are shown standing before a statue of Athena, goddess of wisdom, with incense rising in her honour. Catherine the Great was frequently represented as Athena or Minerva, and the two young men are clearly expressing their devotion to the Empress.

192. *CATHERINE II*

Johann Baptist Lampi the Elder (1751–1830), Austrian,
signed and dated 1793
Oil on canvas, 290.0 x 208.0 cm; 305.0 x 222.0 x 9.0 cm
(framed)
State Hermitage Museum, inv. no. ГЭ–2755

Catherine is depicted in all her glory, in front of a magnificent golden throne, wearing the sashes of the Orders of Saints Andrew, George and Vladimir. Her casual gesture towards a very small medallion of Peter the Great indicates both her respect for her illustrious predecessor and her complete confidence in her own achievements. The eagle and lion symbolize enormous power, while the two statues allude to her prudence and strength.

193. FAMILY TREE OF THE RUSSIAN SOVEREIGNS

Unknown craftsmen, Russian, late 18th or early 19th
century
Wood, velvet and gilt metal, 185.0 x 127.0 x 4.5 cm
State Hermitage Museum, inv. no. ЭРРз–6543

In 1760, Mikhail Lomonosov published *A Short Russian Chronicle of Genealogies* with a chronological list of the Grand Princes and Russian Tsars from Rurik to Peter the Great. This list, which was continued up to Paul I, formed the foundation for the preparation of this family tree. The medals used here were made by Russian and foreign medal makers.

194. *EMPEROR PAUL I*

Stepan Semenovich Shchukin (1762–1828),
Russian, *c*.1797–98
Oil on canvas, 154.0 x 116.0 cm; 169.0 x 130.0 x 6.0 cm
(framed)
State Hermitage Museum, inv. no. ЭРЖ–1733

Paul is wearing the uniform of the Preobrazhensky Regiment and the Orders of St Andrew (sash and star), St Alexander Nevsky (star) and St Anne, First Class (cross with diamonds). The portrait was painted before he was awarded the Maltese Cross in November 1798.

195. PIECES FROM THE BERLIN SERVICE

Royal Porcelain Factory, Berlin, 1776
Porcelain, decorated with overglaze enamels and gilding
State Hermitage Museum, inv. nos.
ЭРФ–9709 а, б, в, tureen, cover and stand,
(a) 7.6 x 16.5 x 12.5 cm, (б) 7.5 x 16.0 x 12.1 cm,
(в) 3.7 x 23.1 x 16.1 cm
ЭРФ–9710 а, б, cup and saucer, (a) 5.0 x 9.7 x 8.1 cm,
(б) 3.3 x 13.1 cm
ЭРФ–9711, vase, 15.5 x 9.5 x 8.0 cm
ЭРФ–9713, oval dish, 4.8 x 31.0 x 40.0 cm
ЭРФ–9715–9717, three plates with openwork rim,
3.6 x 24.7 cm
ЭРФ–9725–9727, three deep plates, 4.6 x 24.2 cm

The Berlin Service was given to Grand Duke Paul by King Frederick the Great of Prussia in 1778. It is decorated with the Russian Imperial eagle and the arms of the duchy of Holstein-Gottorp, which Paul had inherited from his father.

When he became Emperor, Paul commissioned additional items from Russian sources. More pieces were made later. The stamp 'AII' under a crown on the teacup records that it was produced by the Imperial Porcelain Factory, in St Petersburg, during the reign of Alexander II, between 1855 and 1881.

196. EMPEROR PAUL I

Jean-Henri Benner (1776–1836), French, signed and dated 1821
Watercolours and gouache on paper in wooden frame with gilt bronze mounts, 13.6 x 10.1 cm (oval); 20.2 x 16.1 cm (framed)
State Hermitage Museum, inv. no. OPM–164

The miniature depicts Catherine's son, who reigned as Emperor of Russia from 1796 to 1801. Paul is shown wearing the uniform of colonel of the Preobrazhensky Regiment, with the Order of St Andrew and other awards.

197. EMPRESS MARIA FEDOROVNA

Jean-Henri Benner (1776–1836), French, signed and dated 1821
Watercolours and gouache on paper in wooden frame with gilt bronze mounts, 13.7 x 10.2 cm (oval);
20.1 x 16.2 cm (framed)
State Hermitage Museum, inv. no. OPM–165

The Empress Maria (1759–1828) married the Grand Duke Paul in 1776 and they had ten children. Their first and third sons became the Emperors Alexander I (reigned 1801–25) and Nicholas I (reigned 1825–55). Maria is depicted wearing mourning, as a widow, and a diadem made for her by her jeweller Jacob Duval around 1800.

198. EMPEROR ALEXANDER I

Jean-Henri Benner (1776–1836), French, signed and dated 1821
Watercolours and gouache on paper in wooden frame with gilt bronze mounts, 13.9 x 10.1 cm (oval); 19.9 x 15.9 cm (framed)
State Hermitage Museum, inv. no. OPM–166

Alexander I (1777–1825), Paul and Maria's first son, played a major role in the defeat of Napoleon. He is shown wearing some of the decorations awarded for the expulsion of Napoleon from Russia in 1812 and the allied victories over the next three years.

199. GRAND DUKE CONSTANTINE

Jean-Henri Benner (1776–1836), French, signed and dated 1821
Watercolours and gouache on paper in wooden frame with gilt bronze mounts, 13.6 x 10.1 cm (oval); 20.0 x 16.0 cm (framed)
State Hermitage Museum, inv. no. OPM–168

Paul and Maria's second son, Constantine (1779–1831), became general-inspector of cavalry and commander-in-chief of the Polish army in 1815–16. He refused to succeed his brother as Emperor in 1825.

196.

198.

199.

200. GRAND DUKE NICHOLAS, LATER THE EMPEROR NICHOLAS I

Jean-Henri Benner (1776–1836), French, signed and dated 1821
Watercolours and gouache on paper in wooden frame with gilt bronze mounts, 13.6 x 10.1 cm (oval); 19.9 x 15.9 cm (framed)
State Hermitage Museum, inv. no. OPM–170

Paul and Maria's third son, the Emperor Nicholas I (1796–1855), put down an uprising of liberal army officers and their men in St Petersburg in 1825, the year of his accession to power. Nicholas pursued conservative policies that profoundly affected the development of Russia during the 19th century.

201. GRAND DUKE MICHAEL

Jean-Henri Benner (1776–1836), French, signed and dated 1821
Watercolours and gouache on paper in wooden frame with gilt bronze mounts, 13.7 x 10.2 cm (oval); 19.9 x 16.0 cm (framed)
State Hermitage Museum, inv. no. OPM–172

The Grand Duke Michael (1798–1849), Paul and Maria's fourth son, became head of the military schools and commander-in-chief of the Guard and Grenadier regiments. He took part in the Turkish war and the suppression of the Polish rebellion in 1830–31.

202. GRAND DUCHESS MARIA PAVLOVNA

Jean-Henri Benner (1776–1836), French, signed and dated 1821
Watercolours and gouache on paper in wooden frame with gilt bronze mounts, 13.7 x 10.2 cm (oval); 20.0 x 16.0 cm (framed)
State Hermitage Museum, inv. no. OPM–173

Maria (1786–1859) was Paul and Maria's third daughter. She married Charles Frederick, Grand Duke of Saxe-Weimar-Eisenach, in 1804.

203. GRAND DUCHESS CATHERINE PAVLOVNA

Jean-Henri Benner (1776–1836), French, signed and dated 1821
Watercolours and gouache on paper in wooden frame with gilt bronze mounts, 13.7 x 10.2 cm (oval); 19.9 x 16.2 cm (framed)
State Hermitage Museum, inv. no. OPM–174

Paul and Maria's fourth daughter, Catherine (1788–1819), had a short first marriage to George, Duke of Oldenburg, who died of typhoid fever in 1812. Catherine subsequently fell in love with Wilhelm, Crown Prince of Württemberg, who divorced his wife, Charlotte, in order to marry her. Married in 1816, they became King and Queen of Württemberg the same year.

204. *THE DAUGHTERS OF THE EMPEROR PAUL I, THE GRAND PRINCESSES ALEXANDRA PAVLOVNA AND ELENA PAVLOVNA*

Élisabeth Louise Vigée Le Brun (1755–1842), signed and dated 1796
Oil on canvas, 99.0 x 99.0 cm
State Hermitage Museum, inv. no. ГЭ–7747

Alexandra and Elena were Paul's first and second daughters. This portrait, showing Elena holding a miniature of Catherine, was commissioned by the Empress.

205. CATHERINE II'S OFFICER'S UNIFORM OF THE IMPERIAL GUARDS SEMENOVKSY REGIMENT

Russian, 1770–1780s
Silk, metallic thread, bronze stripes and gilding,
(1) outer dress, 200.0 cm (length), 600.0 cm (circum. of hem with train), (2) under dress, 144.0 cm (length), 378.0 cm (circum. of hem)
State Hermitage Museum, inv. nos. (1) ЭРТ–15581, (2) ЭРТ–15582

206. CHILD'S CEREMONIAL COSTUME OF THE GRAND DUKE ALEXANDER

Unknown maker, Russian, 1784
Satin, linen material, flannel, metallic thread, foil and embroidery, (1) 79.0 cm, (2) 75.0 cm
State Hermitage Museum, inv. nos. (1) ЭРТ–15578, (2) ЭРТ–15579

This elegant child's costume of pink and white satin was made for the birthday of Alexander Pavlovich, the elder, beloved grandson of Catherine II, in December 1784.

207. *GRAND DUKES ALEXANDER AND CONSTANTINE AS CHILDREN*

Heyde, signed and dated 1790
Watercolours and gouache on ivory in bronze frame, 16.1 x 11.8 cm; 18.3 x 14.1 cm (framed)
State Hermitage Museum, inv. no. OPM–118

208. GLASS VASE OR BASKET FOR EASTER EGGS WITH SEVEN EASTER EGGS

Potemkin Glass Factory, St Petersburg, dated 1786
The vase blue glass decorated with gilding,
(1) (a) 21.7 x 20.0 cm, (б) 13.7 x 20.8 cm
State Hermitage Museum, inv. nos. (1) ЭРС–1890 а, б, vase and cover, (2) ЭРС–163, egg pendant, (3) ЭРС–2701 to 2706, egg pendants

In 1786, Catherine II presented this specially-commissioned vase or basket with seven Easter eggs inside it to the family of Grand Duke Paul.

Four of the eggs are decorated with the monograms of Paul's wife Maria Fedorovna, daughters Alexandra Pavlovna and Maria Pavlovna, and son and heir Alexander Pavlovich. Two of the others depict 'The Lamb' and a sacrificial altar, and Saints Elizaveta and Veronika.

209. CAMEO OF THE EMPRESS CATHERINE II AS MINERVA

Engraved by the Grand Duchess Maria Fedorovna,
St Petersburg, signed and dated 21 April 1789
Two-layer glass and bronze, 1.3 x 6.9 x 5.3 cm
State Hermitage Museum, inv. no. ЭРС–2250

Grand Duchess Maria Fedorovna was a talented artist. She drew well, made wax models and engraved hardstone, amber and bone. Leading artists and craftsmen, including the medallists Koenig and Leberecht, helped Maria produce her work. This cameo was made as a gift for Catherine II's birthday on 21 April 1789.

210. CAMEO OF THE GRAND DUKE PAUL

Engraved by the Grand Duchess Maria Fedorovna,
St Petersburg, 1790s
Two-layer glass and bronze, 0.9 x 5.5 x 4.4 cm
State Hermitage Museum, inv. no. ЭРС–2251

Maria Fedorovna made a series of cameos with the profile portraits of members of the Imperial family. They were frequently repeated using various techniques and materials, and often used as gifts among members of the Imperial family and their close relatives and friends.

211. *MERCURY AND PARIS*

Drawing by the Grand Princess Catherine Pavlovna (1788–1819), Russian, signed and dated 14 October 1799
Opal glass, graphite pencil and giltwood, 5.0 x 49.0 x 41.0 cm (framed)
State Hermitage Museum, inv. no. ЭРФ–7226

These two drawings were done in a rare technique, using graphite pencil on smooth opal glass. Catherine II encouraged her grandchildren to study art. The St Petersburg artist Ivan Akimovich Akimov taught them drawing. Their best work was sent to the St Petersburg Academy of Arts, to be looked at by the Council of the Academy, and was also displayed in the palace halls.

212. *ALLEGORY OF THE ARTS*

Drawing by the Grand Princess Catherine Pavlovna (1788–1819), Russian, signed and dated 22 March 1800
Opal glass, graphite pencil and giltwood, 5.5 x 57.5 x 47.0 cm (framed)
State Hermitage Museum, inv. no. ЭРФ–6865

213. CEREMONIAL DRESS

St Petersburg, 1780s
Silk, lace, silk threads, mirror glass and embroidery, 200 cm (length of back)
State Hermitage Museum, inv. no. ЭРТ–8584 а, б,

It is possible that this dress belonged to Maria Fedorovna, wife of Catherine II's son, Paul.

214. CEREMONIAL COSTUME OF THE GRAND DUKE ALEXANDER

French (?), 1796
Silk, canvas, satin stitch embroidery and appliqué, 114.0 cm (caftan length), 66.5 cm (breeches)
State Hermitage Museum, inv. nos. ЭРТ–15573 to 15575

This fashionable, ceremonial costume was made for Alexander when he was 19.

215. COVERED CUP DECORATED WITH A PORTRAIT OF CATHERINE II

Meissen Porcelain Factory, Dresden, Germany, late 1770s
Porcelain, decorated with overglaze enamels and gilding, 6.7 x 9.6 x 7.7 cm (cup); 4.8 x 8.2 (cover)
State Hermitage Museum, inv. no. ЭРФ–9743 а, б

The portrait of Catherine is based on an engraving of 1777.

216. CUP AND SAUCER DECORATED WITH A PORTRAIT OF CATHERINE II AND HER MONOGRAM 'EII'

Imperial Porcelain Factory, St Petersburg, c.1785
Porcelain, decorated with overglaze enamels and gilding, 5.8 x 10.1 x 7.8 cm (cup); 3.0 x 13.5 cm (saucer)
State Hermitage Museum, inv. no. ЭРФ–390 а, б

217. COVERED CUP AND SAUCER DECORATED WITH SILHOUETTE PORTRAITS OF THE GRAND DUKES ALEXANDER AND CONSTANTINE

Imperial Porcelain Factory, St Petersburg, late 1780s or early 1790s
Porcelain, decorated with underglaze blue, lustre, overglaze enamels and gilding, (a) 5.6 x 10.5 x 8.4 cm, (б) 4.1 x 8.9 cm, (в) 3.0 x 14.0 cm
State Hermitage Museum, inv. no. ЭРФ–397 а, б, в

218. COVERED CUP AND SAUCER DECORATED WITH THE INSCRIPTION 'KEEP IN ORDER TO REMEMBER' AND THE MONOGRAM 'EP' FOR CATHERINE II AND THE GRAND DUKE PAUL

Imperial Porcelain Factory, St Petersburg, 1780–96
Porcelain, decorated with underglaze blue, overglaze enamels and gilding, (a) 8.1 x 11.0 x 7.1 cm, (б) 4.5 x 7.5 cm, (в) 3.2 x 13.5 cm
State Hermitage Museum, inv. no. ЭРФ–399 а, б, в

THE THISTLE AND THE EAGLE

219. HIGHLAND COSTUME, SWORD, BELT PISTOL, DIRK WITH UTENSILS AND SNUFF SET

Made or supplied by George Hunter, Edinburgh, c.1814–16
Wool, silk, ostrich feathers, steel, gold, silver, copper, bronze, quartz, agate, citrine, amethyst, hessonite, heliodor, ivory, horn, leather, velvet and wood
State Hermitage Museum, inv. nos.
ЭРТ–15882, bonnet, 15.0 x 63.0 cm
ЭРТ–15883, jacket, 80.0 cm (length)
ЭРТ–15884, waistcoat, 57.0cm (length)
ЭРТ–15887, kilt, 64.0 x 197.0 cm
ЭРТ–15888, plaid, 65.0 x 223.0 cm
ЭРТ–15889, plaid, 65.0 x 223.0 cm
З.О–2527/1–2, backsword, 101cm (length)
З.О–4888/1–4, dirk with utensils, 48.5 cm (length)
З.О–644, powder flask, 9.8 cm (length)
З.О–6650, belt pistol, 28.6 cm (length)

This full Highland outfit belonged to the Emperor Alexander I. Catherine's grandson may have acquired it during his visit to London in 1814. Alternatively, it was acquired by Alexander's brother, the Grand Duke Nicholas, during his visit to Edinburgh in 1816–17 and given to Alexander as a present.

LEGACY

220. PLAN AND SECTION OF A PROJECT FOR A PICTURE GALLERY IN THE HERMITAGE

Giacomo Quarenghi (1744–1817), Italian, c.1800
Pen and ink and watercolour on paper, 86.0 x 121.0 x 1.5 cm (framed)
State Hermitage Museum, inv. no. OP–9698

221. *DARIUS OPENS THE TOMB OF NITOCRIS*

Eustache Le Sueur (1616–55), French, c.1649
Acquired from the Crozat collection in 1772
Oil on canvas, 163.0 x 112.0 cm
State Hermitage Museum, inv. no. ГЭ–1242

222. GROUP OF FEMALE MUSICIANS

Master of the Female Half-Lengths, Netherlandish, second quarter of the 16th century
Acquired from John Udny in 1779
Oil on wood, 53.2 x 37.5 x 0.7 cm
State Hermitage Museum, inv. no. ГЭ–435

The open score shows a chanson by the French composer Claudin de Sermisy (*c.*1490–1562), with love lyrics by the French poet Clément Marot (1496–1544), published in 1528. The lines may be translated: 'I will give you joy, my friend, and will take you where your hope is longing to go; while I am alive, I will never desert you; and even in death will my soul keep your memory'.

223. THE APOTHEOSIS OF JAMES I

Sir Peter Paul Rubens (1577–1640), Flemish, 1632–33
Acquired from the collection of Sir Robert Walpole at Houghton Hall, Norfolk, in 1779
Oil on canvas, 89.7 x 55.3 cm
State Hermitage Museum, inv. no. ГЭ–507

Rubens's completed painting was oval. It is still in the Banqueting Hall, along with all the other paintings. They constitute the most important 17th-century group of Baroque paintings in Britain.

224. LANDSCAPE WITH THE FINDING OF MOSES

Etienne Allegrain (1644–1736), French, late 17th or early 18th century
Acquired from the collection of Prince Grigory Potemkin in 1792
Oil on canvas, 88.0 x 114.8 cm
State Hermitage Museum, inv. no. ГЭ–1133

Pharaoh was alarmed at the increasing number of Israelites in Egypt and ordered midwives to kill all newborn Hebrew boys. Moses's mother hid him for three months and then set him adrift, in a basket, on the Nile. The future leader of the Israelites was eventually found by Pharaoh's daughter, who raised him as her son.

225. LANDSCAPE WITH CHRIST ON THE ROAD TO EMMAUS

Claude Lorrain (1602–82), French, dated 1660
Acquired from an unknown Parisian source, with other paintings, on the recommendation of Etienne-Maurice Falconet in 1771
Oil on canvas, 99.5 x 133.5 cm
State Hermitage Museum, inv. no. ГЭ–1229

226. JACOB BURYING LABAN'S IMAGES

Sébastien Bourdon, French, early 1640s
Acquired from the collection of Sir Robert Walpole at Houghton Hall, Norfolk, in 1779
Oil on canvas, 100.0 x 140.0 cm
State Hermitage Museum, inv. no. ГЭ–3682

In the bible, God ordered Jacob to go to Bethel and build an altar to him. Before he departed, Jacob told his family to get rid of the images of other gods they had acquired and hid them. As a reward for his obedience, God later appeared to Jacob, named him Israel and gave him the land of Canaan.

227. ST SEBASTIAN TENDED BY ST IRENE

Antonio Bellucci (1654–1726), Italian, 1720
Acquired from John Udny in 1779
Oil on canvas, 110.0 x 123.0 cm
State Hermitage Museum, inv. no. ГЭ–1546

St Sebastian was a Roman soldier in the service of the pagan Emperor Diocletian (284–305), who was shot by archers because of his devotion to the Christian faith. He survived and was tended and healed by St Irene. Sebastian continued to practise his faith and was finally killed by Diocletian.

SCULPTURE

228. HEAD OF ATHENA

Roman, first half of 1st century AD
Acquired from the collection of John Lyde Brown,
London, in 1787
Marble, 93 x 30 x 49 cm
State Hermitage Museum, inv. no. ГР–1725 (A.47)

Based on Greek examples of the 5th century BC.

229. BOY WITH GARLAND OF BEADS ON HIS HEAD

Roman, 1st century AD
Acquired from the collection of John Lyde Brown,
London, in 1787
Marble, 38.0 cm
State Hermitage Museum, inv. no. ГР–1754 (A.79)

Jewellery represented on the heads of Roman
children is believed to have had a religious or
ritualistic meaning.

230. THREE NYMPHS

Roman, 1st century AD
Acquired from the collection of John Lyde Brown,
London, in 1787
Marble, 43.0 x 41.0 cm
State Hermitage Museum, inv. no. ГР–1712 (A.34)

This relief was found on the island of Ischia near
Naples. It was part of a fountain dedicated to the
Nymphs of Nitrodiae. Their cult was connected
with a thermal spring on the island, believed to have
curative powers.

231. MITHRAS KILLING THE BULL

Roman, 2nd century AD
Acquired from the collection of John Lyde Brown,
London, in 1787
Marble, 37.0 x 39.0 cm
State Hermitage Museum, inv. no. ГР–1711 (A.33)

The cult of the Indo-Persian god Mithras was
popular throughout the Roman Empire, especially
amongst soldiers. This relief represents the eternal
struggle between good and evil, and the victory of
the Heavenly Powers, personified by Mithras, over
Earthly ones, symbolized by the bull.

232. BUST OF ANTINOUS IN THE GUISE OF DIONYSUS

Roman, second quarter of 2nd century AD
Acquired as part of Count Ivan Shuvalov's collection
in 1784 and displayed in the Grotto of the Imperial
residence at Tsarskoye Selo
Marble, 39.5 cm
State Hermitage Museum, inv. no. ГР–1705 (A.27)

233. BUST OF ARTEMIS

Roman, mid-2nd century AD
Acquired from the collection of John Lyde Brown,
London, in 1787
Marble, 41.0 cm
State Hermitage Museum, inv. no. ГР–3007 (A.107)

234. BUST OF EMPEROR PHILIP THE ARAB

Roman, mid-3rd century AD
Acquired from the collection of John Lyde Brown,
London, in 1787
Marble, 72.0 cm
State Hermitage Museum, inv. no. ГР–1709 (A.31)

This bust comes from the 'crisis of the 3rd century',
when soldier emperors of undistinguished birth
frequently succeeded one another after military *coups*.
Philip (*c.*204–49) was an Arab of non-Roman origin
from what is now Syria, who became a Praetorian
prefect under the Emperor Gordian III. He is said
to have killed Gordian in 244. Philip himself was
overthrown and killed following a rebellion led by
his successor Decius in 249.

235. CABINET FOR CARVED GEMSTONES

Doors, workshop of David Roentgen, German, 1786–87;
Christian Meyer (cabinet); Heinrich Gambs (bottom
portion), Russian, early 19th century
Mahogany, oak and gilded bronze, 183.0 x 61.0 x
56.0 cm
State Hermitage Museum, inv. no. Элр–155

236. ARCHITECTURAL FANTASY

Charles-Louis Clérisseau, (1721–1820), French, 1760s
Gouache, brown ink and black chalk on paper,
36.0 x 31.6 cm
State Hermitage Museum, inv. no. OP–2511

In 1773, Catherine II commissioned a series of
drawings from Clérisseau. The Empress was greatly
annoyed when Clérisseau sent her a vast quantity of
drawings and a huge bill. Nevertheless, she purchased
over 1000 of his drawings, some of which were
displayed in her rooms.

237. ARCHITECTURAL FANTASY

Charles-Louis Clérisseau (1721–1820), French, 1760s
Gouache, brown ink and black chalk on paper,
33.6 x 26.1 cm
State Hermitage Museum, inv. no. OP–2512

This watercolour is a version of one of Clérisseau's
favourite subjects – the ruins of a spacious Roman
hall with the remains of a collapsed arch.

ENGRAVED GEMSTONES

Most of the items itemized below are cameos.
Cameos have raised, three-dimensional decoration.
Gems with decoration cut below their surfaces are
called intaglios.

CLASSICAL CAMEOS

238. *DIONYSUS IN A CHARIOT DRAWN BY TWO CENTAURS*

Made in Alexandria, possibly in the workshop of
Sostratos, 1st century BC
Acquired from the collection of Lord Algernon Percy,
second son of the 1st Duke of Northumberland, in 1786
Sardonyx and gold, 31 x 2.3 cm
State Hermitage Museum, inv. no. ГР–12669

Dionysus, or Bacchus, was the god of wine. Alexandria was an important centre of gem-engraving
around the time of Cleopatra. This cameo and the
next two may be connected with the Roman general
Mark Anthony, the lover of Cleopatra, who proclaimed himself a new Bacchus.

239. *DIONYSUS*

Made in Alexandria, possibly in the workshop of
Sostratos, 1st century BC
Acquired from the collection of Lord Algernon Percy,
second son of the 1st Duke of Northumberland, in 1786
Sardonyx and gold, 2.5 x 1.4 cm
State Hermitage Museum, inv. no. ГР–12664

240. *SACRIFICE TO DIONYSUS*

Made in Alexandria, 1st century BC
Sardonyx and gold, 3.0 x 2.3 cm
State Hermitage Museum, inv. no. ГР–12704

This is the right-hand part of a large multi-figure
composition.

241. *ABDUCTION OF GANYMEDE BY THE EAGLE OF ZEUS*

Made in Alexandria, 1st century BC
Acquired with the Duc d'Orléans' collection of gem-
stones in 1787
Three-layered sardonyx and gold, 3.3 x 3.0 cm
State Hermitage Museum, inv. no. ГР–12686

242. *APOLLO AND ARTEMIS*

Possibly made in the workshop of Protarch, Alexandria,
1st century BC
Sardonyx and gold, 2.3 x 2.2 cm
State Hermitage Museum, inv. no. ГР–12684

The Greek engraver Protarch, who worked in Alexandria and then in Rome, was one of the outstanding
masters of 'the golden age of ancient engraving'.

243. *DOE SUCKLING TELEPHUS*

Made in Asia Minor, 1st century BC
Sardonyx and gold, 1.2 x 1.8 cm
State Hermitage Museum, inv. ГР–12633

The infant Telephus, son of Hercules, was abandoned
on a mountain and his life was saved by a deer.

244. *SACRIFICE TO CYBELE*

Made in Asia Minor (?), 1st century BC
Sardonyx and gold, 2.7 x 1.8 cm
State Hermitage Museum, inv. no. ГР–12673

Cybele was the state deity of Phrygia. Her cult
spread throughout Asia Minor, Greece and Italy.

245. *MAENAD*

Made in Asia Minor (?), 1st century BC or 1st century AD
Sardonyx and gold, 3.3 x 2.9 cm
State Hermitage Museum, inv. no. ГР–12721

246. *SACRIFICE TO PRIAPUS*

Made in the Eastern Mediterranean, 1st century BC
Acquired with the Duc d'Orléans' collection of gem-
stones in 1787
Sardonyx and gold, 2.7 x 1.7 cm
State Hermitage Museum, inv. no. ГР–12668

247. *PSYCHE ENSLAVED BY VENUS*

Made in Rome, 1st century BC or 1st century AD
Acquired, with other items, from the collection of
Joseph Angelo de France (d.1761), general director of
the Imperial collection in Vienna, in 1794
Sardonyx and gold, 2.8 x 1.9 cm
State Hermitage Museum, inv. no. ГР–12675

Venus was jealous of Pysche and asked her son
Cupid to punish her.

248. *CASTOR AND POLLUX RIDING HORSES*

Made in Rome, 1st century BC or 1st century AD
Sardonyx and gold, 1.8 x 2.6 cm
State Hermitage Museum, inv. no. ГР–12689

249. *CUPIDS ON DOLPHINS*

Made in Rome, 1st century BC or 1st century AD
Sardonyx and gold, 1.5 x 2.1. cm
State Hermitage Museum, inv. no. ГР–12631

250. *PERSEUS AND ANDROMEDA*

Made in Rome, 1st century BC or 1st century AD
Acquired from the collection of the German painter
Anton Raphael Mengs in Rome in 1780
Sardonyx and gold, 2.8 x 3.1 cm
State Hermitage Museum, inv. no. ГР–12685

This cameo represents Perseus after he freed
Andromeda from the dreadful sea monster. It was
highly rated by art historian Johann Winckelmann.
Catherine noted it had 'pride of place in the museum
and sits in the lowest level of the Imperial rooms'.

251. *LIVIA*

Made in Rome by a son of Dioscurides, 1st century AD
Acquired with the Duc d'Orléans' collection of gem-
stones in 1787
Sardonyx and gold, 4.0 x 3.1 cm
State Hermitage Museum, inv. no. ГР–12654

252. EMPEROR TIBERIUS

Made by Evtikh, son of Dioscurides, in Rome,
1st century AD
Sardonyx and gold, 2.5 x 2.1 cm
State Hermitage Museum, inv. no. ГР–12653

253. GERMANICUS

Made by a son of Dioscurides in Rome, 1st century AD
Acquired with the Duc d'Orléans's collection of gem-
stones in 1787
Sardonyx and gold, 2.4 x 1.7 cm
State Hermitage Museum, inv. no. ГР–12652

Germanicus was the nephew and adopted son of the
Emperor Tiberius and the father of the Emperor
Caligula.

254. EMPRESS AGRIPPINA

Made in Rome, 1st century AD
Acquired with the Duc d'Orléans's collection of gem-
stones in 1787
Sardonyx and gold, 3.9 x 2.8 cm
State Hermitage Museum, inv. no. ГР–12739

Julia Agrippina, or Agrippina the Younger
(AD 15/16–59), was the sister of the Emperor
Caligula, fourth wife of the Emperor Claudius and
mother of the Emperor Nero.

255. MASK OF SILENUS

Made in Rome, 1st century AD
Acquired from the collection of Jean-Baptiste
Casanova, Dresden, in 1792
Opaque blue glass and gold, 4.6 x 3.8 cm
State Hermitage Museum, inv. no. ГР–12604

This and the following two pieces may have been
used to decorate horse harnesses or armour. Such
pieces were often given to soldiers as rewards for
showing courage and valour in battle.

256. MASK OF MEDUSA

Made in Rome, 1st century AD
Acquired from the collection of Jean-Baptiste
Casanova, Dresden, in 1792
Opaque blue glass and gold, 5.0 cm
State Hermitage Museum, inv. no. ГР–12624

257. SPHINX

Made in Rome, 1st century AD
Acquired from the collection of Jean-Baptiste
Casanova, Dresden, in 1792
Opaque green glass and gold, 2.6 cm
State Hermitage Museum, inv. no. ГР–12612

LATER CAMEOS AND INTAGLIOS

258. EAGLE HOLDING A HARE IN ITS TALONS

South Italian, 1240–60
Acquired from the collection of Jean-Baptist Casanova,
Dresden, in 1792
Sardonyx and gold, 3.9 x 2.9 cm
State Hermitage Museum, inv. no. K–2141

This is a typical cameo from the stone-cutting studio
operating at the court of the Emperor Frederick II
in Sicily. An eagle was part of the Emperor's coat of
arms and the image symbolizes his might and power.

259. THE BRAZEN SERPENT

Venetian, 13th century
Sardonyx and gold, 2.8 x 3.4 cm
State Hermitage Museum, inv. no. K–5632

The cameo illustrates the brass serpent that Moses
set up on a pole to heal the Israelites. The Hebrew
inscription reads: 'Every one, when he looketh upon
it, shall live' (Numbers 21: 8).

260. *ADAM AND EVE*

Italian, mid-14th century
Three-layer sardonyx, gold and diamond (inserted later), 3.2 x 2.9 cm
State Hermitage Museum, inv. no. K–5631

261. *KING CHARLES V OF FRANCE*

French, 1370–90
Three-layer sardonyx and gold, 3.4 x 2.9 cm
State Hermitage Museum, inv. no. K–988

Charles V, known as 'the Wise', reigned from 1364 until 1380.

262. *MARCUS CURTIUS LEAPING INTO THE FIERY CHASM TO SAVE ROME*

Milanese, third quarter of 16th century
Acquired with the Duc d'Orléans' collection of gemstones in 1787
Agate and gold, 3.4 x 4.2 cm
State Hermitage Museum, inv. no. K–2498

Marcus Curtius's jump into the chasm that had opened in the Roman Forum is one of the great heroic examples of personal sacrifice for the community or nation.

263. *APOLLO KILLING THE PYTHON*

Attributed to Alessandro Masnago (active 1560–d.1620), Milan or Prague, late 16th century
Acquired, with other items, from the collection of Joseph Angelo de France (d.1761), general director of the Imperial collection in Vienna, between 1781 and 1794
Agate and gold, 5.1 x 5.7 cm
State Hermitage Museum, inv. no. K–483

Based on a print by Etienne Delaune, this cameo was probably made by Alessandro Masnago, court carver of the Holy Roman Emperor Rudolph II.

264. *ST GEORGE KILLING THE DRAGON*

English, second half of 16th century
Three-layer sardonyx and gold, 4.1 x 3.1 cm
State Hermitage Museum, inv. no. K–652

This was probably a 'Lesser George' worn by a Knight of the Garter on a daily basis.

265. *QUEEN ELIZABETH I OF ENGLAND*

Attributed to the workshop of Richard Atsill or Julien de Fontenay, London, *c.*1575–90
Acquired with the Duc d'Orléans' collection of gemstones in 1787
Three-layer sardonyx and gold, 6.2 x 5.4 cm
State Hermitage Museum, inv. no. K–1020

266. *EMPEROR PHILIP II OF SPAIN*

Jacopo da Trezzo (*c.*1514–89), Italian, *c.*1559
Acquired with the Duc d'Orléans' collection of gemstones in 1787
Sardonyx and gold, 3.2 x 2.8 cm
State Hermitage Museum, inv. no. K–1016

Jacopo da Trezzo was a court architect, sculptor and medallist to Philip II.

267. *PENDANT WITH CAMEO OF ANTOINE PERRENOT, CARDINAL GRANVELLE*

After Leone Leoni (1509–90), Italian, *c.*1561
Acquired from the collection of Thomas Martin, London, before 1796
Agate-onyx, gold and diamond, 4.9 x 2.8 cm
State Hermitage Museum, inv. no. K–1012

Antoine Perrenot (1517–86) was a close adviser and minister of the Emperors Charles V and Philip II.

268. KING CHARLES I

Attributed to Thomas Rawlins (c.1620–70), English,
after 1649
Acquired with the Duc d'Orléans' collection of gem-
stones in 1787
Three-layer sardonyx and gold, 2.5 x 2.2 cm
State Hermitage Museum, inv. no. K–986

269. OLIVER CROMWELL

Thomas Simon (1618–85), English, c.1658
Acquired with the Duc d'Orléans' collection of gem-
stones in 1787
Three-layer sardonyx and gold, 2.5 x 2.2 cm
State Hermitage Museum, inv. no. K–1013

**270. PENDANT WITH CAMEO OF HERMAN
BOERHAAVE**

Dutch, late 17th to early 18th century
Paste, gold and enamels, 3.6 x 2.3 cm
State Hermitage Museum, inv. no. K–979

Boerhaave (1668–1738) was a Leiden doctor,
anatomist, botanist, chemist and the author of a
handbook on chemistry.

271. ISAAC NEWTON

Attributed to Christopher Seaton, English, second
quarter of 18th century
Red cornelian and gold, 2.1 x 1.9 cm
State Hermitage Museum, inv. no. И–4042

272. BARON PHILIP VON STOSCH

Lorenz Natter (1703–63), German, 1739
Emerald and gold, 2.6 x 2.2 cm
State Hermitage Museum, inv. no. И–3631

Stosch (1691–1757) was a patron and connoisseur,
whose main interest was engraved gems.

273. CATHERINE II AS MINERVA

Alexander Dmitriev-Mamonov (1758–1803),
St Petersburg, late 1780s
Agate-onyx and gold, 4.0 x 3.4 cm
State Hermitage Museum, inv. no. K–1082

Lieutenant-General Dmitriev-Mamonov shared
Catherine's passion for cameos. He was taught by
the court carver Karl von Leberecht and played an
important role in acquiring the Orléans collection
of cameos in 1787.

**274. FALCONET'S MONUMENT TO PETER
THE GREAT**

William Brown (1748–1825), London, 1782–93
Rock crystal and gold, 5.0 x 3.9 cm
State Hermitage Museum, inv. no. И–3648

**275. ALLEGORY OF VICTORY OVER THE
TURKISH FLEET**

Charles Brown (1749–95), London, 1789–90
Two-layer sardonyx and gold, 5.3 x 6.8 cm
State Hermitage Museum, inv. no. K–1104

**276. CATHERINE II INSTRUCTING HER
GRANDSONS**

William and Charles Brown, London, 1789–91
Agate-onyx and gold, 5.4 x 6.7 cm
State Hermitage Museum, inv. no. K–1124

**277. CATHERINE II CROWNING PRINCE
POTEMKIN WITH A LAUREL WREATH**

William and Charles Brown, London, 1789–92
Three-layer sardonyx, gold and glass, 5.7 x 6.6 cm
State Hermitage Museum, inv. no. K–1125

278. COUNT ALEXANDER LANSKOY

Karl von Leberecht (1755–1827), St Petersburg, 1785
Jasper and gold, 4.0 x 3.5 cm
State Hermitage Museum, inv. no. K–1807

279. SACRIFICE TO MINERVA

Edward Burch (1730–1814), English, exhibited in
London in 1769
Chalcedony and gold, 2.5 x 2.2 cm
State Hermitage Museum, inv. no. И–3956

280. ALEXANDER THE GREAT

Nathaniel Marchant (1739–1816), London, early 1780s
Acquired from the collection of Lord Algernon Percy,
second son of the 1st Duke of Northumberland, in 1786
Sard and gold, 3.1 x 2.5 cm
State Hermitage Museum, inv. no. И–3981

281. CENTAUR AND BACCHANTE

Giovanni Pichler (1734–91), Italian, 1770–90
Acquired from the collection of James Boyd, London,
before 1794
Sardonyx and gold, 2.2 x 2.8 cm
State Hermitage Museum, inv. no. K–1813

282. BACCHUS AND CUPID

By Jean-Baptiste Nicolas Glachant the Younger (1746–
1815), French, second half of 18th century
Acquired, with c.130 other gems, from the collection of
Abraham-Joseph Mihelet d'Ennery, Paris, in 1786
Two-layer sardonyx and gold, 4.6 x 3.8 cm
State Hermitage Museum, inv. no. K–1794

TASSIE COPIES

**283. PASTE AND CAST COPIES OF
CARVED GEMS**

Workshop of James Tassie (1735–99), London, 1780s
Coloured and white glass and paper

In 1766, James Tassie opened his workshop in
London. It produced portrait medallions from
potassium silicate or lead glass using the technology
that he had invented. Tassie's 1775 catalogue offered
3106 casts of cameos from famous collections.

205

In 1781, Catherine II discovered Tassie and, with her financial support, he managed to increase his range to almost 16,000 specimens. Tassie agreed to supply the Empress with each example in two versions: a coloured imitation and a white enamel-like cast. The casts arrived in Russia between 1783 and 1788 in four batches, each accompanied by a handwritten list. All four lists are still preserved in the State Hermitage Museum.

284. FALCON-HEADED HORUS WITH A DOUBLE CROWN SEATED ON A SOLAR DISK

4.1 x 3.4 cm
State Hermitage Museum, inv. no. R–T, 7 a, б

The original agate-onyx scaraboid is now in the State Museums in Berlin.

285. HEAD OF JUPITER

(a) 3.7 x 3.3 cm, (б) 3.6 x 3.2 cm
State Hermitage Museum, inv. no. R–T, 239 a, б

286. BUST OF ATHENA

(a) 4.6 x 3.8 cm, (б) 4.4 x 3.5 cm
State Hermitage Museum, inv. no. R–T, 462 a, б

287. HEAD OF MEDUSA

3.9 x 4.5 cm
State Hermitage Museum, inv. no. R–T, 3296 a

288. BACCHUS

(a) 4.8 x 4.1 cm, (б) 4.6 x 3.8 cm
State Hermitage Museum, inv. no. R–T, 13410 a, б

289. NEPTUNE IN A CHARIOT DRAWN BY HIPPOCAMPI

(a) 5.0 x 4.1 cm, (б) 4.9 x 3.9 cm
State Hermitage Museum, inv. no. R–T, 817 a, б

The original gem is now in the British Museum.

290. VENUS WITH AN EAGLE

(a) 3.6 x 2.9 cm, (б) 3.7 x 3.1 cm
State Hermitage Museum, inv. no. R–T, 358 a, б

After a 1st-century cornelian intaglio in the Duke of Devonshire's collection.

291. THE MARRIAGE OF CUPID AND PSYCHE BY TRYPHON

(a) 3.9 x 4.5 cm, (б) 3.6 x 4.3 cm
State Hermitage Museum, inv. no. R–T, 11128 a, б

The original engraved gem is now in the Museum of Fine Arts, Boston.

292. ALEXANDER PUTTING HOMER'S ILIAD IN A CASKET

(a) 4.0 x 4.7 cm, (б) 4.0 x 4.8 cm
State Hermitage Museum, inv. no. R–T, 3663 a, б

The original gem is now in the Medal Cabinet, Bibliothèque National, Paris.

293. MARCUS CURTIUS LEAPING INTO THE FIERY CHASM TO SAVE ROME

(a) 3.7 x 4.6 cm, (б) 3.7 x 4.6 cm
State Hermitage Museum, inv. no. R–T, 4097 a, б

294. FLORA WITH A BASKET OF FLOWERS ON HER HEAD

(a) 4.4 x 3.1 cm, (б) 4.9 x 3.1 cm
State Hermitage Museum, inv. no. R–T, 609 a, б

295. BUST OF DIDIUS JULIANUS (?)

(a) 4.8 x 4.1 cm, (б) 4.8 x 4.2 cm
State Hermitage Museum, inv. no. R–T, 12103 a, б

296. BUST OF LIVIA

4.7 x 4.0 cm
State Hermitage Museum, inv. no. R–T, 8130 a

297. *JAMES BYRES*

James Tassie, Scottish, signed and dated 1779
8.5 x 6.3 cm
National Museums Scotland, inv. no. A.1881.37.4

James Byres (1733–1817) was one of the most important Scottish guides and art dealers in Rome in the second half of the 18th century.

298. *ADAM SMITH*

James Tassie, Scottish, signed and dated 1787
9.2 x 7.0 cm
National Museums Scotland, inv. no. A.1894.153

Adam Smith (1723–90) was author of *The Wealth of Nations*, the first modern work of economics. He is regarded as the pioneer of political economy.

299. *JAMES GREGORY, MD, OF EDINBURGH UNIVERSITY*

James Tassie, Scottish, signed and dated 1791
9.2 x 6.3 cm
National Museums Scotland, inv. no. A.1881.37.2

James Gregory (1753–1821) became the head of the School of Medicine at the University of Edinburgh in 1790. He was subsequently regarded as the head of the medical profession in Scotland.

300. *JAMES HUTTON, MD*

James Tassie, Scottish, signed and dated 1792
8.9 x 6.0 cm
National Museums Scotland, inv. no. A.1881.37.5

The Edinburgh-born doctor James Hutton (1726–97) played a key role in explaining the formation of geological layers over huge spans of time.

301. CABINET FOR COPIES OF ENGRAVED GEMSTONES

Attributed to F. Roach, London, 1783–90
Oak, spruce, pine, satinwood and other woods, bronze, and imitation porcelain medallions
125.5 x 122.0 x 44.3 cm
State Hermitage Museum, inv. no. Эпр–342

This cabinet was given by Catherine the Great to her favourite, Count Alexander Lanskoy, to house his collection of engraved stones.

ART AGENTS

302. *CATHERINE II*

Copy of marble bust by Jean-Antoine Houdon, Russian, early 19th century (?)
Bronze, 86.0 cm
State Hermitage Museum, inv. no. Н.ск.–501

The original marble bust by Houdon was commissioned by Count Alexander Stroganov and exhibited in Paris, 1773.

303. COUNT ALEXANDER SERGEIEVICH STROGANOV

Attributed to Nicolas Soret (1759–1830), Swiss, 1790s
Enamels on copper in bronze frame, 8.3 x 6.4 cm (framed)
State Hermitage Museum, inv. no. OPM–1231

Soret worked in St Petersburg in 1786–88 and in 1792–99.

FURTHER READING

Vincent Cronin, *Catherine, Empress of All the Russias* (London, 1978).

Isabel de Madariaga, *Catherine the Great: a Short History* (New Haven, 1990).

Henri Troyat, *Catherine the Great* (New York, 1994).

Simon Sebag Montefiore, *Prince of Princes: The Life of Potemkin* (London, 2000).

Virginia Rounding, *Catherine the Great: Love, Sex and Power* (London, 2006).

Simon Dixon, *Catherine the Great* (New York, 2009).

Catherine, Princess Dashkov and Kyril Fitzlyon (tr. and ed.), *The Memoirs of Princess Dashkov* (London, 1958).

A. Woronzoff-Dashkoff, 'Dashkova: A Life of Influence and Exile', *Transactions of the American Philosophical Society*, 97:3, vol. 97, part 3 (Philadelphia, 2008).

National Library of Scotland, *The Caledonian Phalanx: Scots in Russia* (Edinburgh, 1987).

Anthony Cross, *By the Banks of the Neva: Chapters from the Lives and Careers of the British in Eighteenth-Century Russia* (Cambridge, 1997).

Anthony Cross, *St Petersburg and the British: The City through the Eyes of British Visitors and Residents* (London, 2008).

Brian Allen and Larissa Dukelskaya (eds), *British Art Treasures from Russian Imperial Collections in the Hermitage* (New Haven, 1996).

Mikhail Piotrovski, *Treasures of Catherine the Great*, catalogue of an exhibition at the Hermitage Rooms, Somerset House (London, 2000).

Mikhail Piotrovski, *Star of the North: Catherine the Great and the Golden Age of Russian Empire*, catalogue of an exhibition at the Shanghai Museum (Shanghai, 2010).

A. Mineyeva (ed), *Imperial Glass Factory: 225th Foundation Day Anniversary*, catalogue of an exhibition at the State Hermitage Museum (St Petersburg, 2004).

George Heard Hamilton, *The Art and Architecture of Russia* (Harmondsworth, 2nd edition, 1975) ['The Pelican History of Art' series].

Isobel Rae, *Charles Cameron: Architect to the Court of Russia* (London, 1971).

Dmitry Shvidkovsky, *The Empress and the Architect: British Architecture and Gardens at the Court of Catherine the Great* (New Haven, 1996).

Penelope Hunter-Stiebel (ed.), *Stroganoff: The Palace and Collections of a Russian Noble Family* (New York, 2000).

Alexander M. Schenker, *The Bronze Horseman, Falconet's Monument to Peter the Great* (New Haven, 2003).

Igor Sychev, *Russian Bronze* (Moscow, 2003).

Antoine Chenevière, *Russian Furniture: the Golden Age, 1780-1840* (London, 1988).

Tamara Kudriavtseva, *Russian Imperial Porcelain* (St Petersburg, 2003).